Contingencies of Value

Contingencies of Value

Alternative Perspectives
for Critical Theory

Barbara Herrnstein Smith

Harvard University Press

Cambridge, Massachusetts, and London, England   1988

This book is printed on acid-free paper, and its binding
materials have been chosen for strength and durability.

Library of Congress Cataloging-in-Publication Data

Smith, Barbara Herrnstein.
   Contingencies of value.

   Bibliography: p.
   Includes index.
   1. Literature—History and criticism.
2. Value.   3. Aesthetics.   I. Title.
PN45.S4794   1988   809   88-887
ISBN 0–674–16785–6

For Alex

Acknowledgments

For their important contributions to the shaping and sharpening of the ideas in this study, I am grateful to the students who participated in the seminars on Value and Evaluation at the University of Pennsylvania, 1976–85. My thanks also to Thomas D. Cohen, Morse Peckham, and Arkady Plotnitsky for especially productive exchanges relating to these questions over the course of several years. The manuscript benefited from attentive readings of individual chapters by John Fekete, Stephen Jones, Robert A. Pollak, and Lindsay Waters, and from specific tips and encouragements—and/or significant resistances—offered by William Connolly, Clifford Geertz, Thomas A. Green, Joseph Gusfield, Albert O. Hirschman, Joanna Kirkpatrick, Sanford Levinson, Andrew Pickering, Joan Scott, Richard Shweder, Michael Walzer, David Wiggins, and Brackette Williams. Mark Lytal's assistance in the final stages of its preparation was expert and invaluable.

I thank the Guggenheim Foundation, the Luce Foundation, the National Endowment for the Humanities, the Rockefeller Foundation, and the University of Pennsylvania for grants, awards, and leaves that supported the pursuit of this project. I had the good fortune of being able to complete it under the genial conditions provided by the Center for Advanced Study in the Behavioral Sciences, 1985–86, and the Institute for Advanced Study, 1986–87.

An earlier version of Chapter 1 appeared in *Poetics Today* 1, nos. 1–2 (1979); the article originally published as "Contingencies of Value," *Critical Inquiry* 10, no. 1 (1983), is incorporated here—with revisions, additions, and updated references—as Chapters 2 and 3; a portion of

Acknowledgments

Chapter 5 was previously printed in *Life after Postmodernism: Essays on Value and Culture,* edited and introduced by John Fekete (New York: St. Martin's Press, 1987). Permission to use these materials is gratefully acknowledged.

Contents

Contents

Contingencies of Value

1

Fixed Marks and Variable Constancies: A Parable of Value

Evaluating Shakespeare's Sonnets

My text is a passage from the first scene of *King Lear*. The kings of Burgundy and France, for some time rivals in the courtship of Cordelia, are confronted by her abrupt disinheritance. Burgundy, with embarrassed politeness, will decline the offer of her now dowerless hand. The king of France (a better man) will seize it nonetheless, observing:

> Love's not love
> When it is mingled with regards that stand
> Aloof from the entire point . . .

My topic is evaluation: and what I shall suggest here is that it is not like love—or at least not like love so conceived. For evaluation is, I think, always mingled with regards that stand aloof from the entire point: always compromised, impure, contingent; altering when it alteration finds; bending with the remover to remove; always Time's fool.

Our title here is tricky: "*Evaluating* Shakespeare's Sonnets."[1] No agent: *who*'s doing the evaluating? No tense: evaluating *when*? But its form is perhaps proper enough: the agents are innumerable and unspecifiable; the activity is continuous and ongoing; the evaluating of Shakespeare's sonnets has had a past and will have a future. All the evaluatings have been contingent, and all of them will be—which is, I think, as it must and should be. I'll begin by looking at the past.

The sonnets have been the subject of evaluation for more than three and a half centuries and, as such, have exhibited a very mixed, variable, and compromised history. The first evaluatings of them were performed by the poet, in letting them stand: not merely in his not ripping them up, but in the thousand individual acts of approval that the whole complex act of poetic creation must have entailed: each word and line that was not rejected, that was preferred to another, and thus pronounced *good*—or good enough.

It has been noted that the sonnets themselves exhibit considerable self-evaluation and -devaluation: the topos of modesty—"my pupil pen," "my slight Muse," "these poor rude lines"—coexists with large claims of poetic value: such virtue hath his pen, so powerful is his rhyme, that eyes not yet created shall o'er read his lines and, through them Death, to him subscribe. Here we might also note that the poet himself assumes and asks for *biased* readers, readers who will value the poems, he says, "for their love, not their style"; for the poems are sent, he says, "to witness duty, not to show [his] wit"—not as literary achievements, but for what they reflect of his personal feelings. But, we may observe, the feelings that they *do* reflect are not always the sorts of things the biased and implicated reader might wish to know or want to hear: vows of irrational adoration, betrayals of naked resentment, bullying pleas and blackmailing apologies. We do not know how the sonnets were valued and evaluated by their immediate readers—those *thou*'s to whom they were addressed and into whose hands they may have been delivered—though it is an interesting exercise for the modern reader to imagine what it might have felt like to *receive* such embassages as these:

> Being your slave, what should I do but tend
> Upon the hours and times of your desire? . . .

> Farewell, thou art too dear for my possessing,
> And like enough thou know'st thy estimate . . .

> Yet fear her, O thou minion of her pleasure!
> She may detain, but not still keep her treasure . . .

> For I have sworn thee fair, and thought thee bright,
> Who art as black as Hell, as dark as night.

What *could* the value of the sonnets have been for those original readers? Certainly impure, certainly mingled with regards that stood aloof from the entire point, certainly variable: very different, we might imagine, when the poems were received in the midst of a love affair from when perused or disposed of years later—when *all* the lovers were old, and love had long been cold.

But such evaluations are presumably not part of literary history. As

2

"works of literature," the sonnets must be judged insofar as they appeal to their real readers, whom they continue to greet over the shoulders of those *thou*'s to whom they were once addressed. So we move from surmising the vagaries of their private, personal value to the record of their public value and evaluating. But, before we come to their "reputation"—or what Hyder Rollins, in the *Variorium* edition of the sonnets, calls their "vogue"—we should acknowledge an intermediary history of valuings, also variable, also contingent, and notoriously compromised: for example, the simple fact that they were found to be, for whatever motives, ah! *publishable;* worth the printing and presumably, for some purchasers, worth the price; and even, as the thirteen surviving copies of the Quarto attest, for some reasons worth the keeping. Each of these acts—publishing, printing, purchasing, and preserving—is an implicit act of evaluation, though we may think it necessary to distinguish *them,* with their mixed motives, from real literary evaluation, the assessment of intrinsic worth.

The question then becomes whether, and to what extent, the sonnets were found worth the *reading* by their original public audience. We cannot be sure, of course, but, as with any body of poetry, that too must have been a variable matter: for example, the sonnets, individually and as a group, would not have been valued quite the same way by fellow poets as by such readers as might pick them up to pass the time of day.

As we know, there is reason to believe that the Quarto edition was suppressed—possibly by the poet, possibly by others. If so, either way, the suppression was another act of both valuing and devaluing the sonnets: an implicit witness to their having been found, though perhaps good for *something,* still *not* good for something else. Value is impure; evaluation is contingent.

And so it goes. Thirty years later, they were found at least worth the pirating and republishing. Thereafter, especially with Malone's edition in 1780, we can begin to trace the fortunes of the sonnets in the hands of the literary establishment—the editors and anthologists, the critics and scholars, the professors and students of Eng. Lit., down to our own time and this very moment—and, with less assurance, their fortunes in the hands of those myriad inarticulate nonprofessionals for whom, during more than 350 years, the sonnets have figured in some way: the "reading public," those who, for whatever reasons, have treasured or dismissed them, bought them as gifts for friends, read them aloud to lovers, quoted them in letters, or tossed them out when cleaning up the attic.

I shall not chronicle in any detail those fortunes—which, as we

3

know, have been extraordinarily variable and, until fairly recently, fairly dismal. We might recall, however, that the sonnets have been characterized, by men of education and discrimination, as inept, obscure, affected, filled with "labored perplexities and studied deformities," written in a verse form "incompatible with the English language," a form given to "drivelling incoherencies and puling, petrifying ravings." We might recall especially Henry Hallam's remarking of the sonnets that "it is impossible not to wish that Shakespeare had not written them" and that his assessment or distress was shared, at some point in their lives, with some variations, by Coleridge, Wordsworth, and Hazlitt.

Wish Shakespeare had not written them? Lord, man (we may wish to shout back into that abysm of time), did you really *read* them? Well, presumably Hallam did read them, as did Dr. Johnson, Coleridge, Wordsworth, Hazlitt, and Byron (from each of whom I have been quoting here): but whether any of them read the same poems we are reading is another question. Value alters when it alteration finds. The texts were the same, but it seems clear that, in some sense, the *poems* weren't. How else can we account for the—to us, astonishing and perverse—evaluations of them by our eighteenth- and nineteenth-century colleagues? or those of John Crowe Ransom and Yvor Winters, in an age not so remote from ours? The taste of the times? Congenital rigidities of mind? Cultivated frigidities of spirit? To be sure; but in so accounting for them, we cannot thereby *discount* them. Those evaluations were not facile, ill-considered, or perfunctory; they were, we sense, straight from the heart and head; we can still feel Coleridge's shudder and Wordsworth's disdain and Hallam's embarrassed exasperation. Their disgust was as true as anything—except, perhaps, true love.

Well, where are we now?—and *who* are we, anyway? We and our absent counterparts—scholars, teachers, critics, and students of the sonnets: it is clear that we are not quite the reading public, those who now encounter the sonnets in anthologies of "great poetry" or who purchase them in cheap editions with ornate typefaces (but no footnotes) or in expensive editions with goldleaf borders (but still no footnotes) and among whom, we know, many of the sonnets are popular . . . but probably the "wrong" ones—or the right ones, but probably "for the wrong reasons."

Granted *we* are not *them*, it may still be asked where *we* fit in this long fitful history of the sonnets' evaluations. Can it be that we fit at the *end* of it?—that *now, here*, with our authoritative and annotated texts in our hands and, in our heads, the sonnets not only of Petrarch and Sidney but also of Keats, Millay, and Berryman, *we,* untrammeled by historical ignorance, intellectual provincialism, or personal eccentricity, are the ones who can finally provide a *just* assessment of the sonnets' *true* value—as *literature*? Or would we not, rather, be Time's fools—or fools of some sort—to think or claim so?

By way of answer, I should like to give an account of another history of the sonnets' value and evaluating: that is, my own, a history that also culminates here, at this time, and culminates with my solemn and sincere declaration that *I cannot* evaluate Shakespeare's sonnets—which is not to say that I believe the sonnets cannot or should not be evaluated. On the contrary, I believe that they should be, must be, and, in fact, are and will be evaluated, continuously, repeatedly, privately, and publicly, by us and by them and by all who follow. My own incapacity in this regard happens to be a somewhat special case, but I think it is an instructive one for the question at issue.

I cannot evaluate Shakespeare's sonnets partly because I know them too well. It may be thought that one's ability to deliver a just assessment of an artwork is enlarged by experience: we look to the expert, the connoisseur, the man or woman of knowledge—deep knowledge of the thing itself, and broad knowledge of the *kind* of thing it is and of others of its kind. But experience not only deepens and broadens us: it also batters, scars, individualizes, and specializes us; experience is a provincialism of its own, separating us from our fellow creatures. To evaluate a work of art is, among other things, to estimate its potential value for others; but while our ability to make that estimation correctly certainly increases in time with all our general and specific knowledge, it also decreases in time as we become less and less *like* anyone else, and thus less able to predict anyone else's responses on the basis of our own.

But that is not the only or even the basic reason why I cannot evaluate Shakespeare's sonnets. The basic reason is that I am too conscious of how radically variable and contingent their value has been, and remains, for me. I shall not give you a narrative of the history of my own engagement with the poems: a history that spans thirty-five years, during fifteen of which I professed them almost without interruption, sometimes every term, and during two years of which I prepared an edition of them. There is no other work or body of literature that I know so well—though there are no doubt other people who know it better; but the sonnets are so strung through my life, and my life has been so strung through them, that there have been times when I believed I had written them myself. I shall not give you a narrative account of their

5

value for me because the point will be made sufficiently if I indicate its range. And that range is "savage, extreme, rude, cruel," and "not to trust"—which suggests, by the way, that if poetic value is not like true love, it may be a little bit like true lust.

In any case, it would be only slight hyperbole to say that there is not one of Shakespeare's sonnets that has not, at some time, been the occasion of the finest and most intense kind of literary experience of which I am capable; and there is also not one among them that has not, at some time, struck me as being awkward, strained, silly, inert, or dead. Some of the sonnets that are now (i.e., this week or the day before yesterday) my favorites, I once (i.e., last week or ten years ago) thought of as obscure, grotesque, or raw; and some that I once saw as transparent, superficial, or perfunctory have subsequently become, for me, thick with meaning, subtle, and profound. But I have, in the very process of demonstrating to a class or friend the subtlety and profundity of a sonnet, been struck in the midst of my own words by how limp and thin it was, or have seen its power suddenly collapse upon the page into bathos or barbarism. A sonnet that I had never assigned to a class and disdained to comment upon will, during a half-casual rereading, suddenly leap from the page and startle me into awe and recognition—often because, since last reading it, I have lived the poem, lived something like its occasion or something like its motive. Most appalling, there are sonnets that I allude to in class or conversation, only to find that they have disappeared, truly *are not there*, and others that I had not "forgotten" but which, at some reading, I realize were never there before.

I have said nothing here of the form, style, logic, figurative language, or structure of the poems. I can't see them anymore and couldn't, today, "analyze" a Shakespeare sonnet if my life depended on it: all such matters have, for me, been absorbed or reabsorbed into the art of the whole and my experience of it. And, amusingly enough for a card-carrying anti-intentionalist, I now find myself, both in class and in my private musings on the poems, drawn more and more into thinking about the man himself, wondering what he really felt, and speculating about what really happened: What the devil *were* tr unappreciative young man and obsessing mistress really like? and what were they all really *doing* with and to each other?

Sonnet 116 will serve as well as any other to make this a bit more concrete. For a long time, I didn't much like it at all. As a discriminating young snob, I was predisposed to find the value of any poem inversely proportional to the frequency of its appearance in anthologies. More-

6

over, I had heard this one read too often at the wedding ceremonies of friends. It became an embarrassment just to glance at its opening lines, an agony to recall the couplet. And, to cap it, a professor whose *opinions* I valued very highly had once demonstrated in class, with great wit and dash, that the sentiments of 116 were as inane as its logic was feeble and its imagery vague.

So it stood until several years ago, when I was immersed in teaching the plays, editing the poems and rereading the critics, and immersed also in my own life and a second marriage—of true minds, of course, or maybe . . . or maybe not. And, at that point, I discovered an altogether different 116. It was not, as I had previously thought, the expression of the poet as Polonius, intoning sentimental *sententiae* on the virtue of remote virtues but, rather, the poet as Troilus or Hamlet or Lear, in a fury of despair, attempting to sustain the existence, by sheer assertion, of something which everything in his own experience denied. *So* (I might have said then), to be sure, the arguments are frail and the sentiments false and strained: but this is nonetheless a powerful sonnet because, among other things, that very frailty and strain and falseness are expressive of what is strong and true, namely the impulse *not* to know, *not* to acknowledge, not to "admit" what one does know and would wish to be otherwise.

A lovely reading of the poem, I think . . . when I believe it. And it does have the virtue of rescuing, for me, the value of one sonnet: which is to say, of letting me have, as something good, what would otherwise be something bad—which, in the total economy of the universe, must be reckoned as a profit. But, as for evaluating the sonnet: that I cannot do. Not only does its value, for me, depend upon which of two mutually incompatible interpretations I give it (and I still can give it either) but I'm also aware of the fact that I sometimes enjoy it even when I'm giving it the weak interpretation, and sometimes enjoy elements of it when I'm barely giving it any interpretation at all. For example, it's sometimes nice just to experience again the semi-abstract symmetries of its syntax and sound patterns, those boldly balanced mouth-filling clauses: *Love is not love / Which alters when it alteration finds / Or bends with the remover to remove* . . . a pleasure to say. Or again, like Professor Booth, I sometimes *enjoy* "bombast," and can take pleasure in the sheer excesses of the poem, as such.[2] Experienced against a daily background of scrupulously qualified professional precision, in which one has heard one's colleagues or oneself saying, often enough, things like: "Well, it seems to me that, in a sense, it might be possible, under certain circumstances, for some forms of what is commonly referred to as 'love' to have a relatively lengthy duration . . . ," it's really *nice* to hear a good, strong, unqualified absolute or two:

> O no, it is an *ever* fixèd mark
> That looks on tempests and is *never* shaken . . .
> *Love alters not* . . .
> But bears it out even to the edge of *doom*.

It's just an element of the poem, but it's there among the others; and sometimes it just hits the spot. But, of course, nothing hits the spot *all* the time, because the spot is always different.

Now, before I draw the moral that justifies my imposing on you this autobiographical excursion, I should grant the possibility that I am unusually, atypically, even pathologically, unstable in my responses. But I don't want to grant it, and don't really believe it. To be sure, the spectrum of value I've outlined here is mightily "acquainted with shifting change" ("as is false women's fashion," saith the poet); I would maintain, however, that its ranges and extremes are not atypical but, on the contrary, precisely representative. What is peculiar in my relation to the sonnets is not a matter of my temperament but of my profession, one consequence of which is that I have had both the reason and the occasion to read and deal with the same work of literature many times over, in many moods, in many circumstances, over a long span of years— during which time many things (or a sufficient number of them) have happened to me. Aside from professors, poets, and other special types (such as actors and directors), most people, taken one by one, simply do not experience literary works that way; and even professors and poets, because they are mortal, can't experience a great many of them that way.

But out of this peculiarity emerges a kind of universality: for what I have been describing here, a bit melodramatically perhaps, would, I think, be the shape of the experience of anyone who had the reason and occasion to do the same. Moreover, and more pertinently, I think it is also the shape of the entire culture's experience of the sonnets' value, over the entire history of their existence: past, present, and future. In other words, I should like to claim that the two histories I have briefly chronicled here are mirrors and containers of each other: that while the history of the sonnets' value must include, as one brief chapter, the history of their value for me, my personal history is also a picture and parable of the total history of the sonnets' value for all their readers, ever.

This monstrous piece of immodesty, however, amounts to saying no more than I said at the beginning. Evaluation is always compromised because value is always in motion: a never-fixèd mark, whose worth's unknown although his height be taken: "unknown" not because, like true love, it is beyond mortal cognition, but because it is constantly variable and eternally indeterminate.

Critical Problematics

The foregoing discussion was designed, it should be clear, not to raise doubts about my colleagues' powers of discernment but rather to suggest that at least as problematic as the true value of Shakespeare's sonnets are the very concepts of literary value and evaluation. To begin to appreciate the nature and complexity of these problems, we may return briefly to what I referred to as "the reading public" or, more broadly, as all those outside the academy "for whom the sonnets have figured in some way" but the record of whose valuations are not preserved in the annals of literary history. Of course, if we were to chronicle in earnest the *total* history of the sonnets' value, we should have to add to this group all those for whom the sonnets have not figured at all: children and illiterates, for example, plus all those who do not know English, those who do know and read English but have never even heard of the sonnets, those who have *only* "heard of" them—that is, who know the poems exist but have little idea of what they are like—and so forth. My concern here is not only with the well-known social parochialism of academic critics but also with the more fundamental question of what any literary assessment is, in fact, an assessment *of:* not only who does the computing but who and what, implicitly or explicitly, get "taken into account" in the computations and, as a corollary question, the nature of the assumptions presupposed by evaluative statements. For, as I shall suggest later, such statements are neither empty nor idle; on the contrary, they are much richer and perform much more significant social, cultural, and political functions than is commonly supposed.

A related point was implied in my allusion to anthologies: for example, to my own youthful disdain of them. That had been, of course, perverse as well as snobbish of me; there had also been a measure of self-delusion in it, for no one's literary tastes can be formed, sustained, or exercised independently—or, as it might be said, "free of external influence." The problem for the theory of literary value, then, is how

9

they *are* formed, sustained, and exercised; and anthologies themselves may be taken as a metaphor for the operation of various social determinants of literary value. The recommendation of value represented by the repeated inclusion of a particular work in anthologies of "great poetry" not only promotes but goes some distance toward *creating* the value of that work, as does its repeated appearance on reading lists or its frequent citation or quotation by professors, scholars, critics, poets, and other elders of the tribe; for all these acts have the effect of drawing the work into the orbit of attention of potential readers and, by making the work more likely to be experienced at all, they make it more likely to be experienced as "valuable." In this sense, value creates value. We may think here of the young woman who dwelt among untrodden ways, a maid (or violet, or poem) whom there were none to praise and very few to love: unknown, unseen, therefore unpraised, *therefore* without value—unless or until discovered, known, and praised by *someone;* and then "Oh, the difference to me," and the possibility of the difference to others.

One of the most tangled problems touched upon above is the relation of value to meaning or of evaluation to interpretation. For example, I spoke of sonnets that appear and disappear for me by virtue of interpretations of them that suddenly become possible or that were once possible but are no longer so. What I meant to suggest was that comparable appearances and disappearances occur throughout literary history, not only with respect to other individual readers and works but with respect to entire communities of readers and sometimes entire styles, modes, and genres of literature. For, in accord with the changing interests and other values of a community, various potential meanings of a work will become more or less visible (or "realizable"), and the visibility—and hence value—of the work for that community will change accordingly. The problem here can be seen as the interlooping of two circles, the hermeneutic and the evaluative. Our interpretation of a work and our experience of its value are mutually dependent, and each depends upon what might be called the psychological "set" of our encounter with it: not the "setting" of the work or, in the narrow sense, its context, but rather the nature and potency of our own assumptions, expectations, capacities, and interests with respect to it—our "prejudices" if you like, but hardly to be distinguished from our identity (or *who,* in fact, *we are*) at the time of the encounter. Moreover, all three—the interpretation, the evaluation, and the "set"—operate and interact in the same fashion

10

as the hermeneutic circle itself: that is, simultaneously causing and validating themselves *and* causing and validating each other. While these circles are no doubt logically vicious or at least epistemologically compromising, they are also, I believe, both psychologically inevitable and experientially benign. Undue distress at their philosophical status coupled with a failure to appreciate their inevitability will produce misguided and futile attempts to escape from them, as reflected in the familiar searches for "true" or objective value and for uniquely "correct" interpretations or determinate meanings. There is, however, no way out of these circles for the individual reader: only the recognition of their existence and, of course, the pleasure and interest of the particular experiences they yield—and, for the *theorist,* the possibility of describing and explaining the dynamics of their interrelation. Which brings me to the heart and true moral of my parable.

One of the central concepts introduced above was "contingency," and one of the central propositions that both chronicles were meant to exemplify was that literary value is radically relative and therefore "constantly variable." What I should like to emphasize now is, first, that none of the terms here—"contingent," "relative," or "variable"—is equivalent to "subjective," and, second, that my intention was—and is—not to close the doors to inquiry but rather to open them. In aesthetic axiology, the invocation of the term "subjective" has traditionally yielded two dead-end conclusions: either *De gustibus non disputandum est,* which (at least under one understanding of the proverb, itself a matter of dispute) explicitly closes the doors to inquiry, or—less despondent and more energetic but still, I think, misguided—the conviction that there exists and that we must seek to uncover a *converse* to "subjective value," namely "objective value." To suggest that the concept of objective value is vacuous is not, however, to be left with the presumed vagaries of individual taste. The botanist who observed that the growth rate of the plant he was studying *varied* under different conditions would not murmur *De gustibus* and end his research at that point but, on the contrary, begin it. If we recognize that literary value is "relative" in the sense of *contingent* (that is, a changing function of multiple variables) rather than *subjective* (that is, personally whimsical, locked into the consciousness of individual subjects and/or without interest or value for other people), then we may begin to investigate the dynamics of that relativity. Such an investigation would, I believe, reveal that the variables in question are limited and regular—that is, that they occur within

11

ranges and that they exhibit patterns and principles—and that in *that* sense, but only in that sense, we may speak of "constancies" of literary value.

I shall return below to the nature of these constancies. They will be better appreciated, however, if we give some attention first to the problem of literary *evaluation,* what Northrop Frye, in a memorable and influential piece of counteraxiology, referred to as "all those ditherings, vacillatings and reactings that constitute the history of taste": a history, Frye remarked (quite erroneously, I think), in which "there are no facts," and which, he concluded (precipitously and also, I think, illogically), must be firmly ejected from "the systematic and progressive study of literature."[3]

As I have already suggested, "evaluation" is a concept that could embrace a wide range of *forms* of behavior, not all of them overt and certainly not all of them verbal. (Thus, the poet crossing out a line or tossing out a poem is engaged in acts of evaluation, as is the fellow who publishes a volume of the poems and the one who buys a copy of it as a graduation present for his daughter.) Once the range is granted, we may also acknowledge that there are certain forms of evaluation that are, for certain purposes, of particular interest, namely those acts that *are* overt and verbal: that is, explicit statements of value, the sort of act we perform when, provoked by some occasion, we say, "It's the greatest lyric in English," or "What a godawful movie," or "It's even better than his first novel."

Now, traditional value-theory offers a number of competing notions of what we are doing when we make such statements: for example, that we are essentially doing nothing at all, or at least nothing that is philosophically respectable—just giving public vent to private preferences or engaging in what Frye calls "literary chit-chat" and "leisure-class gossip." Or, it has been suggested that we are essentially trying to push people around, telling them what they *should* do or how they should feel when they do it. Or, of course, it has been maintained that, at their best—when delivered by duly qualified persons and supported by duly organized reasons of the proper sort, or when delivered in the form of fine-grained descriptions, thorough analyses, and sufficiently subtle explications—such judgments *are* philosophically respectable and cognitively substantial statements: not merely the expressions of personal preferences or directives to other people but, indeed, valid assessments or demonstrations of *the* value of literary works. I shall not take the time here to explain why I think each of these notions is faulty or inadequate,

12

though it should be noted that there is no reason to suppose that all evaluative statements conform to a single logical or functional type. I also shall not pause here to classify further or to identify by their traditional names the various positions alluded to above—though auto-taxonomy appears to be a preoccupation of axiology.[4] I should, however, like to outline an alternative conception of literary evaluation, one that is in accord with the view of literary *value* as variable and contingent but that also recognizes the considerable social force and significant social functions of all forms of evaluative behavior.

I would suggest, then, that what we may be doing—and, I think, often are doing—when we make an explicit value judgment of a literary work is (a) articulating an estimate of how well that work will serve certain implicitly defined functions (b) for a specific implicitly defined audience, (c) who are conceived of as experiencing the work under certain implicitly defined conditions. I shall briefly elaborate each of the clauses here.

First, when we state the value of a literary work, we are usually not *only* (and certainly not necessarily, and perhaps not at all) declaring its past or present value for *ourselves* but also estimating its probable value for others. Not *all* others, however, but *some* others: the nature and limits of the group may be implied by the context of the evaluation (for example, the set of "others" implied by a book review in *Art News* would be different from the set implied by a review in *Scientific American*—though the two sets might, of course, overlap) and may, in fact, be quite explicitly indicated, as in "A fine book for children between the ages of 8 and 12 who have an interest in animals." If not otherwise characterized, however, that implicitly defined audience would presumably consist of people who are *like ourselves* in the pertinent respects, though it is perhaps worth remarking that some evaluators evidently believe that *everyone* is—or *should* be—like themselves in those respects.

Second, when we allude to a work as great, good, bad, or middling, we usually imply great, good, bad, or middling *for* something and also, thereby, *as* something: that is, with respect to whatever functions or effects works of that kind might be expected or desired to serve or produce. The functions and effects are usually not made explicit; they may not be recognized or even covertly formulated by the evaluator as what *is* desired or expected; and they are likely to differ from one community of audiences to another. Nevertheless, the assumption of certain characteristic functions and effects will not only direct the evaluator's judgment of the work but will also be part of what consti-

13

tutes, for him and presumably for his community, the *classification* of the work as whatever it is classified as: bedtime story, detective novel, nonsense verse, or, of course, "work of literature." Thus, and of special significance, when teachers and academic critics commend a work as "good literature," they are implicitly indicating that it is good *as* whatever teachers and academic critics mean by "literature" and *for* whatever they believe such works *can* or *should* be good for.

Finally, when we judge the value of a work, we usually conceive of it as experienced under certain implicitly defined circumstances: defined, that is, by the conventions and assumptions which, in our community, govern the conception of the circumstances in which a work of that kind is typically (and hence, it may be thought, "properly") experienced. Thus, to draw a vivid parallel example here from music rather than literature, the New Yorker who commends a certain opera and the West African who commends a certain ceremonial drum-piece are each presumably conceiving of the work in question as experienced under specific—and rather different—conditions of performance and reception. (Whether typical in a certain community *is* equivalent to "proper" is, of course, another question.)

A number of lines of inquiry are suggested by the foregoing conception of evaluative behavior. Among them are the exploration of the particular assumptions and conventions that do govern what is implied by evaluative acts, the manner in which those assumptions and conventions arise and are maintained and transmitted, and in response to what variables they change (when they *do* change). Also, recognizing the extent to which evaluation is a form of *social* behavior, we may ask what social occasions provoke or elicit judgmental acts, how the forms of those acts are determined and constrained by the social conditions in which they occur, and what social functions they perform. While it is clear that the answers to such questions will *vary* for various communities, that does not mean that we may look forward to replacing the impasse of individual subjectivity with a higher-level sociological *De gustibus*. For, as I suggested earlier, research does not conclude with the discovery of variability: we must seek to account for the variabilities *themselves* and, once again, we may expect and endeavor to find patterns, principles, regularities, and, in that sense, constancies—here, constancies of evaluative behavior.

It is important at this point that the "constancies" to which I have referred be distinguished from other kinds and conceptions of invariance that are associated with theories of literary or aesthetic value.

14

First, the constancies are not equivalent to what are sometimes referred to as the "universals" of human nature. This is not to say that there are no such universals or that they are not pertinent to the sources of literary value. On the contrary, as I have argued elsewhere, there is reason to believe that the experience of much that we call "aesthetic value" is, to some extent, a function of species-wide mechanisms of perception and cognition and, with regard to the value of literary works, a function of such mechanisms as they relate to what may be universals of verbal behavior. Nevertheless, such presumably biophysiological mechanisms will always operate differentially in different environments and interact with a broad range of other variables (historical, cultural, situational, etc.) and, therefore, the experience of literary and aesthetic value cannot be altogether accounted for, reduced to, or predicted by them.[5]

Second, the constancies are not to be identified with what are sometimes conceived of as the fundamental "traits," recurrent "features," or shared "properties" of valued works. The attempt to locate invariance in the nature (or, latterly, the *structure*) of the works themselves is, I believe, no less misguided than the search for essential or objective value—and is, in fact, only another form of that search, though often presented in contradistinction to it as a matter for "empirical" or "inductive" investigation. It is misguided, however, not only because different features or properties will be valued differently by different audiences, and so on, but, more significantly, because the very *perception* of those presumed properties will itself vary. Thus, when David Hume, in his essay "Of the Standard of Taste," observed with complacency that "the same Homer who pleased at Athens and Rome two thousand years ago is still admired at Paris and London," we have reason to wonder if it is indeed quite "the same" Homer. The constancies are not to be found, then, in the properties of literary works because those properties are *themselves* among the variables of literary value—along with such other fixed marks and putative models of stability and reliability as the unclouded perceptions of all men of discrimination and the enduring values of Western civilization.

The moral of the parable of Shakespeare's sonnets was that, with respect to value, everything is always in motion with respect to everything else. If there *are* constancies of literary value, they will be found *in those very motions:* that is, in the relations among the variables. For, like all value, literary value is not the property of an object *or* of a subject but, rather, *the product of the dynamics of a system.* As readers and critics of

15

literature, we are within that system; and, because we are neither omniscient nor immortal and do have particular interests, we will, at any given moment, be viewing it from *some* perspective. It is from such a perspective that we experience the value of a work and also from such a perspective that we estimate its probable value for others. There is nothing illusory in the experience, however, or necessarily inaccurate in the estimate. From that real (if limited) perspective, at that real (if transient) moment, our experience of the value of the work *is* its value. Or, in the terms I should prefer: our experience of "the value of the work" is equivalent to *our experience of the work in relation to the total economy of our existence.* And the reason our estimates of its probable value for other people may be quite accurate is that the total economy of *their* existence may, in fact, be quite similar to that of our own.

The experiences and activities that constitute the valuing and evaluating of literature are important components of the system out of which literary value arises; indeed, they are what keeps the system "alive"— active and continuous rather than still and stagnant. And while neither of them—that is, neither the valuing of literary works nor the making of value judgments about them—can *as such* be regarded as literary theory, it does not follow that literary theory (or Frye's "systematic and progressive study of literature") should not concern itself with them. On the contrary, it is surely among the tasks of literary theory to explore and describe the dynamics of that system and to relate its operations to everything else that we know about human behavior and culture. The issues that attend the concept of literary value and the activities that constitute literary evaluation are a central part of the network of problems and phenomena that constitute the domain of literary theory, and therefore they must be permitted and encouraged to return from their present exile.

2

The Exile of Evaluation

Fact and Value in the Literary Academy

It is a curious feature of literary studies in America that one of the most venerable, central, theoretically significant, and pragmatically inescapable set of problems relating to literature has not been a subject of serious inquiry for the past fifty years. I refer here to the fact not merely that the study of literary evaluation has been, as we might say, "neglected," but that the entire problematic of value and evaluation has been evaded and explicitly exiled by the literary academy. It is clear, for example, that there has been no broad and sustained investigation of literary evaluation that could compare to the constant and recently intensified attention devoted to every aspect of literary *interpretation*. The past decades have witnessed an extraordinary proliferation of theories, approaches, movements, and entire disciplines focused on interpretive criticism, among them (to recite a familiar litany) New Criticism, structuralism, psychoanalytic criticism, reader-response criticism, reception aesthetics, speech-act theory, deconstruction, communications theory, semiotics, and hermeneutics. At the same time, however, aside from a number of scattered and secondary essays by theorists and critics who are usually otherwise occupied,[1] no one in particular has been concerned with questions of literary value and evaluation, and such questions regularly go begging—and, of course, begged—even among those whose inquiries into other matters are most rigorous, substantial, and sophisticated.

Reasons for the specific disparity of attention are not hard to locate. One is the obvious attachment of problems of interpretation and mean-

ing to the more general preoccupation with language that has dominated the entire century; another, no doubt, is the fact that disciplines
such as linguistics and the philosophy of language are more accessible to
literary scholars than the corresponding disciplines, especially economics and sociology, that are more broadly concerned with the nature of
value and evaluative behavior. The reasons for the general neglect and
exile, however, are more complex, reflecting, among other things, the
fact that literary studies in America, from the time of its inception as an
institutionalized academic discipline, has been shaped by two conflicting and mutually compromising intellectual traditions and ideologies,
namely—or roughly namely—positivistic philological scholarship and
humanistic pedagogy. That is, while professors of literature have sought
to claim for their activities the rigor, objectivity, cognitive substantiality,
and progress associated with science and the empirical disciplines, they
have also attempted to remain faithful to the essentially conservative
and didactic mission of humanistic studies: to honor and preserve the
culture's traditionally esteemed objects—in this case, its canonized
texts—and to illuminate and transmit the traditional cultural values
presumably embodied in them. One consequence or manifestation of
this conflict has been the continuous absorption of "literary theory" in
America with institutional debates over the proper methods and objectives of the academic *study* of literature and, with respect to the topic at
hand, the drastic confinement of its concern with literary evaluation to
debates over the cognitive status of evaluative criticism and its proper
place, if any, in the discipline.

   A bit of history will be helpful here. In accord with the traditional
empiricist doctrine of a fundamental split or discontinuity between fact
and value (or description and evaluation, or knowledge and judgment),
it was possible to regard the emerging distinction within literary studies
between "scholarship" and "criticism" as a reasonable division of labor.
Thus, the scholar who devoted himself to locating and assembling the
historical and philological facts necessary to edit and annotate the works
of, say, Bartholomew Griffin might remark that, although Griffin was no
doubt a less "fashionable" poet than such contemporaries as Spenser
and Shakespeare, the serious and responsible scholar must go about his
work in a serious and responsible manner, leaving questions of literary
merit "to the critics." The gesture that accompanied the remark, however, was likely to signal not professional deference but intellectual
condescension; for the presumably even-handed distribution of the intellectual responsibilities of literary study—the determination of facts to

the scholar and value to the critic—depended on an always question-able and increasingly questioned set of assumptions: namely, that liter-ary value was a determinate property of texts and that the critic, by virtue of certain innate and acquired capacities (taste, sensibility, and so forth, which could be seen as counterparts to the scholar's industry and erudition), was someone specifically equipped to discriminate it.

The magisterial mode of literary evaluation that issued from this set of assumptions (and which, in Anglo-American criticism, characteris-tically reproduced itself after the image—and in the voice—of Dr. John-son and also of such latter-day "master-critics" as Matthew Arnold and T. S. Eliot) was practiced most notably by F. R. Leavis in England and, in the United States, perhaps most egregiously by Yvor Winters. Its reaches and a taste of its once-familiar flavor can be recalled in this passage from Leavis's *Revaluation:*

> There are, of course, discriminations to be made: Tennyson, for example, is a much better poet than any of the pre-Raphaelites. And Christina Rossetti deserves to be set apart from them and credited with her own thin and limited but very valuable distinction . . . There is, too, Emily Brontë, who has hardly yet had full justice as a poet. I will record, without offering it as a checked and deliberated judgment, the remembered impression that her *Cold in the earth* is the finest poem in the nineteenth-century part of *The Oxford Book of English Verse.*[2]

Such unabashed "debaucheries of judiciousness" (as Northrop Frye would later characterize them) were, however, increasingly seen as em-barrassments to the discipline, and the practice of evaluative criticism became more defensive, at least partly in response to the renewed and updated authority given to axiological skepticism.

In the 1930s and 40s, a number of prominent philosophers, among them A. J. Ayer and Rudolph Carnap, began to argue that value judg-ments are not merely distinct from empirically verifiable statements of fact but vacuous pseudostatements, at best suasive and commendatory, at worst simply the emotive expressions of personal sentiment, and in any case neither reflecting nor producing genuine knowledge.[3] For the positivistic literary scholar, such arguments reinforced his impression that the work of his critical colleague was the intellectually insubstantial activity of a dilettante whereas the true discipline of literary studies was exhibited in his own labors, in which he had always sought to achieve a rigor and objectivity as free as possible from the contamination of value ascription. In the institutional struggles that ensued, various maneuvers

19

were developed to secure for "criticism" not only a central place in the discipline but also an intellectual status equal in respectability to that of empirical science and what was commonly referred to as "serious scholarship."

One obvious tactic, still favored in many quarters of the literary academy, was to invoke the humanistic mission of literary studies and turn the fact-value split against the scholars' claim of centrality. Thus, Yvor Winters would maintain that whereas science was value-neutral— or, as he put it, "amoral"—literary studies had moral responsibilities. The function of historical scholarship and philology was, accordingly, ancillary: specifically it was "to lay the groundwork for criticism,"[4] while the important job was, precisely, to evaluate literature. For Winters, this meant to declare, forthrightly and unequivocally, what was good and bad literature (which was to say, "moral" or "decadent" literature) and he did not hesitate, himself, to rank-order not only poets and poems but also literary genres, verse forms, and entire centuries.

Winters had a genius for unequivocality that was imitated, but never matched, by his numerous followers. In any case, a more common tactic, exemplified by a number of the New Critics, was to devise some formulation of critical activity that bridged the fact-value split or at least unobtrusively edged the two sides together. Thus, in 1951, W. K. Wimsatt, Jr., in an important essay titled "Explication as Criticism," observed that it was necessary to find "an escape between the two extremes of sheer affectivism and sheer scientific neutralism," and attempted to demonstrate how evaluation could be assimilated into the typical New Critical production of increasingly exquisite explications and fine-grained analyses: "But then, finally, it is possible to conceive and produce instances where explication in the neutral sense is so integrated with special and local value intimations that it rises from neutrality gradually and convincingly to the point of total judgment."[5]

It may be recalled here that Wimsatt's attempt to expose "the affective fallacy" was directed largely at the "psychological theory of value" developed by I. A. Richards in the 1920s, which Wimsatt charged with amounting to subjectivism and leading to impressionism and relativism. Richards's theory was, however, in effect an updated rehearsal of the eighteenth-century empiricist-normative account and, like the latter, designed to *rebut* axiological skepticism.[6] An adequate theory of criticism, Richards wrote, must be able to answer such questions as "What gives the experience of reading a poem its value?" and "Why is one opinion about works of art not as good as others?"[7] And while the first

of these questions no doubt seemed to Wimsatt altogether different from what, for him, would have been the more proper question of what gives *the poem itself* its value, the second of them makes Richards's normative objectives quite clear. Indeed, he consistently put his psychoneurological account of value in the service of canonical judgments and repeatedly translated it into versions of evaluative absolutism and objectivism. Thus, the remarkable chapter on "Badness in Poetry" in *Principles of Literary Criticism* concludes its excruciating examination of the failure of a sonnet by Ella Wheeler Wilcox to produce a "high level or organization" of "adequate [neural] impulses" with Richards's observation that, although "those who enjoy [the sonnet] certainly seem to enjoy it to a high degree," nevertheless, with good and bad poetry, as with brandy and beer, the "actual universal preference of those who have tried both fairly is the same as superiority in value of one over the other. Keats, by universal qualified opinion, is a more efficient poet than Wilcox, and that is the same as saying his works are more valuable."[8] The invocation of an "actual" universality coupled with such question-begging hedges as "fairly" and "qualified" is, as we shall see, characteristic of traditional empiricist-normative accounts. It was not, one suspects, its alleged relativism that made Richards's theory so unabsorbable by the literary academy, but rather the raw jargon and unedifying physiology that attended it.

The boldest move in the mid-century effort to give disciplinary respectability and cognitive substance to criticism was, of course, Northrop Frye's call upon it to redefine itself as a project that banished evaluation altogether. In his "Polemical Introduction" to *The Anatomy of Criticism,* Frye insisted that if criticism was ever to become a "field of genuine learning" (significantly exemplified by "chemistry and philology"), it would have to "snip off and throw away" that part that had "no organic connection with it," namely evaluation.[9] For Frye, the shifting assessments and rank-orderings made by critics were not only a noncumulative accumulation of subjective judgments, but also irrelevant to "real criticism," since he believed, echoing and endorsing T. S. Eliot, that "the existing monuments of literature form an ideal order among themselves." "This," Frye commented, "is criticism, and very fundamental criticism. Much of this book attempts to annotate it" (*AC*, p. 18).

In what proved to be a memorable passage, he derided "all the literary chit-chat which makes the reputations of poets boom and crash in an imaginary stock-exchange," and observed: "This sort of thing cannot be part of any systematic study, for a systematic study can only progress; whatever dithers or vacillates or reacts is merely leisure-class gossip. The history of taste is no more a part of the *structure* of criticism than the Huxley-Wilberforce debate is a part of the structure of biological science" (*AC*, p. 18). In view of Frye's Platonic conception of literature and positivistic conception of science, it is not surprising that he failed to recognize that his analogy here cuts both ways. For not only could the Huxley-Wilberforce debate be seen as very much a part of the "structure" of biological science (which, like that of any other science, including any science of literature, is by no means independent of its own intellectual, social, and institutional history), but, since the "order" of the "existing monuments of literature" is the distinctly sublunary product of, among other things, evaluative practices, any truly systematic study of literature would sooner or later have to include a study of *those practices*. In other words, the structure of criticism cannot be so readily disengaged from the history of taste because they are mutually implicating and incorporating.

Joining as it did both an appeal to scientific objectivity and a humanistic conception of literature while at the same time extending the promise of a high calling and bright future to a project pursued in the name of "criticism," Frye's effort to banish evaluation from literary study was remarkably effective, at least to the extent of haunting a generation of literary scholars, critics, and teachers, many of whom are still inclined to apologize for making overt value judgments, as if for some temporary intellectual or moral lapse.[10] It was hardly the last word on the subject, however, and as late as 1968 we find E. D. Hirsch, Jr. attempting to rehabilitate the cognitive status of evaluative criticism in an essay significantly titled "Evaluation as Knowledge." In the essay, Hirsch argues that the value judgment of a literary work, when properly directed to the work itself and not to a "distorted version of it," closely coordinated with a correct interpretation of its objective meaning, and rationally justified with reference to specific criteria, *does* constitute a genuine proposition and, therefore, like a "pure description," does "qualify as objective knowledge."[11] Since just about every concept engaged by Hirsch's argument is at issue in contemporary epistemology and critical theory, it is not surprising that it did not settle the question of the intellectual status of evaluative criticism—for Hirsch or anyone else.[12]

The debate over the proper place of evaluation in literary studies remains unresolved and is, I believe, unresolvable in the terms in which it has been formulated. Meanwhile, although evaluative criticism remains intellectually suspect, it certainly continues to be practiced as a magisterial privilege in the classrooms of the literary academy and granted admission to its journals as long as it comes under cover of other presumably more objective types of literary study, such as historical description, textual analysis, or explication. At the same time, however, the fact that literary evaluation is not merely an aspect of formal academic criticism but a complex set of social and cultural activities central to the very nature of literature has been obscured, and an entire domain that is properly the object of theoretical, historical, and empirical exploration has been lost to serious inquiry.

Although I confine my comments here primarily to the literary academy in the United States and to Anglo-American critical theory, the situation—and its intellectual and institutional history—has not been altogether different in continental Europe. The dominance of language- and interpretation-centered theories, movements, and approaches, for example, is clearly international, and versions of the positivist/humanist conflict have shaped the development of literary studies in Europe as well. Certain exceptions are, however, instructive. When, in the 1920s and 30s, East European theorists also sought to transform literary studies into a progressive, systematic science, the problematic of value and evaluation was not excluded from the project. For example, the historically variable functions of texts and the interrelations among canonical and noncanonical works and other cultural products and activities were recognized and documented by, among others, Jurij Tynjanov and Mikhail Bakhtin, and Jan Mukařovský's explorations of the general question of aesthetic value were both original and substantial.[13] Also, studies in the sociology of literature, especially in France and Germany, and the project of reception aesthetics have concerned themselves with aspects of literary evaluation.[14] It should be noted, however, that the study of value and evaluation remained relatively undeveloped in the later work of formalists and structuralists,[15] while Marxist literary theory has only recently begun to move from minimal revisions of orthodox aesthetic axiology toward a radical reformulation.[16] It may be added that, although the theoretical perspective, conceptual structures, and analytic techniques developed by Jacques Derrida are potentially of great interest here (especially in conjunction with the renewed attention to Nietzsche), their radical axiological implications remain largely unexplored and, insofar as it has been appropriated by Anglo-American critical theory, deconstruction has been put almost entirely in the service of antihermeneutics, which is to say that it has been absorbed by our preemptive occupation with interpretive criticism.[17] Recent moves in the direction of opening the question of value and evaluation in the literary academy have come primarily from those who have sought to subject its canon to dramatic revaluation, notably feminist critics. Although their efforts have been significant to that end, they have not amounted as yet to the articulation of a well-developed noncanonical theory of value and evaluation.[18]

The Politics of Evaluative Criticism

One of the major effects of prohibiting or inhibiting explicit evaluation is to forestall the exhibition and obviate the possible acknowledgment of divergent systems of value and thus to ratify, by default, established evaluative authority. It is worth noting that in none of the debates of the 1940s and 50s was the traditional academic canon itself questioned, and that where evaluative authority was not ringingly affirmed, asserted, or self-justified, it was simply assumed. Thus, Frye himself could speak almost in one breath of the need to "get rid of . . . all casual, sentimental and prejudicial value judgments" as "the first step in developing a genuine poetics," and of "the masterpieces of literature" which are "the materials of literary criticism" (*AC,* pp. 18, 15). The identity of those masterpieces could, it seemed, be taken for granted or followed more or less automatically from "the direct value-judgment of informed good taste" or "certain literary values . . . fully established by critical experience" (*AC,* pp. 27, 20).

In a passage of particular interest, Frye wrote: "Comparative estimates of value are really inferences, most valid when silent ones, from critical practice . . . The critic will find soon, and constantly, that Milton is a more rewarding and suggestive poet to work with than Blackmore. But the more obvious this becomes, the less time he will want to waste belaboring the point" (*AC,* p. 25). In addition to the noteworthy correlation of validity with silence (comparable, to some extent, to Wimsatt's discreet "intimations" of value), two other aspects of Frye's remarks here repay some attention. First, in claiming that it is altogether obvious that Milton, rather than Blackmore, is "a more rewarding and suggestive poet [for the critic] to work with," Frye begged the question of *what kind of work* the critic would be doing. For surely if one were concerned with a question such as the relation of canonical and noncanonical texts

24

in the system of literary value in eighteenth-century England, one would find Blackmore just as rewarding and suggestive *to work with* as Milton. Both here and in his repeated insistence that the "material" of criticism must be "the masterpieces of literature" (he refers also to "a feeling we have all had that the study of mediocre works of art remains a random and peripheral form of critical experience"—*AC*, p. 17), Frye exhibits a severely limited conception of the potential domain of literary study and of the sorts of problems and phenomena with which it could or should deal. In this conceptual and methodological confinement, however (which betrays the conservative force of the ideology of traditional humanism even in the laboratories of the new progressive poetics), he has been joined by just about every other member of the Anglo-American literary academy during the past fifty years.

The second point of interest in Frye's remarks is his significant conjoining of Milton with Blackmore as an illustration of the sort of comparative estimate that is so obvious as not to need belaboring. Blackmore, we recall, was the author of an ambitious epic poem, *The Creation*, notable in literary history primarily as the occasion of some faint praise from Dr. Johnson and otherwise as a topos of literary disvalue; its function—indeed, one might say its *value*—has been to stand as an instance of bad poetry. This handy conjunction, however (and similar ones, such as Shakespeare and Edgar Guest, John Keats and Joyce Kilmer, T. S. Eliot and Ella Wheeler Wilcox, that occur repeatedly in the debates outlined above), evades the more difficult and consequential questions of judgment posed by genuine evaluative diversity and conflict: questions that are posed, for example, by specific claims of value made for noncanonical works, such as modern texts, especially highly innovative ones, and such culturally exotic works as oral or tribal literature, popular literature, and so-called ethnic literature, and *also* by claims and judgments of literary value made by or on behalf of what might be called *noncanonical audiences*, such as all those readers who are not now students, critics, or professors of literature and perhaps never were and never will be within the academy or on its outskirts.

Perhaps because the latter claims and judgments touch on personally as well as ideologically sensitive matters of social stratification, their political significance is even more resistant to recognition than claims of value made for noncanonical works. What is being missed and obscured here is the fact that there is a politics of personal *taste* as well as a politics of institutional evaluation and explicit evaluative criticism. This resistance is displayed, moreover, not only by conservative members of the

25

literary academy but also by those who are otherwise most concerned to indicate the political implications of these issues; and the revulsion of academics and intellectuals at the actual literary preferences, forms of aesthetic enjoyment, and general modes of cultural consumption of nonacademics and nonintellectuals—including those whose *political* emancipation they may otherwise seek to promote—has been a familiar feature of the cultural-political scene since at least the 1930s. It will not do, of course, simply to label this "snobbery" or "elitism," for it is the product of multiple and quite complexly related psychological, sociological, and ideological elements which, moreover, are played out differently under different historical, social, and institutional conditions and therefore require very careful analysis.[19] It is clear, however, that oppositional cultural theory and conservative humanism have repeatedly generated strictly parallel (and, indeed, often indistinguishable) accounts to explain the tastes of other people in such a way as to justify the academic intellectual's revulsion at them.

The historical-psychological-ideological complex operating here might be referred to as "The-Other's-Poison Effect," meaning not only that one man's meat is sometimes the other's poison but that one man sometimes gets sick just *watching* the other fellow eat his meat and, moreover, that if one of them is also a cultural theorist (left-wing or conservative as otherwise measured), he or she may be expected to generate an account of how the other fellow is himself actually being poisoned by the meat he likes and eats. It is no surprise, perhaps, that the often self-consciously *historicist* accounts referred to here operate in strict complicity with the *universalist* accounts developed by Hume, Kant, and the tradition of aesthetic axiology examined in Chapters 3 and 4, below.

The evasion mentioned above is dramatized when conflicts of judgment arising from fundamental and perhaps irreconcilable diversity of interest are exhibited in a currently charged political context. A specific example will illustrate my point here. In 1977 a study of Langston Hughes's poetry was published by Onwuchekwa Jemie, a Nigerian-born, American-educated poet and critic, at that time associate professor of English and Afro-American literature at the University of Minnesota. In one section of his study, Jemie discussed Hughes's poetic cycle "Madame" in relation to Eliot's "The Love Song of J. Alfred Prufrock" and Ezra Pound's "Hugh Selwyn Mauberly," comparing various formal and thematic aspects of the three works. He observed, for example, that each of them is "consistent in language, tone and attitude with the socio-psychological milieu which it explores: the ghetto dialect and sassy humor [in Hughes's work], the cynical polished talk of literary London [in Pound], and the bookish ruminations of Prufrock's active mind in inactive body," and then concluded pointedly: "In short, to fault one poem for not being more like the other, for not dealing with the matter and in the manner of the other, is to err in judgment."[20] Soon after its publication, a reviewer of Jemie's book in the London *Times Literary Supplement* took it very much to task for, among other things, its "painfully irrelevant comparisons," citing the passage quoted above.[21] And, a few weeks later, there appeared in *TLS* an extraordinary letter to the editor from Chinweizu, himself a Nigerian-born, American-educated writer and critic. Responding to the review and particularly to the phrase, "painfully irrelevant comparisons," he shot back:

> Painful to whom? Irrelevant to whom? To idolators of white genius? Who says that Shakespeare, Aristophanes, Dante, Milton, Dostoevsky, Joyce, Pound, Sartre, Eliot, etc. are the last word in literary achievement, un-equalled anywhere? . . . The point of these comparisons is not to thrust a black face among these local idols of Europe which, to our grave injury, have been bloated into "universality"; rather it is to help heave them out of our way, clear them from our skies by making clear . . . that we have among our own the equals and betters of these chaps . . . In this day and age, British preferences do not count in the Black World. As Langston Hughes put it half a century ago: "If white people are pleased, we are glad. If they are not, it doesn't matter."[22]

This brief episode in the history of literary evaluation illustrates, among other things, what genuine evaluative conflict sounds like. (It also illustrates that, contrary to Frye's assertion, the history of taste is not "a history where there are no facts," though we have barely begun to recognize either how to chronicle its episodes and shape its narrative or how to assess its significance not only for "the structure of criticism" but also for the structure of "literature.") I would suggest that it is, also among other things, the very possibility of that sound that is being evaded in Anglo-American literary studies and, furthermore, that when the sound reaches the intensity that we hear in Chinweizu's letter, the literary academy has no way to acknowledge it except, perhaps, in the language of counter-outrage.[23]

An Alternative Project

It is clear that, with respect to the central pragmatic issues as well as theoretical problems of literary value and evaluation, American critical theory has simply painted itself out of the picture. Beguiled by the humanist's fantasy of transcendence, endurance, and universality, it has been unable to acknowledge the most fundamental character of literary value, which is its mutability and diversity. And, at the same time, magnetized by the goals and ideology of a naïve scientism, distracted by the arid concerns of philosophic axiology, obsessed by a misplaced quest for "objectivity" and confined in its very conception of literary studies by the narrow intellectual traditions and professional allegiances of the literary academy, it has foreclosed from its own domain the possibility of investigating the dynamics of that mutability and understanding the nature of that diversity.

The type of investigation I have in mind here would not seek to establish normative "criteria," to devise presumptively objective evaluative procedures, or to discover grounds for the "justification" of critical judgments or practices. It would not, in short, be a literary *axiology* or, in effect, the counterpart for evaluative criticism of what a literary hermeneutics offers to be for interpretive criticism. It would seek, rather, to clarify the nature of literary—and, more broadly, aesthetic—value in conjunction with a more general rethinking of the concept of "value"; it would explore the multiple forms and functions of literary evaluation, covert as well as overt, nonverbal as well as verbal, institutional as well as individual; it would account for the features of literary and aesthetic judgments in relation to the multiple social, political, circumstantial, and other constraints and conditions to which they are responsive; it would chronicle "the history of taste" in relation to a more general model of historical cultural dynamics and specific local conditions; and it would devise descriptions and accounts of all the other phenomena and activities involved in literary and aesthetic evaluation in relation to our more general understanding—as it is and as it develops—of human culture and behavior.

The sort of inquiry suggested here (which obviously could not be pursued within the confines of literary study or critical theory as they are presently conceived and demarcated) might be expected to make its accounts internally consistent, externally connectible, and amenable to continuous extension and refinement; for it is thus that the theoretical power and productivity of those accounts would be served and secured.

28

This is not, however, to imagine a monolithic intellectual project that would offer to yield an ultimately comprehensive, unified, and objective account of its subject; for to imagine it thus would, of course, be to repeat, only on a grander scale, elements of the raw positivism and naïve scientism that have been responsible, in part, for both the exile of evaluation and the confinements of modern critical theory. What is desirable, rather, is an inquiry pursued with the recognition that, like any other intellectual enterprise, it would consist, at any given time, of a set of heterogeneous projects; that the conceptual structures and methodological practices adopted in those projects would *themselves* be historically and otherwise contingent, reflecting, among other things, prevailing or currently interesting conceptual structures and methods in related areas of inquiry; that whatever other value the descriptions and accounts produced by any of those projects might and undoubtedly would have (as, for example, indices of twentieth-century thought to future historians), their specific value as descriptions and accounts would be a function of how well they made intelligible the phenomena within their domain to whoever, at whatever time, and from whatever perspective, had an interest in them; and that its pursuit would be shaped by—that is, energized and transformed in response to—those various, historically emergent interests, and its descriptions and accounts variously interpreted and employed accordingly.[24] The present study is designed to suggest a theoretical framework for such an inquiry.

3

Contingencies of Value

Contingency and Interdependence

All value is radically contingent, being neither a fixed attribute, an inherent quality, or an objective property of things but, rather, an effect of multiple, continuously changing, and continuously interacting variables or, to put this another way, the product of the dynamics of a system, specifically an *economic* system. It is readily granted, of course, that it is in relation to such a system that commodities such as gold, bread, and paperback editions of *Moby-Dick* acquire the value indicated by their market prices. It is traditional, however, both in economic and aesthetic theory as well as in informal discourse, to distinguish sharply between the value of an entity in that sense (that is, its *exchange value*) and some other type of value that may be referred to as its *utility* or *use value* or, especially with respect to so-called nonutilitarian objects such as artworks or works of literature, as its *intrinsic value.* Thus, it might be said that whereas the fluctuating price of a particular paperback edition of *Moby-Dick* is a function of such variables as supply and demand, production and distribution costs, the publisher's calculation of corporate profits, and so forth, these factors do not affect the value of *Moby-Dick* as experienced by an individual reader or its intrinsic value "as a work of literature." These distinctions, however, are not as clear-cut as they may appear.

Like its price in the marketplace, the value of an entity to an individual subject is *also* the product of the dynamics of an economic system: specifically, the personal economy constituted by the subject's needs, interests, and resources—biological, psychological, material, experien-

30

tial, and so forth. Like any other economy, moreover, this too is a continuously fluctuating or shifting system, for our individual needs, interests, and resources are themselves functions of our continuously changing states in relation to an environment that may be relatively stable but is never absolutely fixed. The two kinds of economic system described here are, it should be noted, not only analogous but also interactive and interdependent, for part of our environment *is* the market economy and, conversely, the market economy is composed, in part, of the diverse personal economies of individual producers, distributors, consumers, and so forth. At the same time, it must be emphasized that any particular subject's "self"—or that in behalf of which he or she may be said to act with "self-interest"—is also variable, being multiply and differently configurable in terms of different roles, relationships, and, in effect, identities (citizen, parent, woman, property owner, teacher, terrestrial organism, mortal being, etc.), in relation to which different needs and interests acquire priority (and, as may happen, come into conflict) under different conditions.

The traditional discourse of value—including a number of terms I have used here, such as "subject," "object," "needs," "interests," and indeed "value" itself—reflects an arbitrary arresting, segmentation, and hypostasization of the continuous process of our interactions with our environments or what could also be described as the continuous interplay among multiply configurable systems. While it would be difficult to devise (and perhaps impossible to sustain) a truly Heraclitean discourse that did *not* reflect such conceptual operations, we may nevertheless recognize that, insofar as such terms project images of discrete acts, agents and entities, fixed attributes, unidirectional forces, and simple causal and temporal relationships, they obscure the dynamics of value and reinforce dubious concepts of noncontingency: that is, concepts such as "intrinsic," "objective," "absolute," "universal," and "transcendent." It is necessary, therefore, to emphasize a number of other interactive relationships and forms of interdependence that are fragmented by our language and commonly ignored in critical theory and aesthetic axiology.[1]

First, as I have already suggested, a subject's experience of an entity is always a function of his or her personal economy: that is, the specific "existence" of an object or event, its integrity, coherence, and boundaries, the category of entities to which it "belongs," and its specific "features," "qualities," or "properties" are all the variable products of the subject's engagement with his or her environment under a particular

31

set of conditions. Not only is an entity always experienced under more or less different conditions, but the various experiences do not yield a simple cumulative (corrected, improved, deeper, more thorough or complete) knowledge of the entity because they are not additive. Rather, each experience of an entity frames it in a different role and constitutes it as a different configuration, with different "properties" foregrounded and repressed. Moreover, the subject's experiences of an entity are not discrete or, strictly speaking, successive, because recollection and anticipation always overlay perception, and the units of what we call "experience" themselves vary and overlap.

Second, what we speak of as a subject's "needs," "interests," and "purposes" are not only always changing, but they are also not altogether independent of or prior to the entities that satisfy or implement them; that is, entities also produce the needs and interests they satisfy and evoke the purposes they implement. Moreover, because our purposes are continuously transformed and redirected by the objects we produce in the very process of implementing them, and because of the complex interrelations among human needs, technological production, and cultural practices, there is a continuous process of mutual modification between our desires and our universe.[2]

Of particular significance for the value of "works of art" and "literature" is the interactive relation between the *classification* of an entity and the functions it is expected or desired to perform. In perceiving an object or artifact in terms of some category—*as*, for example, "a clock," "a dictionary," "a doorstop," "a curio"—we implicitly isolate and foreground certain of its possible functions and typically refer its value to the extent to which it performs those functions more or less effectively. But the relation between function and classification also operates in reverse: thus, under conditions that produce the "need" for a doorstopping object or an "interest" in Victorian artifacts, certain properties and possible functions of various objects in the neighborhood will be foregrounded and both the classification and value of those objects will follow accordingly. As we commonly put it, one will "realize" the value of the dictionary *as* a doorstop or "appreciate" the value of the clock *as* a curio.[3] (The mutually defining relations among classification, function, and value are nicely exhibited in the *OED*'s definition of "curio" as "an object of art, piece of bric-a-brac, etc. valued as a curiosity," which is, of course, something like—and no less accurate than—defining *clock* as "an object valued as a clock.") It may be relevantly noted here that human beings have evolved as distinctly opportunistic creatures and that our survival, both as individuals and as a species, continues to be enhanced by our ability and inclination to reclassify objects and to "realize" and "appreciate" novel and alternate functions for them—which is also to "misuse" them and to fail to respect their presumed purposes and conventional generic classifications.

The various forms of interdependence emphasized here have considerable bearing on what may be recognized as the economics of literary and aesthetic value. The traditional—idealist, humanist, genteel—tendency to isolate or protect certain aspects of life and culture, among them works of art and literature, from consideration in economic terms has had the effect of mystifying the nature—or, more accurately, the dynamics—of their value. In view of the arbitrariness of the exclusion, it is not surprising that the languages of aesthetics and economics nevertheless tend to drift toward each other and that their segregation must be constantly patrolled.[4] (Thus, an aesthetician deplores a pun on "appreciation" appearing in an article on art investment and warns of the dangers of confusing "the uniqueness of a painting that gives it scarcity value . . . with its unique value as a work of art.")[5] To those for whom terms such as "utility," "effectiveness," and "function" suggest gross pragmatic instrumentality, crass material desires, and the satisfaction of animal needs, a concept such as use value will be seen as irrelevant to or clearly to be distinguished from aesthetic value. There is, however, no good reason to confine the domain of the utilitarian to objects that serve only immediate, specific, and unexalted ends or, for that matter, to assume that the value of artworks has altogether nothing to do with pragmatic instrumentality or animal needs.[6] The recurrent impulse and effort to define aesthetic value by contradistinction to all forms of utility or as the negation of all other nameable sources of interest or forms of value—hedonic, practical, sentimental, ornamental, historical, ideological, and so forth—is, in effect, to define it out of existence; for when all such utilities, interests, and other particular sources of value have been subtracted, nothing remains. Or, to put this in other terms: the "essential value" of an artwork consists of everything from which it is usually distinguished.

To be sure, various candidates have been proposed for a pure, nonutilitarian, interest-free, and, in effect, value-free source of aesthetic value, such as the eliciting of "intrinsically rewarding" intellectual, sensory, or perceptual activities, or Kant's "free play of the cognitive faculties." The question remains, however, whether a strict accounting of any of these seemingly gratuitous activities would not bring us, sooner or later, to their interest, utility, and thus value in some—and perhaps many—senses for those who pursue them.

Three points may be made here. First, in speaking of certain objects and activities as "intrinsically rewarding" or done "for their own sake," what we usually mean is that the rewards involved (a) are not predictable or quantifiable; (b) are likely to be heterogeneous and ongoing rather than specific and terminal; and, in the case of an object (for example, a painting or a child), (c) are produced more or less uniquely by that object as distinct from any other of its kind. Of course, the provision of a variety of ongoing satisfactions is itself a contingent utility, and uniqueness is itself contingent (not everyone would derive irreplaceable satisfaction from that painting or that child). Second, although we may be individually motivated to engage in various ludic, aesthetic, or artistic activities only for the sake of the ongoing pleasure they provide (or other, less readily nameable or specifiable, ongoing satisfactions), our doing so may nevertheless yield a long-term profit in enhanced cognitive development, behavioral flexibility, or other kinds of advantage for survival, and our general tendency to *find* pleasure in such activities may, accordingly, be the product or by-product of our evolutionary development.[7] Third, the occasioning of "intrinsically rewarding" activities (or "experiences") obviously cannot be confined to "works of art" and therefore cannot, without circularity, be said to constitute the defining "aesthetic function" of the objects so labeled.[8] Indeed, since there are no functions performed by artworks that may be specified as generically unique and also no way to distinguish the "rewards" provided by art-related experiences or behavior from those provided by innumerable other kinds of experience and behavior, any distinctions drawn between "aesthetic" and "nonaesthetic" (or "extra-aesthetic") value must be regarded as fundamentally problematic.

It should be noted in passing that, except for allusions to other usages, "art" and "aesthetic" in the present study are equivalent, respectively, to "that which is *called* 'art' in the indicated discourse(s)" and "that which is *related to* that which is called 'art' (etc.)." Their use here is, in short, thoroughly nominalistic. Indeed, the point needs some emphasis in view of the fact that essentialist and circular usages of these terms are key operators in contemporary aesthetic axiology.

"Aesthetic" has, of course, a number of currently viable senses in addition to the nominalistic one just noted. For example, following Baumgarten and early nineteenth-century usage as influenced by Kant, it can also indicate a certain type of cognitive activity and/or sensory experience, specifically the type elicited by artworks either uniquely or among other things. At the same time, it can indicate a certain type of property of any object: specifically, the type of "purely formal" property which, according to Kant's analysis, uniquely elicits the sorts of experiences which, if all else is in order, constitute genuine judgments of taste. A combination or conflation of these three senses issues in the familiar recursive use of the term to name certain types of experience *and* certain types of objects *and* certain types of properties of objects, so that "aesthetic" comes to be roughly equivalent to "relating to certain cognitive/sensory experiences, these being the ones elicited by objects that have certain formal properties, these being the ones that identify objects as artworks, these being the kinds of works that elicit certain cognitive/sensory experiences, these being . . . ," and so forth around again.[9] The academic aesthetician trained to flourish in this sort of circle can spend his or her professional career describing (a) the nature of the "experiences" that are produced by those objects that are readily identifiable as works of art by virtue of their having the properties that elicit such experiences, and (b) the nature of the "properties," unquestionably possessed by what are unquestionably works of art, that elicit the experiences that only artworks can elicit. (This is a parody, but not by much.)

In addition to the circularities thus generated, these academic exercises also perpetuate a thoroughly unproblematized conception of art, which is to say an essentialist definition of the *label* "art." The aesthetician who takes for granted the identity of those objects—"works of art"—that exemplify the possession of "aesthetic properties," or, in an only slightly more sophisticated move, who acknowledges the fact of historical and variable usage only to dismiss its force with an appeal to some "core" of examples "that would be acknowledged as works of art by everyone," thereby effaces both the historicity and cultural specificity of the term "art" and also the institutionally and otherwise contingent variability of the honorific labeling of cultural productions. Since the "core" examples cited will always be drawn from the Western academic canon (typically a handful of classic forms, works, and figures recurrently invoked in just these discourses: for example, sculpture, tragedy, symphony; Homer, Rembrandt, Mozart; *King Lear, Don Giovanni*, and, to indicate that there are modern masterpieces too, *Guernica*), and will also typically be attended by the tacit presumption of canonical audiences experiencing those works under canonical conditions plus the tacit exclusion of noncanonical (that is, non-Western, nonacademic,

35

nonadult, or non-high-culture) *audiences* and noncanonical (for example, folk, tribal, or mass-mediated) *conditions of production and reception*, it is no surprise that "essentially aesthetic experiences" always conform to those typical of the Western or Western-educated consumer of high culture and that "essentially aesthetic properties" and "essential aesthetic value" always turn out to be located in all the old familiar places and masterpieces.

Matters of Taste

Suggestions of the historical or cultural contingency of aesthetic value are commonly countered by evidence of apparent noncontingent value: the endurance, for example, of certain classic canonical works (the invocation of Homer being a topos of the critical tradition) and, if not quite Pope's "gen'ral chorus of mankind," then at least the convergent sentiments of all people of education and discrimination. Certainly any theory of aesthetic value must be able to account for continuity, stability, and apparent consensus as well as for drift, shift, and diversity in matters of taste. The tendency throughout formal aesthetic axiology, however, has been to explain each in a quite different way: specifically, to explain the constancies of value and convergences of taste by the inherent qualities of certain objects and/or some set of presumed human universals, and to explain the variabilities of value and divergences of taste by historical accident, cultural distortion, and the defects and deficiencies of individual subjects.

This *asymmetrical* type of explanation recalls—and is, in intellectual history, of a piece with—the tendency in traditional philosophy of science to explain the credibility of so-called rational or true beliefs (for example, that the earth revolves around the sun) by the fact that they *are* rational or true, and the credibility of other beliefs (for example, that the sun revolves around the earth) by special historical, institutional, social, psychological, or otherwise "external" factors. I appropriate here the characterization of this tendency by two of its critics, Barry Barnes and David Bloor, who offer in opposition to it a postulate for historians and sociologists of science that states, in part, that "the incidence of all beliefs without exception . . . must be accounted for by finding the specific, local causes of their credibility."[10]

The classic development of this account of *taste* is found in Hume's essay "Of the Standard of Taste," where the "catholic and universal beauty" is seen to be the result of the relation which nature has placed between the form and the sentiment . . . We shall be able to ascertain its influence . . . from the durable admiration which attends those works that have survived all the caprices of mode and fashion, all the mistakes of ignorance and envy.

The same Homer who pleased at Athens two thousand years ago, is still admired at Paris and London. All the changes of climate, government, religion and language have not been able to obscure his glory . . .

It appears then, that amidst all the variety and caprice of taste, there are certain general principles of approbation and blame, whose influence a careful eye may trace in all the operations of the mind. Some particular forms or qualities, from the original structure of the internal fabric, are calculated to please, and others to displease; *and if they fail of their effect in any particular instance, it is from some apparent defect or imperfection in the organ.*

Many and frequent are the defects . . . which prevent or weaken the influence of those general principles.[11]

We shall return to this passage in the next chapter, where, together with Kant's *Critique of Judgment,* Hume's essay will be examined in connection with the general structure of axiological argumentation. For the present, we may observe that two linked notions are central to the account of tastes in traditional aesthetic axiology: first, the idea that certain objects or forms please us "naturally" by virtue of certain human universals; and second, the belief that a *norm* and thus "standard" of correct and defective taste can be derived accordingly. This set of notions obliged—or, rather, permitted—Hume, as it did and still does many others, to conclude that, in matters of taste, most people in the world are substandard or deviant. Perhaps, from a certain perspective, they are. But that still leaves us with a very peculiar sort of norm, and perhaps it can be seen otherwise.

Before turning to that alternative conceptualization, we may recall here I. A. Richards's remarkable explanation of how the very fact that someone is capable of taking pleasure in a sonnet by Ella Wheeler Wilcox is evidence of that person's inability to survive in a complex environment and therefore of his or her biological unfitness (and note as well the general observations on popular culture and the mass media to which Richards is led):

Those who have adequate impulses . . . are not appeased [by the sonnet's conclusion]. Only for those who make certain conventional, stereotyped maladjustments instead does the magic work.

. . . At present bad literature, bad art, the cinema [*sic*], etc. are an

37

influence of the first importance in fixing immature and actually inapplicable attitudes toward most things . . .

. . . The strongest objection to, let us say, the sonnet we have quoted is that a person who enjoys it, through the very organization of his responses which enables him to enjoy it, is debarred from appreciating many things which, if he could appreciate them, he would prefer.[12]

We can readily recognize the familiar moves of axiologic logic in Richards's proposal, set forth here with egregious circularity, that the Other's enjoyment of his bad meat is possible only because of something suboptimal about his physiology, some problem in the organization of his responses that keeps him from "appreciating" certain "things"— really or objectively good meat, presumably, though Richards avoids saying so explicitly—that he would prefer if his responses were properly organized. Whether the debility is attributed to defective "organs" or defective "organization," to innate deficiencies or the "influence" of popular culture and the mass media, the privileging of the self through the pathologizing of the Other remains the key move and defining objective of axiology.

An alternative view of these matters is, however, possible. Specifically, the array of individual preferences that Hume and Richards regarded as reflecting the proper operation of healthy organs of taste and also the individual preferences that they interpreted as so many instances of personal pathology could *both* be seen as functions of interactions among the following variables:

a) various psychophysiological structures, mechanisms, and tendencies that are *relatively* uniform among human beings;

b) other psychophysiological structures, mechanisms, and tendencies that vary quite widely among individuals;

c) such more or less obvious particulars of personal identity and history as gender, age, the particular physical and social environment into which one was born, ethnic and national culture, formal and informal education, and so forth;

d) other more subtle, volatile, and, accordingly, less readily specifiable or measurable particulars of personal identity, including individual "temperament," "mood" on any given occasion, and current "interests"—each of which, it might be noted, is itself a product of the interactions of the other variables listed here; and, finally,

e) innumerable social, cultural, institutional, and contextual variables operating at every level of analysis, from broad though culturally specific ways of classifying objects to the most subtle and minute contextually specific circumstances of individual encounters with them.

38

The traditional axiological tendency, noted above, to provide two different kinds of explanation for human preferences—one for canonical tastes and the stability of preferences (convergence on an objective norm, the intrinsic value of certain objects) and another for deviant tastes and the mutability of preferences (defective organs, mists, mistakes, the "whirligig of fashion," and so forth)—would be replaced by a single account that explained all these phenomena symmetrically. That is, in accord with such an account, evaluative divergences and the exhibition of so-called bad taste would be seen as the product of the *same* dynamics—the playing out of the same *kinds* of variables, but with different specific values—that produce evaluative convergences and the exhibition of so-called good taste. These points can be elaborated further with regard to human preferences generally—that is, "tastes" for anything, from artworks to lifestyles and from types of food to types of explanation or even types of logic.

Within a particular community, the tastes and preferences of subjects will sometimes be conspicuously *divergent* or indeed idiosyncratic; that is, members of the community will tend to find more satisfaction of a certain kind (aesthetic, erotic, consummatory, or whatever) in quite *different* items from some array of comparable items and will also tend to select among them accordingly. This occurs when and to the extent that the satisfactions in question are themselves functions of types of needs, interests, and resources that vary individually along a relatively *wide* spectrum, are relatively *resistant*—if not altogether intractable—to cultural channeling, and are especially *responsive* to differences of circumstantial context. Conversely, their tastes and preferences will tend to be *convergent*—that is, they will tend to find satisfactions of certain kinds in the *same* items or types of items and to select them accordingly—to the extent that the satisfactions in question are functions of types of needs, interests, and resources that vary individually within a relatively *narrow* spectrum, are relatively *tractable* to cultural channeling, and remain fairly *stable* under a variety of conditions.

Insofar as satisfactions (again, "aesthetic" or any other: erotic, for example) with regard to some array of objects are functions of needs, interests, and resources of the *first* kind, individual preferences for those objects will appear "subjective," "eccentric," "stubborn," and "capricious." Insofar as they are functions of the *second*, preferences will seem so obvious, "natural," and "rational" as not to appear to be matters of taste at all. Indeed, it is precisely under these latter conditions that the value of particular objects will appear to be inherent, that distinctions or gradations of value among them will appear to reduce to differences in

39

the "properties" or "qualities" of the objects themselves, and that explicit judgments of their value will appear to be—and for many, but not all, purposes will be—"objective." In short, here as elsewhere, *a co-incidence of contingencies among individual subjects who interact as members of some community will operate for them as noncontingency and be interpreted by them accordingly.*

Because we are speaking here not of two opposed sets of discrete determinants (or "contraints" or "forces") but of the possibility of widely differing specifications for a large number of complexly interacting *variables,* we may expect to find a continuous exhibition of every degree of divergence and convergence among the subjects in a particular community over the course of its history, depending in each instance on the extent of the disparity and uniformity of each of the relevant contingencies and on the strength of various social practices and cultural institutions that control the exhibition of extreme "deviance."[13] It may be noted in passing that the normative mechanisms within a community that suppress divergence—and thereby obscure as well as deny the contingency of value—will always have, as their counterpart, a *counter*mechanism that permits a recognition of that contingency and a more or less genial acknowledgment of the inevitability of divergence: hence the ineradicability, in spite of the efforts of establishment axiology, of what might be called folk-relativism: *"Chacun a son goût,"* *"De gustibus . . . ,"* "One man's meat is another's poison," and so forth.

As the preceding account suggests, the prevailing structure of tastes and preferences within some community (and consequent illusion of a consensus based on objective value) will always be implicitly threatened or directly challenged by the divergent tastes and preferences of some subjects within the community (for example, those not yet adequately acculturated, such as the young, and others with "uncultivated" tastes, such as provincials and social upstarts), as well as by most subjects who are outside it or, more significantly, on its periphery and who thus have occasion to interact with its members (for example, exotic visitors, immigrants, colonials, and members of various minority or marginalized groups). Consequently, institutions of evaluative authority will be called upon repeatedly to devise arguments and procedures that validate the community's established tastes and preferences, thereby warding off barbarism and the constant apparition of an imminent collapse of standards and also justifying the exercise of their own normative authority.

40

Both informally, as in the drawingrooms of men of cultivation and discrimination or in the classrooms of the literary academy, and formally, as in Hume's essay and throughout the central tradition of Western critical theory, that validation typically takes the twofold form of, first, *privileging absolutely*—that is, "standard"-izing, making a standard out of—not simply the preferences of the members of the group but, more significantly and also more powerfully because more invisibly, *the particular contingencies that govern their preferences*; and, second but simultaneously, *discounting or pathologizing* not merely other people's tastes but, again more significantly and effectively, *all other contingencies.*

Thus, it is assumed or maintained:

a) that the particular *functions* that the established members of the group expect and desire the class of objects in question (for example, "works of art" or "literature") to perform are their proper or intrinsic functions, all other expected, desired, or emergent functions being inappropriate, irrelevant, and extrinsic—abuses of the true nature of those objects or violations of their authorially intended or generically intrinsic purposes;

b) that the particular *conditions* (circumstantial, technological, institutional, and so forth) under which the members of the group typically interact with those objects are suitable, standard, or necessary-for-their-proper-appreciation, all other conditions being exceptional, peculiar, irregular, unsuitable, or substandard; and, most significantly of course,

c) that the particular *subjects* who constitute the established and authorized members of the group are of sound mind and body, duly trained and informed, and generally competent, all other subjects being defective, deficient, or deprived: suffering from crudenesses of sensibility, diseases and distortions of perception, weaknesses of character, impoverishment of background-and-education, cultural or historical biases, ideological or personal prejudices and/or undeveloped, corrupted, or jaded tastes.

A few points deserve special notice here. The first is that communities (and drawingrooms) come in all sizes and that, insofar as the provincials, colonials, and other marginalized groups mentioned above—including the young—constitute social communities in themselves, they also tend to have prevailing structures of tastes and may be expected to control them in much the same ways as do more obviously "establishment" groups. ("Folk-relativism" is neither confined to the folk nor always exhibited by them.)

Second, with regard to (c) above, we may recall the familiar

41

specifications of the "ideal" critic as one who, in addition to possessing various exemplary natural endowments and cultural competencies, has, through exacting feats of self-liberation, freed himself of all forms of particularity and individuality, all special interests (or, as in Kant, all interests whatsoever), and thus of all bias—which is to say, one who is "free" of everything in relation to which any experience or judgment of value occurs. In these respects, it may be added, the ideal critic of aesthetic axiology is the exact counterpart of the "ideal reader" of literary hermeneutics.

Finally, we may note that the privileging of a particular set of *functions* for artworks or works of literature (cf. (a), above) is often itself justified on the ground that the performance of such functions serves some higher individual, social, or transcendent good, such as the psychic health of the reader, the brotherhood of mankind, the glorification of God, the project of human emancipation, or the survival of Western civilization. Any selection from among these alternate—and clearly to some extent mutually exclusive—higher goods, however, would itself require justification in terms of some yet *higher* good, and there is no absolute stopping point for this theoretically infinite regress of judgments and justifications. This is not to say that certain functions of artworks do not serve higher (or at least more general, comprehensive, or longer-range) goods better than others. It is to say, however, that our selection among higher goods, like our selection among any array of goods, will always be contingent.[14]

Processes of Evaluation

It follows from the conception of value outlined above that evaluations are not discrete acts or episodes punctuating experience but indistinguishable from the very processes of acting and experiencing themselves. In other words, for a responsive creature, to exist is to evaluate. We are always, so to speak, calculating how things "figure" for us— always pricing them, so to speak, in relation to the total economy of our personal universe.[15] Throughout our lives, we perform a continuous succession of what are, in effect, rapid-fire cost-benefit analyses, estimating the probable "worthwhileness" of alternate courses of action in relation to our always limited resources of time and energy, assessing, reassessing, and classifying entities with respect to their probable capacity to satisfy our current needs and desires, and to serve our emergent interests and long-range plans and purposes. We tend to become most conscious of our own evaluative behavior when the need to select among an array of alternate "goods" and/or to resolve an internal "contest of sentiments"[16] moves us to specifically verbal or other symbolic forms of accounting: thus we draw up our lists of pros and cons, lose sleep, and bore our friends by overtly rehearsing our options, estimating the risks and probable outcomes of various actions, and so forth. Most of these "calculations," however, are performed intuitively and inarticulately, and many of them are so recurrent that the habitual arithmetic becomes part of our personality and comprises the very style of our being and behavior, forming what we may call our principles or tastes— and what others may call our biases and prejudices.

I have been speaking up to this point of the evaluations we make for ourselves. We do not, however, move about in a raw universe. Not only are the objects we encounter always to some extent pre-interpreted and pre-classified for us by our particular cultures and languages; they are also pre-evaluated, bearing the marks and signs of their prior valuings and evaluations by our fellow creatures. Indeed, pre-classification is itself a form of pre-evaluation, for the labels or category names under which we encounter objects not only, as I suggested earlier, foreground certain of their possible functions, but also operate as signs—in effect, as culturally certified endorsements—of their more or less effective performance of those functions.

Like all other objects, works of art and literature bear the marks of their own evaluational history, signs of value that acquire their force by virtue of various social and cultural practices and, in this case, certain highly specialized and elaborated institutions. The labels "art" and "literature" are, of course, commonly signs of membership in distinctly honorific categories. The particular functions that may be endorsed by these labels, however, are, unlike those of "doorstops" and "clocks," neither narrowly confined nor readily specifiable but, on the contrary, exceptionally heterogeneous, mutable, and elusive. To the extent— always limited—that the relation between these labels and a particular set of expected and desired functions is stabilized within a community, it is largely through the normative activities of various institutions: most significantly, the literary and aesthetic academy which, among other things, develops pedagogic and other acculturative mechanisms directed at maintaining at least (and, commonly, at most) a *sub*population of the community whose members "appreciate the value" of works of art and literature "as such." That is, by providing them with "necessary backgrounds," teaching them "appropriate skills," "cultivating their interests," and generally "developing their tastes," the academy produces generation after generation of subjects for whom the objects and texts thus labeled do indeed perform the functions thus privileged, thereby ensuring the continuity of mutually defining canonical works, canonical functions, and canonical audiences.[17]

Artistic Creation as a Paradigm of Evaluative Activity

It will be instructive at this point (and also for later analysis) to consider the very beginning of a work's valuational history—that is, its initial evaluation by the artist (here, the author)—for it is not only a prefiguration of all the subsequent acts of evaluation of which the work will become the subject but is also a model or paradigm of all evaluative activity generally. I refer here not merely to that ultimate gesture of authorial judgment that must exhibit itself negatively—that is, in the author's either letting the work stand or ripping it up—but to the thousand individual acts of approval and rejection, preference and assessment, trial and revision, that constitute the entire process of literary composition. The work we receive is not so much the achieved consummation of that process as its enforced abandonment: "abandonment" not because the author's techniques are inadequate to her goals, but because the goals themselves are inevitably multiple, mixed, mutually competing and thus mutually constraining, and also because they are inevitably unstable, changing their nature and relative potency and priority during the very course of composition. The completed work is thus always, in a sense, a temporary truce among contending forces, achieved at the point of exhaustion, that is, the literal depletion of the author's current resources or, given the most fundamental principle of the economics of existence, at the point when she simply has something else—more worthwhile—to do: when, in other words, the time and energy she would have to give to further tinkering, testing, and adjustment are no longer compensated for by an adequately rewarding sense of continuing interest in the process or increased satisfaction in the product.

It is for comparable reasons that we, as readers of the work, will later let our own experience of it stand: not because we have "fully appreciated" the work, not because we have exhausted all its possible sources of interest and hence of value, but because we, too, ultimately have something else—more worthwhile—to do. The reader's experience of the work is pre-figured—that is, both calculated and pre-enacted—by the author in other ways as well: for, in selecting this word, adjusting that turn of phrase, preferring this rhyme to that, she is all the while testing the local and global effectiveness of each decision by impersonating in advance her various presumptive audiences, who thereby themselves participate in shaping the work they will later read. Every literary work—and, more generally, artwork—is thus the product of a complex evaluative feedback loop that embraces not only the ever-shifting economy of the artist's own interests and resources as they evolve during and in reaction to the process of composition, but also all the shifting economies of her assumed and imagined audiences, including those who do not yet exist but whose emergent interests, variable conditions of encounter, and rival sources of gratification she will attempt to predict—or will intuitively surmise—and to which, among other things, her own sense of the fittingness of each decision will be responsive.[18]

The inevitable evaluative and prefigurative aspects of literary composition, or of what is commonly referred to as "the creative process" in relation specifically to aesthetic/cultural production, mark significant continuities not only between "creative" and "critical" activities but also between "artistic" and "scientific" production, and thereby make quite problematic the traditional effort to maintain clear distinctions among any of these. I shall return in Chapter 5 to the relation between the simultaneously critical and productive processes of artistic composition and some characteristic aspects of scientific activity.[19]

The description, above, of the evaluative processes of the author and, analogously, the individual reader, may be extended even further. For it also describes all the other diverse forms of evaluation by which the work will be subsequently marked and its value reproduced and transmitted: that is, the innumerable implicit acts of evaluation performed by those who, as may happen, publish the work, purchase, preserve, display, quote, cite, translate, perform, allude to, and imitate it; the more explicit but casual judgments made, debated, and negotiated in informal contexts by readers and by all those others in whose personal economies the work, in some way, "figures"; and the highly specialized institutionalized forms of evaluation exhibited in the more or less professional activities of scholars, teachers, and academic or journalistic critics: not only their full-dress reviews and explicit rank-orderings, evaluations, and revaluations, but also such activities as the awarding of literary prizes, the commissioning and publishing of articles about certain works, the compiling of anthologies, the writing of introductions, the construction of department curricula, and the drawing up of class reading lists. All these forms of evaluation, whether overt or covert, verbal or inarticulate, and whether performed by the common reader, professional reviewer, big-time bookseller, or small-town librarian, have functions and effects that are significant in the production and maintenance or destruction of literary value, both reflecting and contributing to the various economies in relation to which a work acquires value. And each of the evaluative acts mentioned, like those of the author and the individual reader, represents a set of individual economic decisions, an adjudication among competing claims for limited resources of time, space, energy, attention—or, of course, money—and also, insofar as the evaluation is a socially responsive act or part of a social transaction, a set of surmises, assumptions, or predictions regarding the personal economies of other people.

Although it is important to recognize that the evaluation of texts is not confined to the formal critical judgments issued within the rooms of the literary academy or upon the pages of its associated publications, the activities of the academy certainly figure significantly in the production of literary value. For example, the repeated inclusion of a particular work in literary anthologies not only promotes the value of that work but goes some distance toward creating its value, as does also its repeated appearance on reading lists or its frequent citation or quotation by professors, scholars, and academic critics. For, as noted in Chapter 1, all these institutional acts have the effect, at the least, of drawing the work into the orbit of attention of a population of potential readers; and, by making it more accessible to the interests of those readers while at the same time shaping and supplying the very interests in relation to which they will experience the work, they make it more likely both that the work will be experienced at all and also that it will be experienced as valuable.

The converse side to this process is well known. Those who are in positions to edit anthologies and prepare reading lists are obviously those who occupy positions of some cultural power; and their acts of evaluation—represented in what they exclude as well as in what they include—constitute not merely recommendations of value, but, for the reasons just mentioned, also determinants of value. Moreover, since they will usually exclude not only what they take to be inferior literature but also what they take to be nonliterary, subliterary, or paraliterary, their selections not only imply certain "criteria" of literary value, which may in fact be made explicit, but, more significantly, they produce and maintain certain definitions of "literature" and, thereby, certain assumptions about the desired and expected functions of the texts so classified and about the interests of their appropriate audiences, all of which are usually not explicit and, for that reason, less likely to be questioned, challenged, or even noticed. Thus the privileging power of evaluative authority may be very great, even when it is manifested inarticulately.[20] The academic activities described here, however, are only a small part of the complex process of literary canonization.

The Dynamics of Endurance

When we consider the cultural re-production of value on a larger time-scale, the model of evaluative dynamics outlined above suggests that both (a) the "survival" or "endurance" of a text and, it may be, (b) its achievement of high canonical status not only as a "work of literature" but as a "classic" are the product neither of the objectively (in the Marxist sense) conspiratorial force of establishment institutions nor of the continuous appreciation of the timeless virtues of a fixed object by succeeding generations of isolated readers but, rather, of a series of continuous interactions among a variably constituted object, emergent conditions, and mechanisms of cultural selection and transmission. These interactions are, in certain respects, analogous to those by virtue of which biological species evolve and survive and also analogous to those through which artistic choices evolve and are found "fit" or fitting by the individual artist. The operation of these cultural-historical dynamics may be briefly indicated here in quite general terms.

At a given time and under the contemporary conditions of available materials and technology or techniques, a particular object—let us say a verbal artifact or text—may perform certain desired/able[21] functions quite well for some set of subjects. It will do so by virtue of certain of its "properties" as they have been specifically constituted—framed, foregrounded, and configured—by those subjects under those conditions and in accord with their particular needs, interests, and resources—and also perhaps largely as pre-figured by the artist who, as described earlier, in the very process of producing the work and continuously evaluating its fitness and adjusting it accordingly, will have multiply and variably constituted it.

47

Two related points need emphasis here. One is that the current value of a work—that is, its effectiveness in performing desired/able functions for some set of subjects—is by no means independent of *authorial* design, labor, and skill. To be sure, the artist does not have absolute control over that value, nor can its dimensions be simply equated with the dimensions of his artistic skill or genius. But the common anxiety that attention to the cultural determinants of aesthetic value makes the artist or artistic labor *irrelevant* is simply unfounded. The second point is that what may be spoken of as the "properties" of a work—its "structure," "features," "qualities," and of course its "meanings"—are not fixed, given, or inherent in the work "itself" but are at every point the variable products of particular *subjects'* interactions with it. Thus, it is never "the *same* Homer."[22] This is not to deny that some aspect, or perhaps many aspects, of a work may be constituted in similar ways by numerous different subjects, *among whom we may include the author:* to the extent that this duplication occurs, however, it will be because the subjects who do the constituting are themselves similar, not only or simply in being human creatures (and thereby, as it is commonly supposed, "sharing an underlying humanity" and so on) but in occupying a particular universe that may be, for them, in many respects recurrent or relatively continuous and stable, and/or in inheriting from one another, through mechanisms of cultural transmission, certain ways of interacting with texts and "works of literature."

To continue, however, the account of the cultural-historical dynamics of endurance. An object or artifact that performs certain desired/able functions particularly well at a given time for some community of subjects, being perhaps not only "fit" but exemplary—that is, "the best of its kind"—under those conditions, will have an immediate survival advantage; for, relative to (or in competition with) other comparable objects or artifacts available at that time, it will not only be better protected from physical deterioration but will also be more frequently used or widely exhibited and, if it is a text or verbal artifact, more frequently read or recited, copied or reprinted, translated, imitated, cited, commented upon, and so forth—in short, culturally re-produced—and thus will be more readily available to perform those or other functions for other subjects at a subsequent time.

Two possible trajectories ensue:

1. If, on the one hand, under the changing and emergent conditions of that subsequent time, the functions for which the text was earlier valued are no longer desired/able or if, in competition with comparable

48

works (including, now, those newly produced with newly available materials and techniques), it no longer performs those original functions particularly well, it will, accordingly, be less well maintained and less frequently cited, recited, etc., so that its visibility as well as interest will fade and it will survive, if at all, simply as a physical relic. It may, of course, be subsequently valued specifically *as* a relic (for its archeological or "historical" interest), in which case it *will* be performing desired/able functions and pursue the trajectory described below. It may also be subsequently "rediscovered" as an "unjustly neglected masterpiece," either when the functions it had originally performed are again desired/able or, what is more likely, when different of its properties and possible functions become foregrounded by a new set of subjects with emergent interests and purposes.

2. If, on the other hand, under changing conditions and in competition with newly produced and other re-produced works, it continues to perform *some* desired/able functions particularly well, even if not the same ones for which it was initially valued (and, accordingly, by virtue of *other* newly foregrounded or differently framed or configured properties—including, once again, emergent "meanings"), it will continue to be cited and recited, continue to be visible and available to succeeding generations of subjects, and thus continue to be culturally re-produced. A work that has in this way survived for some time can always move into a trajectory of extinction through the sudden emergence or gradual conjunction of unfavorable conditions of the kind described above. There are, however, a number of reasons why, once it has achieved canonical status, it will be more secure from that risk.

For one thing, when the value of a work is seen as unquestionable, those of its features that would, in a noncanonical work, be found alienating—for example, technically crude, philosophically naïve, or narrowly topical—will be glozed over or backgrounded. In particular, features that conflict intolerably with the interests and ideologies of subsequent subjects (and, in the West, with those generally benign "humanistic" values for which canonical works are commonly celebrated)—for example, incidents or sentiments of brutality, bigotry, and racial, sexual, or national chauvinism—will be repressed or rationalized, and there will be a tendency among humanistic scholars and academic critics to "save the text" by transferring the locus of its interest to more formal or structural features and/or by allegorizing its potentially alienating ideology to some more general ("universal") level where it becomes more tolerable and also more readily interpretable in

49

terms of contemporary ideologies. Thus we make texts timeless by suppressing their temporality. (It may be added that to those scholars and critics for whom those features are not only palatable but for whom the value of the canonical works consists precisely in their "embodying" and "preserving" such "traditional values," the transfer of the locus of value to formal properties will be seen as a descent into formalism and "aestheticism," and the tendency to allegorize it too generally or to interpret it too readily in terms of "modern values" will be seen not as saving the text but as betraying it.)

Second, in addition to whatever various and perhaps continuously differing functions a work performs for succeeding generations of individual subjects, it will also begin to perform certain characteristic cultural functions by virtue of the very fact that it *has* endured—that is, the functions of a canonical work as such—and be valued and preserved accordingly: as a witness to lost innocence, former glory, and/or apparently persistent communal interests and "values" and thus a banner of communal identity; as a reservoir of images, archetypes, and topoi—characters and episodes, passages and verbal tags—repeatedly invoked and recurrently applied to new situations and circumstances; and as a stylistic and generic exemplar that will energize the production of subsequent works and texts (upon which the latter will be modeled and by which, as a normative "touchstone," they will be measured). In these ways, the canonical work begins increasingly not merely to *survive within* but to *shape and create* the culture in which its value is produced and transmitted and, for that very reason, to perpetuate the conditions of its own flourishing. Nothing endures like endurance.

To the extent that we develop within and are formed by a culture that is itself constituted in part *by* canonical texts, it is not surprising that those texts seem, as Hans-Georg Gadamer puts it, to "speak" to us "directly" and even "specially": "The classical is what is preserved precisely because it signifies and interprets itself; [that is,] that which speaks in such a way that it is not a statement about what is past, as mere testimony to something that needs to be interpreted, but says something to the present as if it were said specially to us . . . This is just what the word 'classical' means, that the duration of the power of a work to speak directly is fundamentally unlimited."[23] It is hardly, however, as Gadamer implies here, because such texts are uniquely self-mediated or unmediated and hence not needful of interpretation but, rather, because they have already been so thoroughly mediated—evaluated as well as interpreted—*for* us by the very culture and cultural institutions through which they have been preserved and by which we ourselves have been formed.

What is commonly referred to as "the test of time" (Gadamer, for example, characterizes "the classical" as "a notable mode of 'being historical,' that historical process of preservation that through the constant proving of itself sets before us something that is true")[24] is not, as the figure implies, an impersonal and impartial mechanism; for the cultural institutions through which it operates (schools, libraries, theaters, museums, publishing and printing houses, editorial boards, prize-awarding commissions, state censors, and so forth) are, of course, all managed by *persons* (who, by definition, are those with cultural power and commonly other forms of power as well); and, since the texts that are selected and preserved by "time" will always tend to be those which "fit" (and, indeed, have often been *designed* to fit) *their* characteristic needs, interests, resources, and purposes, that testing mechanism has its own built-in partialities accumulated in and thus *intensified* by time. For example, the characteristic resources of the culturally dominant members of a community include access to specific training and the opportunity and occasion to develop not only competence in a large number of cultural codes but also a large number of diverse (or "cosmopolitan") interests. The works that are differentially reproduced, therefore, will tend to be those that gratify the exercise of such competencies and engage interests of that kind: specifically, works that are structurally complex and, in the technical sense, information-rich—and which, by virtue of those qualities, may be especially amenable to multiple reconfiguration, more likely to enter into relation with the emergent interests of various subjects, and thus more readily adaptable to emergent conditions. Also, as is often remarked, since those with cultural power tend to be members of socially, economically, and politically established classes (or to serve them and identify their own interests with theirs), the texts that survive will tend to be those that appear to reflect and reinforce establishment ideologies. However much canonical works may be seen to "question" secular vanities such as wealth, social position, and political power, "remind" their readers of more elevated values and virtues, and oblige them to "confront" such hard truths and harsh realities as their own mortality and the hidden griefs of obscure people, they would not be found to please long and well if they were seen *radically* to undercut establishment interests or *effectively* to subvert the ideologies that support them. (Construing them to the latter ends, of course, is one of the characteristic ways in which those with anti-

establishment interests participate in the cultural re-production of ca-nonical texts and thus in their endurance as well.)

Two final points should be added here. First, it should be noted that "structural complexity" and "information-richness" are, of course, subject-relative as "qualities" and also experientially subject-variable. Since we differ individually in our tolerance for complexity in various sensory/perceptual modalities and also in our ability to process informa-tion in different codes, what is interestingly complex and engagingly information-rich to one subject may be intolerably chaotic to another and slickly academic to yet a third. Moreover, these tolerances and competences are themselves the complex and variable products of cul-turally specific conditions. For these reasons, and *pace* the more naïvely ambitious claims of "empirical aesthetics," such features cannot operate as "objective" measures of aesthetic value.[25]

Second, it is clear that the needs, interests, and purposes of culturally and otherwise dominant members of a community do not exclusively or totally determine which works survive. The antiquity and longevity of domestic proverbs, popular tales, children's verbal games, and the entire phenomenon of what we call "folklore," which occurs through the same or corresponding mechanisms of cultural selection and re-production as those described above specifically for "texts," demonstrate that the "en-durance" of a verbal artifact (if not its achievement of *academic* canonical status as a "work of literature"—many folkloric works do, however, perform all the functions described above as characteristic of canonical works *as such*) may be more or less independent of institutions con-trolled by those with political power. Moreover, the interests and pur-poses of the latter must always operate in interaction with non- or antiestablishment interests and purposes as well as with various other contingencies and "accidents of time" over which they have limited, if any, control, from the burning of libraries to political and social revolu-tion, religious iconoclasms, and shifts of dominance among entire lan-guages and cultures.

As the preceding discussion suggests, the value of a literary work is continuously produced and re-produced by the very acts of implicit and explicit evaluation that are frequently invoked as "reflecting" its value and therefore as being evidence of it. In other words, what are com-monly taken to be the *signs* of literary value are, in effect, its *springs*. The endurance of a classic canonical author such as Homer, then, owes not to the alleged transcultural or universal value of his works but, on the contrary, to the continuity of their circulation in a particular culture. Repeatedly cited and recited, translated, taught and imitated, and thoroughly enmeshed in the network of intertextuality that continuously *constitutes* the high culture of the orthodoxly educated population of the West (and the Western-educated population of the rest of the world), that highly variable entity we refer to as "Homer" recurrently enters our experience in relation to a large number and variety of our interests and thus can perform a large number of various functions for us and obviously has performed them for many of us over a good bit of the history of our culture. It is well to recall, however, that there are many people in the world who are not—or are not yet, or choose not to be—among the orthodoxly educated population of the West: people who do not encounter Western classics at all or who encounter them under cultural and institutional conditions very different from those of American and European college professors and their students. The fact that Homer, Dante, and Shakespeare do not figure significantly in the personal economies of these people, do not perform individual or social functions that gratify their interests, *do not have value for them,* might properly be taken as qualifying the claims of transcendent universal value made for such works. As we know, however, it is routinely taken instead as evidence or confirmation of the cultural deficiency—or, more piously, "deprivation"—of such people. The fact that other verbal artifacts (not necessarily "works of literature" or even "texts") and other objects and events (not necessarily "works of art" or even artifacts) have performed and do perform for them the various functions that Homer, Dante, and Shakespeare perform for us and, moreover, that the possibility of performing the totality of such functions is always distributed over the totality of texts, artifacts, objects, and events—a possibility continuously realized and thus a value continuously "appreciated"—commonly cannot be grasped or acknowledged by the custodians of the Western canon.

4

Axiologic Logic

No illusion is more powerful than that of the inevitability and propriety of one's own beliefs and judgments. The conviction of the necessity of one's convictions survives the most strenuous opposition and extensive contradiction. Indeed, it feeds off them: self-privileging operates not merely as a self-sustaining mechanism but as a productive one, generating new perceptual and conceptual articulations—new beliefs, descriptions, interpretations, judgments, and justifications—even from "evidence" and "arguments" to the contrary. Since the self, even as it is transformed by its interactions with the world, also transforms how that world seems to itself, its system of self-securing is not thereby unhinged nor is it "corrected" by cosmopolitanism. Rather, in enlarging its view "from China to Peru," it may become all the more imperialistic, seeing in every horizon of difference new peripheries of its own centrality, new pathologies through which its own normality may be defined and must be asserted.

The project of axiology—that is, the justification of the claim of certain norms, standards, and judgments to objective validity, which is to say the demonstration of the noncontingency of the contingent—must, by the definition of it just given, fail. And, in a sense, it always does fail. That is, all axiological arguments, no matter what their epistemological tradition or explicit logical method, whether empiricist or rationalist, positivist or phenomenological, and also no matter what the domain—aesthetic, cognitive, or moral—of the judgments and standards at issue, enact a characteristic array of ultimately self-canceling moves. Nevertheless, the axiological account of the phenomena of human preferences

54

has been and remains the dominant one in Western thought. The structure of argumentation in the two classic axiologies of Western critical theory, Hume's essay "Of the Standard of Taste" and Kant's *Critique of Judgment*, will be examined here, as will also the persistence, dominance, and indeed historical success of the logic they exemplify.

Hume's Natural Standard

Hume's essay opens with what had already become, and remains, the preferred gambit of axiological argumentation, namely an urbane—and here, pointedly cosmopolitan—acknowledgment of the diversity of individual judgments:

> The great variety of Taste, as well as of opinion, which prevails in the world, is too obvious not to have fallen under every one's observation . . . Those who can enlarge their view to contemplate distant nations and remote ages, are still more surprised at the great inconsistence and contrariety. We are apt to call *barbarous* whatever departs widely from our own taste and apprehension; but soon find the epithet of reproach retorted upon us. And the highest arrogance and self-conceit is at last startled, on observing an equal assurance on all sides, and scruples, amidst such a contest of sentiment, to pronounce positively in its own favor.[1]

We see already, however, in the very terms of the move, the shadow of what will come, as "variety" becomes "contest," a zero-sum game with winners and losers. For it is, of course, precisely that "scruple" that must be removed and that "arrogance and conceit" that must be justified.

Hume's next move is to grant even more expansively the cultural diversity of judgments. Indeed, he observes that "from the very nature of language" apparent agreement may cover disagreement, and illustrates the point as follows:

> The admirers and followers of the Alcoran [i.e., the Koran] insist on the excellent moral precepts interspersed throughout that wild and absurd performance. But it is to be supposed, that the Arabic words, which correspond to the English, equity, justice, temperance, meekness, charity, were such as . . . must always be taken in a good sense . . . But would we know, whether the pretended prophet had really attained a just sentiment of morals, let us attend to his narration, and we shall soon find, that he bestows praise on such instances of treachery, inhumanity, cruelty, revenge, bigotry, as are utterly incompatible with civilized society. (*ST*, p. 5)

55

Having before us an example of sentiments "utterly incompatible with civilized society," we are prepared for the pivotal turn: "It is natural for us to seek a *Standard of Taste*; a rule by which the various sentiments of men may be reconciled; at least a decision afforded confirming one sentiment, and condemning another" (*ST*, p. 5). What makes that search *natural* is a question that remains unanswered in the essay, as is also the question of whose interests are served by either a reconciliation of divergent sentiments of taste or a decision confirming one sentiment and condemning another. One answer—but itself problematic—is suggested by the analogies, recurrent in Hume and elsewhere in the critical tradition, between the exercise of judgment in matters of taste and the use of instruments of measurement (clocks, watches, scales, yardsticks) in the pursuit of such affairs as trade, navigation, engineering, and property settlements. The analogy appeals to our recognition that, in the latter affairs, where disruptions and confusions would result from divergent units, instruments, or procedures of measurement, a standard that regularizes or "reconciles" them benefits all parties concerned. For such purposes, it is certainly advantageous (and in that sense "natural") for those affected to seek a standard, and they commonly find it by *establishing* it: for example, by selecting and arbitrarily privileging a unit identified with some commonly accessible and/or relatively durable reference point (such as the meridian at Greenwich or a metal rod deposited in the National Bureau of Standards), with respect to which measurements are conventionally (and only in the relevant community, of course) determined as "correct."

When the analogy is thus drawn out, however, the inadequacy of the answer is evident, for it not only reminds us of the arbitrariness (in the sense of conventionality or un-"naturalness") of other standards and norms, but it leaves us with the question of what communal good is served by establishing a standard of *taste*. A different sort of answer to the initial question is implied in the second part of Hume's observation and emerges with increasing force as the essay unfolds: for what appears to be perhaps even more desirable than "a rule by which . . . sentiments . . . may be reconciled" is one that affords "a decision . . . confirming one sentiment and condemning another," which is a different matter. For in the latter case, what is implemented by the standard is not—or at least not self-evidently—a general interest or communal goal but the evaluative authority of some members of the community over others.

The latter point is important and will receive further discussion below. I continue here, however, to follow Hume's argument. The search for the standard of taste is represented as not only natural and in the service of peace, justice, and convenience, but also as heroic, for it must do battle with despair and impotence, that is, axiological skepticism: "a species of philosophy, which cuts off all hopes of success in such an attempt, and represents the impossibility of ever attaining any standard of taste" (*ST*, p. 6). The skeptic's argument, as Hume presents it, is as follows: whereas in questions of empirical knowledge there is an external standard of correctness, namely conformability to "real matter of fact," in questions of taste "sentiment has a reference to nothing beyond itself, and is always real, wherever a man is conscious of it" (ibid.). Therefore, the skeptic concludes, "every individual ought to acquiesce in his own sentiment, without pretending to regulate that of others," a conclusion which, Hume points out, is in accord with "common sense"; and, he adds, if the skeptic is right, then "the proverb has justly determined it to be fruitless to dispute concerning tastes" (ibid.)—in short, *De gustibus.*

Because of what is at stake, however, this apparently genial conclusion cannot be the last word. Hume's initial move against it is to invoke "a certain [other] species of common sense, which opposes it, or at least serves to modify and restrain it":

> Whoever would assert an equality of genius and elegance between Ogilby and Milton, or Bunyan and Addison, would be thought to defend no less an extravagance, than if he had maintained a mole-hill to be as high as Teneriffe, or a pond as extensive as the ocean. Though there may be found *persons*, who give the preference to the former authors; *no one* pays attention to such a taste; and *we* pronounce, without scruple, the sentiment of these pretended critics to be absurd and ridiculous. (*ST*, p. 7; emphasis added)

This drawingroom vignette has considerable rhetorical force, and some version of it occurs repeatedly—or is spontaneously recreated—as a triumphant clincher in arguments against axiological skepticism. Three points, however, aside from that remarkable sequence of pronouns, may be noted immediately. The first, which I shall not pursue further here, is that Hume's skeptic is wrong, but not in the ways or for the reasons that Hume indicates: rather, in concluding from the non-objectivity of taste that all judgments of taste are "equally valid," the skeptic falls into the significant error discussed in Chapters 5 and 7 as the Egalitarian Fallacy, as does thereby Hume. The second, a more obvious point though its implications are often evaded, is the embar-

57

rassment of the argument by the examples, a not infrequent occurrence in axiological demonstrations where the force of supposedly self-evident evidence is continuously being historically undermined by precisely those operations of historical (and other) contingency that are thereby being denied. It is not irrelevant that the embarrassment is discreetly glossed over by Hume's twentieth-century editor who, alluding to this moment in the argument, tacitly substitutes "Shakespeare's poetry" and "doggerel" for Hume's equivocal examples, evidently counting on the vividness and direction of *that* contrast to hold up somewhat longer (*ST,* p. xx). The force of *any* such contrast, however, is just as historically and otherwise contingent as that of any other.[2] For example, someone might "give the preference" to doggerel over Shakespeare's poetry to illustrate the nature and effects of certain verse forms. To object that such a purpose is "atypical" or "not what people usually have in mind" when they say one work is better than another is only to restate the contingency of the value *typically* asserted: its dependence, in other words, on the performance of a particular—*assumed,* "had in mind," if not stated—set of functions. The third and most important point is Hume's explicit recouping for "us" of the privilege that was only temporarily set aside in the opening paragraph of the essay as "the highest arrogance and conceit," namely the privilege, when "pretended critics" with "absurd and ridiculous sentiments" contest our own judgments, to "pronounce positively in [our] own favor"—"*without scruple.*" As noted above, the removal of that scruple and the justification of that privilege are central motives of the construction of the Standard of Taste—and, it may be added here, of the entire axiological project per se.

In view of certain objections that the foregoing analysis recurrently elicits, two additional points may be made here. One is that much of the force of Hume's argument in this passage depends on his crucial but complex switch of the skeptical and/or philistine claims he undertakes to rebut. Thus, affirming an "equality of genius and elegance" *between two authors* is not the same as observing in general terms that one author is "just as good as" (or even "better than") another, and very different from observing an "equality of taste" *among all critics.* Hume obscures these differences when he moves from the specific examples to speak of the absurdity of someone's "giving the preference to the former authors," where it is not clear whether this means someone's (a) stating his own preference for Ogilby over Milton and Bunyan over Addison, or (b) stating that Ogilby and Bunyan are—objectively and absolutely, as it were—better than Milton and Addison, or (c) stating that the former are equal or superior to the latter in "elegance" and "genius." In the first case, where the judgment or claim is weakest or most highly qualified (as in "Well, m'Luds, the fact o' the matter is I'd rather read Bunyan than Addison any day"), "we" may find the preference contemptible or hard to imagine, but the only thing that is thereby demonstrated is that tastes can diverge quite widely, and, since no one ever claimed otherwise, the example proves nothing. In the last two cases, where the claim or judgment is most unqualified (as in "Unquestionably, gentlemen, Ogilby is as great a genius as Milton"), what is revealed is how ridiculous an opinion will be to "us" in view of what "we" all believe to be necessarily and self-evidently otherwise, a response that is evidence not, of course, of the necessity or rightness of our convictions but only of the strength of our illusion to that effect.

The other point is that, although claims of equality of value among authors or works may indeed become harder to maintain as the *terms* of the comparison become more *specific,* this is *not,* as is commonly maintained, because the claims are more readily seen as "factually" correct or incorrect as they come closer to being "descriptions" but, rather, because the more specific terms call into play the strong operation of linguistic conventions and thus, in effect, another form of communal consensus. The question then becomes why or how such terms (or what are called "aesthetic predicates") operate with specific meaning and effect, and, in particular, whether it is a matter of their correctly naming the "objective features" of artworks; it becomes, in short, nothing other than the issue of the viability of the traditional correspondence-to-reality theory of language, truth, and validity. Although that issue is too broad and complex for consideration at this point (I will discuss it in Chapter 5), it may be noted here that Madame A's sense of the self-evident absurdity of Lord B's saying that Ogilby is as great a genius as Milton, or of Mistress C's saying that Bunyan is as elegant a writer as Addison, cannot be separated from how, *within specific verbal communities that coincide to a large degree with specific social classes,* each one of them has learned to *use* the words "genius" and "elegance."

We have yet to consider the central axiological move of Hume's argument, which is to ground the standard of taste in (naturally, one might say) *nature:* specifically, the presumed psychophysiological nature of all human beings. Thus, granting that the skeptic is correct in maintaining that beauty is not an objective property of things but only a sentiment produced in us by objects (or, as he indicates later, certain of their

59

formal qualities), Hume observes that there is nevertheless "a catholic and universal beauty" that results from "the relation which nature has placed between the form and the sentiment." The core of the argument, then, is that by virtue of our "structure," "organs," or "machine," certain "forms and qualities" *naturally* produce "feelings of pleasure or displeasure" in us, and these feelings are simultaneously the source of all general rules of art and the empirical underpinnings for the standard of taste.

No sooner is this claim put into place, however, than it must be qualified; for, it seems, men do not always feel in accord with the common feelings of men or, as Hume puts it: "But though all the general rules of art are founded only on experience, and on the observation of the common sentiments of human nature, we must not imagine, that, on every occasion, the feelings of men will be conformable to these rules" (*ST*, p. 8). And not only "not . . . on *every* occasion" but on very few occasions; for, as the next wave of qualifications insists, these feelings require "the concurrence of many favorable circumstances" to make them "play . . . according to their general and established principles." If we want to "make an experiment" and "try the force of any beauty or deformity" (either, it appears, in order to test which of the two it is or, assuming "we" already know that, to give ourselves clear evidence of the relation between "the form" and "the sentiment"), "we must choose with care a *proper* time and place, and bring the fancy to a *suitable* situation and disposition. A *perfect* serenity of mind, a recollection of thought, a *due* attention to the object; if any of these circumstances be wanting, our experiment will be fallacious, and we shall be unable to judge of the catholic and universal beauty" (*ST*, pp. 8–9, emphasis added).

In view of how difficult it is to arrange the conditions under which the natural and common feelings of men will exhibit themselves ("The least exterior hindrance to such small springs, or the least internal disorder, disturbs their motion, and confounds the operation of the whole machine"—*ST*, p. 8), Hume suggests that we not depend on this experiment for evidence of the natural relation between forms and sentiments, but turn instead to another, more reliable crucible, namely the test of time.[3] Hence the familiar passage:

> We shall be able to ascertain its influence . . . from the durable admiration which attends those works that have survived all the caprices of mode and fashion, all the mistakes of ignorance and envy.

The same Homer who pleased at Athens and Rome two thousand years ago, is still admired at Paris and at London. All the changes of climate, government, religion, and language, have not been able to obscure his glory . . .

It appears, then, that amidst all the variety and caprice of taste, there are certain general principles of approbation or blame, whose influence a careful eye may trace in all operations of the mind. Some particular forms or qualities, from the original structure of the internal fabric are calculated to please, and others to displease; and if they fail of their effect in any particular instance, it is from some apparent defect or imperfection in the organ.

Many and frequent are the defects . . . (*ST,* pp. 9–10)

As I pointed out in Chapter 3, the passage is a memorable instance of the sort of *asymmetrical explanation* of preferences that is one of the definitive marks of axiological logic: intrinsic qualities of objects plus universal, underlying principles of human nature are invoked to explain stability and convergence; historical accident and error and the defects and imperfections of individual subjects are invoked to explain their divergence and mutability—and also, thereby, to explain the failure of the universal principles to operate universally.

Hume goes on to enumerate and elaborate the defects at great length, introducing the familiar catalogue (already given vivid expression in, among other places, Pope's *Essay on Criticism*) with an analogy, also a commonplace of the tradition, between "the perfect beauty" as agreed upon by men "in a sound state of the organ" and the "true and real color" of objects as they appear "in daylight, to the eye of a man in health" (*ST,* p. 10). This analogy too, however, ultimately controverts the point it was designed to support. For, whereas standardized usage with respect to color-labels can be explained (or, if one likes, "justified") by the overwhelming *numerical* predominance of persons with the sort of color-vision which we *therefore* call "normal," it appears from the very length of the catalogue of defects provided by Hume that, in his words, "the generality of men labor under some imperfection [of the organs of taste]"—and, indeed, that a man with healthy organs is "so rare a character" that "a true judge in the fine arts is difficult to discover even in the most polished ages" (*ST,* p. 17).

Hume acknowledges the difficulty as follows: "But where are such critics to be found? By what marks are they to be known? How distinguish them from pretenders? These questions are embarrassing; and seem to throw us back into the same uncertainty from which, during the course of this Essay, we have endeavored to extricate ourselves" (*ST,*

61

p. 17). He extricates himself here by firmly begging the question and casually substituting one dubious universal for another: "But if we consider the matters aright, these are questions of fact, not of sentiment . . . It is sufficient for our present purpose, if we have proved, that the taste of all individuals is not upon an equal footing, and that some men in general, however difficult to be particularly pitched upon, will be acknowledged *by universal sentiment* to have a preference above others" (*ST*, pp. 17–18; emphasis added). But this alleged universal acknowledgment of the "preference" of some art *critics* above others must encounter the same difficulties as the initially alleged universal acknowledgment of the superiority of some art *works* above others, and the argument thus moves us inexorably toward the same uncertainties from which it was designed to extricate us. For the same exceptions to the general rule would have to be acknowledged and explained, the same defects would have to be imputed to those people who do not, in fact, prefer those critics preferred by universal sentiment,[4] and the same questions would have to be raised or begged all over again.

The characteristic difficulties encountered by axiological logic are exhibited most dramatically in the concluding pages of the essay, where Hume grants that the skeptic's *De gustibus* view is "unavoidable" in certain cases. Since, however, these presumably special cases (or exceptions to the rule) are defined by a principle that must embrace *all* cases, Hume is edged toward a total turnabout, which he almost—but not quite—executes:

> But not withstanding all our endeavors to fix a standard of taste, . . . there still remain two sources of variation, which . . . will often serve to produce a difference in the degrees of our approbation or blame. The one is the different humors of particular men; the other, the particular manners and opinions of our age and country . . . Where there is such a diversity in the internal frame or external situation as is entirely blameless on both sides, . . . in that case a certain degree of diversity in judgment is unavoidable, and we seek in vain for a standard, by which we can reconcile the contrary sentiments. (*ST*, pp. 19–20)

The qualification that keeps this from being a total reversal—for, after all, what other sources of difference are there besides those of the "internal frame" and "external situation"?—is the phrase "as is entirely blameless on all sides." But this qualification also introduces a new normative consideration, here a moral one; for how—on what basis, in reference to what standard, grounded on what other universal—do we know or decide that something in the internal frame or external situation is *blamable* or not? And so the argument moves again toward that infinite regress of norm and justification, and justification of justification, toward which the essay repeatedly slips and into which all axiologies typically tumble.

As we have seen, each piece of evidence for the existence of "general principles of approbation and blame" must be repeatedly hedged and severely qualified: the universality of the appeal of certain authors is not quite universal; the underlying shared psychophysiological structure of all human beings is usually defective; and "the whole machine" by virtue of which certain feelings are naturally produced by certain forms can operate only under very special conditions and, even then, very unreliably. Moreover, when the evidence is restated with all its necessary hedges, acknowledged qualifications, and rigorously detailed specifications in place, its claim to foundational status collapses; for it then becomes equivalent to a statement of the *conditionality* of aesthetic preferences and also the conditionality of their *convergence*, which is of course the very opposite of an *unconditioned* (unchanging, fixed, absolute, objective) foundation for a standard of taste.

The point evidently needs emphasis, for it is often argued that these qualifications and specifications show that Hume recognized and "already allowed for" the various exceptions to his rules mentioned here. To be sure; what such arguments fail to recognize, however, is that when the qualifications and specifications are in place, the universals are no longer universals, the unconditional foundations are no longer unconditional, and whatever standards are built upon them lose the force of *absolutes*. Hume's claim is that there is empirical, factual evidence for a natural norm of taste. When restated with the conceded qualifications, however, the foundation of that norm, the alleged fact that some objects, by the very structure of the mind, are naturally calculated to please and others to displease, becomes the limp truism, *some objects tend to please or displease some people under some conditions,* that is, the simple observation of the simple fact that people have preferences— or the not much more interesting truism, *different objects please different people differently, and please the same people differently under different conditions,* that is, the simple observation of the simple fact of diversity, none other than the very one which Hume noted, at the beginning of the essay, as "too obvious not to have fallen under every one's observation." Neither of these commonplace observations can be a foundation for deciding which tastes are "normal" or "defective," or which judgments are "correct" or "absurd"; on the contrary, it is always in the face of the fact of the diversity of preferences that the axiological argument seeks to discover underlying normative principles—principles, that is, that validate the privileged status of *some* of those preferences. As in Hume's essay, however, so also in any other instance of axiological logic: the argument always either dissolves into infinite regresses, or is supported in circular or bootstrap fashion by unacknowledged self-privileging a priori norms, or amounts to an axiologically impotent restatement of the diversity and conditionality of all preferences and the contingency of all value.

Hume's essay is, to my mind, more interesting and theoretically richer than any other text in the classic axiological tradition, not excepting Kant's *Critique of Judgment*—though this, of course, is a matter of taste. As I have sought to indicate, however, the essay also appears to be deeply at odds with itself. The *but*s that recur at the beginning of a good number of the paragraphs quoted above are characteristic of the entire essay, which moves repeatedly from some strong general statement to an acknowledgment and examination of the exceptions and thence to a qualified but highly unstable recovery of the initial generalization, requiring further acknowledgment and accounting for (or discounting of) further exceptions, and so on. Given that this structure governs not only the major line of argument but every subsidiary element of it, recurring throughout the essay and sometimes several times within a single paragraph, it may be suspected that strong but antagonistic forces were operating here: specifically, it seems, the power of Hume's temperamental skepticism and cosmopolitan personal history continuously conspired to subvert, but was in turn subverted by, both the momentum of his traversing the already well-established (and in some ways quite "natural") routes of axiological logic and also his perspectives and interests as an eighteenth-century man of letters and member of polite society. The significance of these possibilities will be considered again below in connection with the more general taste for axiologic logic displayed throughout the history of Western critical theory.

Kant's Pure Judgments

The topics that dominate the first part of the *Critique of Judgment* continue to define the domain of formal aesthetics and the text itself remains scriptural within it. What is most instructive about Kant's analysis for our present purposes, however, is the extent to which its axiological argument duplicates or mirrors that of Hume in the essay discussed above. The interest here is not the evidence of any specific "influence" or "derivation" (Kant's close and exercized reading of Hume is a commonplace of the history of philosophy), but the generality and apparent inevitability of the logical moves set into motion by the defining objectives of axiology. Certain distinctly Kantian features of the argument should, however, be indicated at the outset.

First, Kant's objective is considerably more circumspect than Hume's, for he offers not to justify the claim to objective validity of certain ("our") judgments of taste but only to inquire into the conditions of the possibility of the rightfulness of such a claim. Second, "the judgment of taste" (*das Geschmacksurteil*) as initially identified by Kant has the quite confined sense of the specific act of mental discrimination expressed in the specific verbal statement *"Es ist schön"* and is subsequently subjected by the internal imperatives of the analysis itself to even more exacting specifications. Indeed, and that is the third point here, it should be remembered that the characteristic mode of a Kantian analysis is consummate reflexivity, so that "*initially* identified" and "*subsequently* subjected" are not really appropriate for describing its course: in a sense, it is no surprise that a genuine judgment of taste, as Kant defines it, can be said to rightfully claim universal validity, for the very process of his definition of it consists of his successively distinguishing it from anything that could *not* make that claim. As we shall see, however, the question remains whether, having rigorously refined out everything in the definition, occasion, and execution of the judgment of taste that might compromise the rightfulness of its claim to universal validity, Kant is left with anything at all.

Like Hume, Kant begins by acknowledging the wide diversity of tastes and also notes the apparently intractable diversity of at least certain judgments:

> To one [man], violet color is soft and lovely; to another, it is washed out and dead. One man likes the tone of wind instruments, another that of strings. To strive here with the design of reproving as incorrect another man's judgment which is different from our own . . . would be folly. As regards the pleasant, therefore, the fundamental proposition is valid: *everyone has his own taste* [that is, his own sense of taste: *ein jeder hat seinen eigenen Geschmack (der Sinne)*].[5]

As in Hume's essay, however, this acknowledgment is only a foil to the major point and contrast that follows, here set up by the observation that "everyone" would agree that, if "reproved" for not doing so, he *ought* to say not just "It is pleasant" but "It is pleasant *to me*." This is apparently an "ought" of linguistic propriety: that is, saying it would make explicit what is, according to Kant, presupposed by the use of the term *pleasant*. Or to put this another way, in not adding the first-person qualification, the speaker fails to make explicit the merely personal force (or reference or applicability) which, according to Kant, is involved in someone's saying that something is pleasant, as pointedly opposed to a judgment of "the *beautiful*" which claims not merely personal but objective—in the sense of universal subjective—validity:

> It would (on the contrary) be laughable if a man who imagined anything to his own taste thought to justify himself by saying: "This object (the house we see, the coat that person wears, the concert we hear, the poem submitted to our judgment) is beautiful *for me*" . . . [For] if he gives out anything as beautiful, he supposes in others the same satisfaction; he judges not merely for himself, but *for everyone* . . . Here, then, we cannot say each man has his own particular taste. For this would be as much as to say that there is no taste whatever, i.e. no aesthetical judgment which can make a rightful claim upon everyone's assent. (sect. 7, emphasis added)

In addition to the swift dismissal of the other alternative in the last turn here (that is, Kant's question-begging elimination of the possibility that there may indeed be no aesthetical judgment that can make the claim at issue), what is notable in this passage is how much the force of the argument owes to presumed empirical facts about *linguistic* usage or convention, bolstered by what appears to be the tacitly universalized testimony of personal introspection or, as it might be called now, "linguistic intuition": "Further, this claim to universal validity so essentially belongs to a judgment by which we describe anything as *beautiful* that, if this were not thought in it, it would never come into our thoughts to use the expression at all" (sect. 8).

Although Kant's expressivist conception of the relation of language to thought may have prevented his recognition of it ("judgment" in the *Critique* can mean both a mental discrimination and an overt verbal statement because, it appears, the latter is, for Kant, simply an "expression"—*Ausdruck*—of the former), the force of any appeal to linguistic propriety, usage, or convention is, of course, itself historically and otherwise contingent. Thus, someone could always say: "Well, that may be what everyone meant by *schön* in 1790, at least in the salons of Königsberg, but hardly anyone means that anymore; these days nobody would laugh and only a handful of professors of philosophy would even be given pause if someone said 'You and your friends may not like my wife's poetry, but it's beautiful to me' or 'This coat may be shabby and old-fashioned, but I've had it since my student days and it's beautiful to me.' " It is also questionable (though empirically indeterminable) whether, when people refer to something as "beautiful," it always or even typically does—or ever did—come into their thoughts that everyone ought to agree with them. Although it may be suspected that Kant was accurately reporting the implicit provincial universalism of the drawingroom conversation with which he was familiar, the point remains that the historicity of linguistic convention (and, thereby, of linguistic "intuition") and the contingency of usage deprive such observations of any epistemic authority or axiological force.[6]

We may turn now to the major lines of Kant's analysis of judgments of taste. Though notoriously angular and elusive in its discursive articulation, its skeletal logic may be paraphrased as follows. If we assume that everyone has the same cognitive apparatus, then if someone's judgment regarding some object were to reflect only the operations of that apparatus, uncontaminated by any other kind of personally individuating mental activity or sensation and also uncontaminated by any circumstantially contingent factors, then that judgment would necessarily be the same as anyone else's under any conditions. It follows that, if someone's judgment of some object as "beautiful" has really been produced only by the operations of this (assumedly) uniformly shared cognitive apparatus as elicited by that object, then such a judgment could rightfully claim to be universally valid.

Kant defers to the end of the "Analytic of the Beautiful" the crucial question of whether the assumption of a uniform cognitive machine is itself well grounded. Up to that point, he is concerned to specify the exacting conditions that would have to obtain if the logic outlined above was, otherwise, to "take." His explicit objective and method in detailing these specifications is, of course, neither to characterize the phenomenological nature of aesthetic experiences nor to determine (empirically, as it were) the properties of the objects that elicit such experiences, but to determine strictly through transcendental logic the conditions of possibility required by the hypothesis just outlined.[7] What concerns Kant, in other words, is not what certain objects, experiences, and judgments *are* like but, rather, what they *must be* like for the demonstration to work.

What they must be like is very pure. Much of the "Analytic of the Beautiful" is devoted to demonstrating that there can be and is a sensa-

67

Subjective
but not subjective

tion which, while *necessarily* subjective (because it *is* a sensation), is nevertheless so decisively independent of anything individual, personal, private, or peculiar to the subject having that sensation that it is, in effect, *not* subjective. After several other candidates are examined and rejected, the sensation/judgment[8] of the beautiful turns out to meet the requirements, but only when it is free of concepts and also "troubled and interrupted by no foreign sensation" (sect. 14). (As Kant explains, a sensation/judgment of the beauty of some object can rightfully claim objective validity when—but *only* when—it is independent of any identification of the object's meaning, purpose, or even existence and is thus also free of emotion, interest, desire, and such compromising gratifications as might be offered by the object's charm, perfection, ethical goodness, or practical utility.) Further analysis reveals that these specifications can be met only when the judgment of beauty has been truly elicited by a pure reflection on the pure sensation of the pure operation of the mental faculties responding to pure form.

Purity

Although he emphasizes that mistakes of judgment can occur (and indeed must occur, for otherwise it would be hard to say why we do not in fact always agree with each other's judgments of taste), Kant dismisses surprisingly casually the idea that there could be any great difficulties involved in arriving at or identifying the required state of purity. Thus, he suggests at one point that we can readily confirm our conviction that our sensation of beauty is a *true* one by a bit of experimental introspection: "He [i.e., the man who believes he is laying down a judgment of taste] can be quite certain of this for himself by the mere consciousness [*das blosse Bewusstsein*] of the separating off everything belonging to the pleasant and the good from the satisfaction which is left" (sect. 8). The kinds of purity that Kant's logic posits as necessary for objective judgments of taste do not, however, appear possible at all, at least not for sublunary creatures. On the contrary, it appears that we never do and never could encounter pure forms and qualities purely: neither in what are labeled "works of art" (including those of abstract expressionism, *art povera,* or any other allegedly purist or minimalist style), nor in even the most pared-down "stimuli" presented in the most rigorously controlled experiments of contemporary empirical aesthetics, nor in the most highly focused and intensely gratifying or arousing "nonaesthetic" or "extra-aesthetic" experiences, including sexual, ritual, and drug-induced ones. Rather, that which Kant called "sensation" (*Empfindung*) and which we still, informally, call "sensation" and/or "perception" is now understood as the always complexly contingent product of a global interaction in which the subject selects and configures elements of her environment in relation to the current state of her own system as that system has been produced by her own quite individual history.[9] This means that, no matter how "simple" the "stimulus" or "pure" the "form," the human creature always experiences it through her total sensory/perceptual/cognitive system and in relation to *memory, context,* and *meaning:* in relation, that is, to (a) the structural traces of prior perceptions and actions with regard to "stimuli" or "forms" of that and related kinds, (b) the circumstantial conditions of the interaction itself, including, where relevant, social conditions (and, in a sense, social conditions are always relevant), and (c) all the other cognitive and integrative aspects of the interaction that would be in place for any creature that develops in a cultural and linguistic universe and experiences its world accordingly.[10] Contrary to the key requirements of Kant's analysis, then, our interactions with our environments are always and inevitably multiply contingent and highly individuated for every subject: our "sensations" and "perceptions" of "forms" or of anything else are inseparable from—or, as it might be said, thoroughly contaminated by—exactly who we are, where we are, and all that has already happened to us, and there is therefore nothing in any aspect of our experience of anything that could ever be, in the required sense, pure.[11]

The need for purity produced by the imperatives of Kant's logic generates a recurrent drawing of distinctions and subdistinctions throughout the "Analytic of the Beautiful." Since every specification of the kind of object, experience, or judgment that exemplifies the posited purity is seen to admit of contaminating exceptions, Kant must engage in a repeated *refining* process of first distinguishing the exceptions from the real thing, then bracketing them out, then distinguishing and bracketing out the contaminating exceptions from what remains, and so forth.[12] It appears, however, that Kant is not left with that pure residue which the analysis/demonstration requires but, rather, that the exceptions exhaust the possibilities and the residue is nothing at all.

Kant's repeatedly refined and ultimately refined-out-of-existence *specifications* of the conditions under which judgments of taste would be validated by his own logic recall the continuously expanded and ultimately extended-to-everything *qualifications* which, as we have seen, Hume was obliged to attach to the operation of the standard of taste to make it empirically responsible. Although proceeding from two traditionally opposed positions, then, both end up axiologically empty-

handed. As Hume's detailing of the conditions affecting human preferences becomes richer and more subtle, his claim that there is an
objective standard of taste grounded in nature becomes weaker; as
Kant's specifications of what would make a judgment of taste totally
objective become tighter, purer, and more foolproof, his demonstration
becomes more remote from the conditions of any sublunary world and
more irrelevant to any sublunary axiology. Before any further comment
can be made on this parallel in reverse, however, the final and crucial
theoretical move played out in the "Analytic of the Beautiful" must be
considered.

As Kant here insists, the existence of a universal cognitive apparatus
is the keystone of his axiological edifice: "Hence it is only under the
presupposition that there is a common sense [*Gemeinsinn*, meaning not
everyday reasoning or ordinary beliefs but, as he explains, our common
capacity for shared cognition] . . . it is only under this presupposition, I
say, that the judgment of taste can be laid down" (sect. 20). In the
passage that follows, he demonstrates the *necessity* of a universal
knowing-machine on the ground of its being presupposed by the *necessarily* universal communicability of knowledge—which is, for Kant,
equivalent to the objectivity of knowledge:

> Cognitions and judgments must . . . admit of universal communicability;
> for otherwise there would be no harmony between them and the object,
> and they would be collectively a mere subjective play of the representative
> powers, exactly as scepticism desires.
>
> . . . Since now this accordance itself must admit of universal communica-
> bility, and consequently also our feeling of it . . . , and since the universal
> communicability of a feeling presupposes a common sense, we have
> grounds for assuming the latter. And this common sense is assumed . . .
> simply as the necessary condition of the universal communicability of our
> knowledge, which is presupposed in every logic and in every principle of
> knowledge that is not skeptical. (sect. 21)

In short, if everyone's cognitive faculties did not operate in the same
way, then the objectivity of knowledge itself would not be possible, and
everyone knows that knowledge is objective . . . except, as everyone
knows, skeptics. So, there must be a universal knowing-machine, because otherwise skepticism would be right and the entire argument of
the "Analytic" (and perhaps even more than that) would be wrong.

It is clear from the perplexity or inconclusiveness of the conclusion of
the "Analytic of the Beautiful" that Kant recognizes the tautologous
nature of the entire demonstration. The recognition is hedged and to

some extent obscured, however, by the salvaging alternative left in its wake: <u>that is, the suggestion that even if the claims of taste to universal validity cannot be ultimately justified, it may yet be Reason's labyrinthine way to have them *seem* justifiable so that a higher good, namely the institution of a perhaps illusory but nevertheless inspirational—and, therefore, properly regulatory—ideal of unanimity or consensus, can thereby be effected:</u>

> Whether there is in fact such a common sense . . . or whether a yet higher principle of reason makes it only into a regulative principle for producing in us a common sense for higher purposes; whether, therefore, taste is an original and natural faculty or only the idea of an artificial one yet to be acquired, so that a judgment of taste with its assumption of a universal assent in fact is only a requirement of reason for producing such harmony of sentiment; whether the *ought*, i.e. the objective necessity of the confluence of the feeling of any one man with that of any other, only signifies the possibility of arriving at this accord, and the judgment of taste only affords an example of the application of this principle—these questions we have neither the wish nor the power to investigate as yet . . . (sect. 22, emphasis added)

The claim of judgments of taste to universal validity being, it appears, ultimately ungroundable, what remains is only the claim itself, which is where the analysis/demonstration began—but not quite; for, though not rightful by transcendental necessity, the claim can be justified *in another way*, which turns out to be the same way that the ultimately uninstantiable Standard of Taste was justified in Hume's essay: that is, as an ideal norm or regulative principle by which "harmony of sentiment" may be produced—or, at least, when "tasteless persons propose to avoid blame" by invoking the proverbial *De gustibus* (sect. 56), persons with taste will have Reason's own rational rebuttal in hand.[13]

Kant is able to salvage the otherwise thoroughly compromised claim of judgments of taste to universal validity by invoking the higher good that such claims serve. That invocation, however, only displaces one axiological question with another and leads into the usual infinite regressions. For one may always ask how high and how good that higher good is, and also *for whom* it is good at all. Is it (that is, unanimity, consensus, "the confluence of any one man's feeling with that of any other") a good in itself? Is universal concordance self-evidently better than diversity, or even better in all cases than conflict? Is prior agreement indeed presupposed by human communication? And is it, as Kant does not question here and as Hume did not question in regard to the Standard of Taste, good for *everyone*?

Or is it not the case, rather, that all these questions may be answered negatively and that the invocation of an ideally achievable consensus is not only not good for everyone but tends inevitably to operate to the advantage of the majority and those with de facto social power and to the disadvantage of the more "different," "idiosyncratic," "singular," and otherwise innovative and/or marginal members of any community? We are evidently concerned here, however, not with logic but with social politics or, perhaps, with the inseparability of the two.

Logical Tastes and The Other's Poison

The relative concreteness of the passage from section 56 of the *Critique of Judgment* cited above may appear, with its evocation of drawingroom upstarts and putdowns, somewhat incongruous juxtaposed to the abstract rigors of the "Analytic of the Beautiful." The drawingroom, however—and, in our own era, the classroom—is never too far out of sight in the discourses of the axiological tradition. For, as we have seen, what is at stake in the axiological project is always the contested legitimacy of someone's evaluative authority; and, though not all the battles are fought out in drawingrooms or classrooms, they are inevitably fought out in social arenas and along lines of authority and power defined by social, institutional, and economic categories: age and gender, class and political status, teacher versus student, censor versus citizen, bureaucrat versus artist, art producer versus art distributor versus art consumer, and so forth.[14]

The arguments of Hume's essay and Kant's analysis are transparently circular and altogether self-canceling—at least, as the present analysis attests, it now appears so to some of us. Nevertheless, the logic they exhibit and to a great extent share has been continuously perpetuated, appropriated, and recreated for at least the past two hundred years and continues to dominate disciplinary aesthetics and critical theory. What, one might ask, could account for such peculiar taste in logic? The political answer to that question—that is, that aesthetic axiology has operated as an official ideology serving the interests of established evaluative authority—is obviously available but not, I think, adequate. To be sure, Hume's asymmetrical account of human preferences and Kant's specifications of purity have been invoked repeatedly to rule out

72

the tastes and discount the claims of upstarts and philistines. It must be remarked, however, that corresponding asymmetrical accounts have also been invoked repeatedly to *challenge* established evaluative authority and to claim, through a duplicate or mirror logic, an "equal" legitimacy for officially substandard or deviant tastes. Though the latter invocations have perhaps not operated so decisively, we must nevertheless acknowledge that the value of aesthetic axiology has never consisted wholly in its justification of elite preferences and established cultural power. It appears rather that, like other dominant discourses, it has developed an account of the "phenomena" that has continuously served, for those who have reproduced and appropriated it, a number and variety of fundamental interests: not only social and political interests but other equally significant though perhaps less readily namable ones, among them what we may think of as vested *cognitive* interests.

It is clear, for example, that the success of eighteenth-century aesthetics in justifying elite patterns of cultural consumption depended on the coherence of its norm-and-deviation account of human preferences with *other* current knowledge and beliefs, including contemporary conceptions of cultural history, psychophysiology, genetics, and the causality of human behavior. Extending the point, we might say that the more general success of axiologic logic seems to be a product of its continuous coherence with and participation in our favored—most comfortable, most familiar, and in some ways most functional—cognitive styles: that is, the repertoire of conceptual/discursive steps, moves, and turns that Derrida identifies as Western metaphysics or logocentrism. The contemporary deconstruction of the latter and its displacement, in some places, by other cognitive styles are discussed in the next chapter. We may anticipate the point here, however, by observing that there are intellectual fashions as well as aesthetic ones and, it appears, tastes for logic as well.[15]

Also, and no less importantly, the arguments of the axiological tradition evidently confirm and are confirmed by the deeply felt intuition of the manifest rightness of certain judgments and utter absurdity of others, and, in aesthetics, the almost palpable experience of the beauty of certain objects and deformity of others: intuitions and experiences that become no less deeply felt and palpable when confronted by the apparent contrary intuitions and experiences of other people. Indeed, it may be here that we reach the fundamental principle or mechanism of axiologic logic. If we thereby also reach a fundamental principle of all cognitive process, namely the will to epistemic self-maintenance—a

73

conservativism that may be even deeper than that of politics or, in the literal sense, economic self-interest—then, as we have learned to suspect from other evidence, Reason and rationalization are not altogether distinct. The question, clearly a major one for contemporary theory in all disciplines, cannot be pursued here as such, but a number of related points may be briefly indicated.

First, it is important to recognize that "intuitions" (of rightness, wrongness, absurdity, and so forth) have no special claim to epistemic authority, being different from other convictions only in being less readily formulated or explicated in terms of other current explanatory accounts and, it seems, in having been acquired more *informally*. While intuitions are therefore no less historically and otherwise contingent than other beliefs, they may be exceptionally powerful—that is, less responsive to changed conditions and less readily modified by new conceptual formulations—precisely because, in having been learned more informally and thus imperceptibly, they are especially resistant to the reflection that they were *learned* at all or could have been learned otherwise.[16]

Second, the sense of gratification or distress, rapture or revulsion one can experience in relation to artworks and other cultural objects seems to be simultaneously *socially engendered* and *physically inscribed*. The complex dynamics involved here recall what I have described as The-Other's-Poison Effect: not only would one man's meat poison the other, but just looking at the meat—and, even more, watching the man eat it—would make the other sick. Thus, Hume alludes to the *pain* experienced by a person "conversant in the highest excellence of the kind" when confronted by the coarse daubings and vulgar ballads that "would affect the mind of a peasant or Indian with the highest admiration" (*ST,* p. 14), and it is reported that Theodor Adorno had a "visceral distaste for mass culture."[17] But, of course, the authenticity of the pain does not vouch for the accuracy of the diagnosis. This is worth emphasizing in the view of the fact that The-Other's-Poison Effect may join aesthetic axiology to yield the conviction that the other man is himself being poisoned by the meat he is eating, that his eating and enjoying it is evidence that he has already been poisoned by something else, and/or that his eating it is poisoning everyone in the community: in theories, that is, that interpret the consumption of non-elite culture as a cause and sign of broader social corruption and cultural decline.

We may recall here the familiar diagnoses by academic critics and journalists of the cultural symptomatology of rock music, television, commercial films, and romance fiction and their degenerative effects on the educationally lower classes, and the accounts by Frankfurt School theorists and others of the central role of the mass media (and, recently, of "postmodern" art, architecture, and writing) in marking and hastening the decay of Western civilization. In relation to each, Marxist cultural critics join Arnoldian humanists in deploring the novel/alien cultural productions of the late twentieth century and also in depicting them in apocalyptic terms.[18]

The issues here are obscured by the familiar and commonly unquestioned categories of cultural criticism itself. Thus, by way of simultaneously apologizing for and excusing Adorno's virulent "insensitivity" to "negro jazz" (that is, his horror at what he saw—or heard—as its fraudulent affirmations, sadomasochism, frantic sexuality, deepening of alienation, and so on), Martin Jay remarks that it was the result of Adorno's "failure to make the appropriate distinction" between "the commercial variety churned out by Tin Pan Alley" and "the less popular variety rooted in black culture itself."[19] But this, of course, begs the key questions of the nature of popular culture and aesthetic value, and is historically questionable in every element. Who, or what kinds of people, "churned out" the jazz of Tin Pan Alley? Were their motives and constraints any more *simply* or *exclusively* "commercial" than those of other contemporary composers and performers? Was Tin Pan Alley music *not* "rooted" in some culture(s), including "black culture itself"? What, in short, *is* "the appropriate distinction" to be made?

The ideological complexity of these accounts and diagnoses is suggested by Pierre Bourdieu's important postaxiological analysis, *Distinction: A Social Critique of the Judgement of Taste.* According to that analysis, patterns of cultural consumption emerge in highly stratified societies in accord with a "symbolic logic" of social distinction that operates simultaneously to identify and also to maintain class differences. The logic is itself based on distinction: "legitimate" (that is, elite or canonical) culture and the elective tastes of the socially dominant classes define themselves and acquire their distinguishing features in contradistinction to the ("ordinary," "vulgar," "barbaric") tastes of the socially dominated.[20] In particular, the ascetic ideals of disinterest, disembodiment, purity, and autonomy that are associated with "the Kantian aesthetic" and exhibited in aristocratic tastes emerge as a symbolic counterpart and active sign of the objective and subjective distance of members of the dominant classes from practical urgency and economic necessity, whereas the inverse—that is, the "popular aesthetic," which favors

75

substance over form, quantity over quality, and utility, immediate consumption, and bodily sensation over the "detached gaze" of aesthetic contemplation—is the symbolic counterpart and objective product of the socioeconomic status, history, and trajectory of members of the dominated classes (*Distinction,* pp. 41–65).

Bourdieu points out that tastes cluster predictably and correlate highly with social strata largely because tendencies and competences in the consumption of cultural goods are learned in the course of a life history that itself depends crucially on class origins and on the specific types of formal and informal education thereby made possible. So much would, perhaps, be granted by any contemporary sociological account.[21] What he emphasizes, however, is that, because these learned patterns of cultural consumption tend to be experienced as internal preferences and interpreted as evidence of different *natural* inclinations and competences, taste also functions to legitimate the power of the socially dominant. Specifically, the cultural objects and practices favored by the dominant classes (these include types of clothing, sports activities, food preparation, and so on, as well as music and other artforms) are legitimated as intrinsically superior by the normative institutions controlled by those very classes; at the same time, the tastes of the dominant *for* those objects and practices are interpreted as evidence of their own natural superiority and cultural enlightenment and thus also their right to social and cultural power. Moreover, this doubly legitimating interpretation is accepted and reproduced not only by those who benefit most directly from it but by everyone, including those whose subordination it implicitly justifies.[22]

It would follow from Bourdieu's analysis that all normative theories of culture, including those mounted from or in the name of the political left, serve vested tastes and vested interests: that is, deeply inscribed individual aesthetic and cultural tastes and also, though indirectly, the more general class stratifications that those tastes identify and maintain. Among the questions we are thereby (and otherwise) led to ask are whether nostalgic/apocalyptic accounts of popular and mass culture may not represent a reactionary response to the increasing contemporary destratification of cultural arenas and practices, and a misdiagnosis of the cognitive dislocation, dissonance, and nausea—literally, disgust—experienced as a result by high-culture cultural critics. We may also ask whether the familiar images of contemporary cultural degeneration—narcissism, hedonism, videots, zombies, one-dimensional men, and so on—may not be products of the increased occasion that the mass media give for close contact with The Other and pollution by his meat (his music on one's radio, his reading on one's drugstore bookracks, his revels and revelings on one's television screen and thus in one's very home) and the increasing unavoidability of mingling with The Other in the midst of his cultural consumptions in public spaces such as streets, malls, and terminals: that is, on sites and grounds that not only fail to segregate classes and cultures but also fail to confer distinction on the high-culture cultural critic's preferences or authority on his politico-philosophical justifications of them. It seems that wherever systems of more or less strictly segregated hierarchical strata begin to break down and *differentiations* become more numerous, rapid, complex, less predictable, and less controllable, the resulting emergences, mixtures, and minglings will look, from the perspective of those in the historically upper strata, like flattenings, falls, and collapses—in short, like *losses of distinction*.[23] It is certainly to some extent destratification itself that has put The Other in our company and classrooms and his meat on our plate and palate. If, as perhaps all would agree, the sense of the decline of civilization is the by-product (or "other side of the coin") of the successful—if, from some perspectives, noisome—expansion of democracy, then it must also be acknowledged that the *politics* of cultural criticism is a very complex matter indeed.

Aesthetic axiology and latter-day normative theories have preempted alternative theoretical explorations of the dynamics of taste, and thereby also inhibited and postponed other practical—including pedagogic—responses to the problems of cultural change. We can hardly hope to understand the social mechanisms and political consequences of popular culture and the mass media so long as we regard any contact with them as pollution, complicity, or "lax" tolerance; nor can we move toward adequate analyses of their complex and differentiated effects so long as we begin and end with assumptions of mental and moral torpor, cultural stupefaction, and mass exploitation. Unless cultural criticism moves beyond the self-privileging logic and foregone conclusions of the axiological tradition, it will have no intellectual or practical force beyond assuaging the pain of The Other's Poison.

Three Postaxiological Postscripts

Nature, Culture, and Human Preferences

Contemporary accounts of human preferences are haunted not only by the *aporias* of traditional axiological logic but by other related ideological and conceptual issues. One is the significance of what are called genetic or biological factors as distinct from and opposed to what are called environmental, social, or cultural factors. In the account outlined in this study, all human preferences, and the variations and convergences among them, are referred to the particular values of certain fairly general variables, including historical, social, and institutional conditions *and* psychophysiological structures, mechanisms, and tendencies. The first point to be emphasized here is that the latter, in this account, are seen to operate not as a substratum of underlying "determinants," "forces," or "constraints" but, precisely, as *variables*—that is, they develop and function differently among different human beings and, equally significantly, always interact, for each of us, with the other variables mentioned. With respect to human preferences, nothing is uniform, universal, natural, fixed, or determined in advance, either for the species generally, or for any specific individual, or for any portion or fraction of the species, by whatever principle, sociological or other, it is segmented and classified (gender, age, race, nation, and so forth). In view of the fact that interactions among the relevant variables occur continuously throughout the life history of each individual and at every level of description or analysis, the question of whether some given behavioral variation or convergence among people (for example, erotic preferences, cognitive styles, competences in music, or tastes in logic) is the product of their "genetic" differences or similarities *as distinct from and opposed to* differences or similarities in their "environments" becomes not merely difficult to answer but altogether meaningless in such oppositional terms. In other words, the issue here, as it is commonly framed and argued, poses choices that one need not and *cannot* make.

We have come to recognize that invocations of the "natural" are always ideologically loaded. *All* the terms in play here, however (and this is the second point to be emphasized), "environmental" as well as "genetic," "cultural" and "social" as well as "biological," are implicated in a long history of conceptually problematic dichotomization. Merely shooting out one leg of any of these dichotomies does not, therefore, solve any of the relevant problems; on the contrary, it participates in the continuous deferral of the more difficult but important task of disarming the entire "nature/culture" opposition of its ideological power. The task is not made any easier, of course, by the fact that these dichotomies are reflected in and reinforced by the institutional segregation of the relevant disciplines (for example, psychology and biology versus sociology and anthropology) and by the corollary differences of training, temperament, intellectual identity, political and ideological commitments, and so forth among the practitioners of each. For various reasons, themselves both "social" and "psychological" and also quite complexly interrelated, these disciplinary differences have tended to play themselves out as competition and conflict within academic institutions and also in that arena we call "intellectual history." While one must, for these very reasons, be wary of any facile claims of "synthesis" in this area, recent responses to various intellectual and political pressures—for example, demands on both sides in the debates over sociobiology for richer and better-knit formulations, and the necessity for intellectual collaboration among feminists in different academic disciplines—indicate that the possibility of more integrated perspectives may yet be looked for.[24]

The Developmental Fallacy / teleology / maturation

The fallacy so named here is the quite common idea of a teleologically directed "normal" maturing of aesthetic tastes and judgments and, accordingly, an ultimate "fullness" of development at which point, having moved beyond the dark glass of their "undeveloped" and "immature" likes and dislikes, now-grown children, unless innately defective, pathologically fixated, or culturally deprived or corrupted, will "recognize" the inherent value of canonical artworks and, like their erstwhile teachers and other elders, properly and naturally prefer them. Not restricted to questions of literary or aesthetic judgment, the notion and fallacy are typically found in empiricist or putatively "empirical" accounts of value, whether aesthetic, moral, or other. Thus, in debates over the "objectivity" of some such type of value, great significance will often be attached to the observation that, as it appears, people's preferences tend to emerge in a particular sequence or, as it also appears, *direction*—for example, from rock music to symphonic works, or, in the case of moral tastes, from invocations of ad hoc "fairness" to citings of Universal Principles of Justice—and not the other way around. This apparent uniformity and directionality is routinely offered as evidence of, if not quite the specific "organ" invoked by Hume and others, then at least an innate developmental vector of aesthetic taste (or moral consciousness) and thereby an equivalent natural basis for positing an objective norm and standard of value.[25]

The empirical validity and theoretical significance of such observations are, however, altogether dubious. For one thing, it is questionable whether sequences of that kind are actually duplicated in any but the most limited populations. Thus (to restrict ourselves to aesthetic preferences), the more precisely one specifies the items in such a sequence (from the Grateful Dead to Bach, from Edna St. Vincent Millay to Dante, and so forth) the more limited the population in which the sequence as such is predictable and the more readily the similarities among people can be accounted for not by the "natural" maturing of value-detecting organs but by contingent similarities of education and cultural experience. The question is as much theoretical and interpretive as it is empirical, however, which means, as always, that question-begging formulations are to be expected. Thus, not only is there a strong tendency for the degree of age-correlation and extent of subject-similarity to be exaggerated, but once the (limited) general tendencies have been standard-ized into an axiological norm, the exceptions (babies who like Bach, senior citizens who like rock) will typically be seen not as *qualifying* the claims of universality and inevitability but as special cases of prodigiousness, retardation, regression, or simply as pathological in the usual ways.

It must be emphasized that the issue here is not whether age-correlated changes of aesthetic preference do occur, or whether there really are similarities of taste-change among different people. Our individual sensory/perceptual systems no doubt change as we age[26] and, to the extent that the systemic states and environmental conditions of different subjects are similar, the ways their personal economies change will themselves be similar and so also will be the general nature of the changes in their preferences. The questions at issue are, rather, (a) whether such *changes* are "developments" in the sense of moving from an objectively inferior toward an objectively superior position on some normative scale, (b) whether their occurrence is evidence of an inevitable *telos* of taste, that is, an objectively superior "end-stage," and (c) whether their co-occurrence among different people is evidence of the objective value of the objects preferred at that temporally latest point. The answer to all these questions is *no:* for, even if it were the case that people throughout the world uniformly and universally preferred "X" at age five, "Y" at age twenty-five, and "Z" at age fifty, that *array* of common differences would not be evidence of the objective *superiority* of any particular point on it (whether the superiority of "Z" to "X" or the other way around); nor would it be evidence of the increasing *correctness* of people's preferences as they grow older unless, of course, the preferences of middle-aged adults per se had already been arbitrarily privileged as more "correct." (To better grasp the arbitrariness of the

80

latter, one may imagine a Romantic-type culture, not altogether remote from some aspects of our own, in which the tastes of the fresh and innocent eye, before the closing down of the prison-house shades, were seen as truer and more blessed than those of the effete and jaded connoisseur.) Of course, there are reasons why we (or some of us) commonly privilege the tastes of middle-aged adults as the most natural and desirable ones to have: they are the same as the reasons why Japanese privilege Japanese tastes, Javanese privilege Javanese tastes, and school-children privilege the tastes of their own cliques.

Comparative Pleasure

The idea here, quite common in casual debates on these issues and encountered above in I. A. Richards's reflections on the emotional pathology of the sort of person who prefers a sonnet by Ella Wheeler Wilcox to one by John Keats, is that some people enjoy what they enjoy *more* than others do. This may, of course, be the case as a general proposition, but its invocation on any particular occasion will always be problematic. The notion has been put into play fairly recently by the American sociologist Herbert Gans, and his equivocations on the subject are instructive.

Gans, a genial pluralist, argues in his book *Popular Culture and High Culture* that different groups of people—or, as he calls them, "taste publics"—make "equally valid" choices expressing their own "taste standards," and also that "both [high and popular culture publics] derive emotional and intellectual rewards from their choices."[27] He *also* concedes, however, (a) that "if only the content of the reward is measured, and the person's background and experience is left out, it is possible that individuals from a high culture public derive more reward from their content choice than do persons from a lower culture public . . . ," (b) that the objects of "higher cultures may be better than the lower ones because they may be able to provide greater and perhaps more lasting aesthetic gratification," and (c) that *"if one compared the* [objects of] *taste cultures alone, without taking into account the taste publics who choose them, it would be fair to say that the* [objects of] *higher cultures are better or at least more comprehensive and more informative"* (pp. 171 and 125).

Although Gans's general objective in his study is to establish and support a "to each his own" conception of cultural preferences, it is clear from these last two remarks that he is pressed—perhaps by his own background-and-experience as an intellectual and member of the academy, perhaps by anxious humanist colleagues or critics—to find some way of relating "high" and "low" cultural preferences to each other so that the former can be seen as, in effect, objectively better. The point, of course, and it should have been Gans's point, is that "one" (who?) *cannot* "compare the cultures [i.e., objects of cultural consumption] *alone*" and that, if we do not "take into account" *some* subject or population, even if it is only the high-culture sociologist and some of his friends, then there is no one with respect to whose interests, desires, experiences, and general perspective those objects of cultural consumption *could* be "better," "more comprehensive," or "more informative."[28]

Evidently uncomfortable with his own line of argument here, Gans observes in a footnote, "I believe that all cultures provide genuine gratifications, and I am only suggesting that the higher cultures may do so *more effectively*" (pp. 170–171, emphasis added). The terms of the distinction here recall once again, of course, Richards's observation that a Keats sonnet is better than one by Wilcox (the way brandy is better than beer) because the former is "more efficient"; and, with this suggestion that certain cultural objects are superior in themselves, Gans is backed even further into the corner he evidently wishes to avoid (though he keeps good company there). Moreover, and this is my central point here, the suggestion that *certain* people (such as high-culture publics or, as in Richards, those who are neurologically well organized) "get more" from the art they prefer than *other* people (such as low-culture publics or those with "inadequate impulses") get from *their* preferences is absurd or meaningless. For not only does the question of what they get more *of* remain unanswered or begged,[29] but the facile allusions to "measuring" and "comparing" the "content" of different people's aesthetic "rewards" must sooner or later confront the classic epistemological conundrum of how to determine the quality of other people's experiences. Is my airplane-neighbor reading *Rebecca* enjoying it less than I am enjoying *Emma*? Is there any way (by the difference in our EEG-waves? rates of heartbeat? muscle tone?) it could be demonstrated that the teenager listening to Pink Floyd is not feeling as good as I do when I listen to *Parsifal*?

Gans seems unaware of these difficulties and their implications for his analysis, but one of his suggestions here is especially revealing. The reason that "individuals from a high culture public derive more reward from their content choice than do persons from a lower culture public" may be, he observes, "the training the former have received in the aesthetic standards of their culture. As a result, they *draw more* from culture and are able to *relate* what they have drawn to many other facets of their emotional and intellectual lives" (p. 171, emphasis added). Not only may we ask here, again, what exactly it is that high-culture publics "draw more" *of* from the objects they prefer but, even more significantly, what the active verb "relate" means here and, specifically, whether it is indeed the case, as the formulation suggests, that low-culture publics are less able to experience the objects they prefer in relation to "other facets of their emotional and intellectual lives." May it not be, rather, that what members of the high culture are able to do better than members of low-culture by virtue of "the training [they] . . . have received in the aesthetic standards of their culture" (and for reasons that Gans obscures by his indefatigably upbeat as well as evenhanded descriptions of what makes different "taste publics" different) is to articulate certain quite specific *kinds* of relations in a certain quite specific *idiom?*

Gans, like other academics (egalitarian and otherwise), attempts to give an account of cultural preferences that makes sense of the fact that what looks like aesthetic *education* (and what apparently gratifies those who receive as well as those who administer it) does seem to take place: the fact, for example, that students from working-class and lower-middle-class families, and whose parents and other relatives still watch TV, drink beer, and read pulp magazines or bestsellers, *do* come to "appreciate" and enjoy Shakespeare and Milton. There is no reason to doubt that such acculturation takes place and is, in various ways, desirable, or to question the authenticity of those students' gratifications. The question raised above is, rather, the extent to which *we*, that is, high-culture academics, identify *their* "appreciation" by the fact—and indeed *locate it in the fact*—that those working-class and lower-middle-class students have also learned to articulate their experiences of high-culture objects through the descriptive categories and interpretive and evaluative idiom *of the high culture:* learned, for example, to speak of stanzas, lines, images, metaphors, characters, and plots; learned to make inter-textual connections and to identify allusions and influences; learned to ascribe meanings in terms of general themes and oppositions; and learned to evaluate authors in terms of the "irony" and "imagination" they exhibit just as, in Hume's time, members of high-culture publics learned to evaluate authors in terms of their "elegance" and "genius." What obscures these processes is the powerful illusion, very likely shared by those students and their professors, that in learning to use that idiom they have literally moved from darkness into light and that, compared to their current experiences of French films, Milton, and Remy Martin V.S.O.P., their former experiences (and their own family-members' current experiences) of TV, beer, and bestsellers were thinner, cruder, less connected, less reflective, less discriminating, and not as good *as experiences.* That illusion also obscures the fact (and rich field for postaxiological exploration) that there are extensive demotic languages of popular criticism: that is, discourses of description, evaluation, comparison, and discrimination of films, TV shows, beer, sports, rock music, and so forth that are well known to "the fans" and used among them with considerable communicative subtlety, force, and social effectiveness. The epistemological conundrum, however (that is, the puzzle of how to find out how The Other's meat tastes to *him*), remains uncrackable, and other questions are raised for normative cultural criticism and its associated pedagogic and missionary imperatives, including whether the quality of other people's lives or cultures is appropriately or usefully measured by the extent to which either the objects of their experience duplicate our own or their articulation of those experiences are produced in the idioms of our own cultural discourses.

5

Truth/Value

The preoccupation of formal value-theory with specifically *verbal* forms of evaluation, and the corresponding preoccupation of traditional critical theory and disciplinary aesthetics with debates over the "validity," "verifiability," and "truth-value" of aesthetic judgments, have obscured the operation and significance of the institutional and other less overt and explicit forms of judgment discussed in Chapter 3. Because the issues in these debates remain current, however, and also because evaluative discourse, as such, is of interest in relation to contemporary analyses of language and truth, *verbal judgments,* as such, require our attention here. In later sections of this chapter, I will be concerned with the recurrent question of how to acknowledge, assess, and compare the value of verbal judgments in the absence of such classic parameters as objectivity, correctness, and truth-value, and also with the implications of the present analysis and other contemporary formulations, including those of deconstruction, for classic questions of truth and error in intellectual history. It will be useful to approach these issues, however, through an examination of the strictly dualistic *typology* of judgments that is invoked recurrently in relation to them and which, it appears, is fundamental to traditional axiology.

Judgment Typology and MacIntyre's Fall

It is a commonplace of traditional value theory that there are two fundamentally distinct types of evaluative discourse, one exemplified by statements such as "I like it," "I want to do it," or "I think so," the other by statements such as "It is beautiful," "It is right," or "It is true," the first expressing a subjective and merely personal preference (or desire or opinion), the second constituting an impersonal judgment of the value (aesthetic, moral, or cognitive) of something and claiming universal validity. A key instance (and perhaps the founding one) of the distinction was developed by Kant in the opening pages of the *Critique of Judgment*. A lay version of it is the familiar observation that, since one can say "It's good, but I don't like it" and "I like it though I know it's no good," it must be because we intuitively recognize and/or "our language embodies" a fundamental difference between personal feelings and objective value.[1]

These distinctions also operate crucially in Alisdair MacIntyre's *After Virtue*, an axiologically nostalgic meditation on the decline of moral discourse and practice in modern times.[2] Early in his first chapter, MacIntyre contrasts two kinds of reply to the question "Why should I do so-and-so?" Reply #1 has a form such as *"Because I wish it,"* whose "reason-giving force," MacIntyre observes, is confined to "the personal context of the utterance." It "depends on certain characteristics possessed [by the speaker] at the time of hearing or otherwise learning of the utterance by [the listener]" (*AV*, p. 9). (These confining contexts and characteristics are exemplified, in the discussion, by situations where the speaker is "a police or army officer" who has "power or authority" over the listener, or where the listener "love[s] or fear[s] or want[s] something from" the speaker.) In contrast to this, the reason-giving force of Reply #2, which has a form such as *"Because it is your duty,"* is said by MacIntyre *not* to be so confined but, on the contrary, to be altogether unconditional, quite independent of who utters it or, he adds, even whether it is uttered at all. He continues:

> Moreover the appeal [of a statement such as "Because it is your duty"] is to a type of consideration which is independent of the relationship between speaker and hearer. Its use presupposes the existence of *impersonal* criteria—the existence, independently of the preferences or attitudes of speaker and hearer, of standards of justice or generosity or duty. *The particular link between the context of utterance and the force of the reason-giving which always holds in the case of expressions of personal preferences or desire is severed in the case of moral and other evaluative utterances.* (*AV*, p. 9, emphasis in last sentence added)

According to MacIntyre, the emotive theory of value judgments—which he explains as the view that expressions such as "It is good" really mean "I like it and urge it on or recommend it to you"—"is dedicated to characterizing as equivalent in meaning two kinds of expression which . . . derive their distinctive function in our language in key part from the contrast and difference between them. I have already suggested that there are good reasons for distinguishing between what I called expressions of personal preference and evaluative (including moral) expressions" (*AV*, p. 13). Therefore, he concludes, the emotive theory is really "a theory about the *use*—understood as purpose or function—of members of a certain class of expressions rather than about their *meaning*—understood as including all that Frege intended by 'sense' and 'reference' " (*AV*, p. 13).

MacIntyre goes on to posit the remarkable hypothesis on which the major argument of *After Virtue* is subsequently constructed:

> Clearly the argument so far shows that when someone utters a moral judgment such as "This is right" or "This is good," it does not mean the same as "I approve of this; do so as well" or "Hurrah for this!" . . .
> . . . [If it could be demonstrated] that in *using* such sentences *to say* whatever they *mean*, the agent was in fact *doing* nothing other than *expressing his feelings or attitudes and attempting to influence the feelings and attitudes of others* . . . it would follow that the meaning and the use of moral expressions were, or at the very least had become, radically discrepant with each other. Meaning and use would be at odds in such a way that meaning would tend to conceal use. We could not safely infer what someone who uttered a moral judgment was doing merely by listening to what he said. Moreover the agent himself . . . might be assured that he was appealing to independent impersonal criteria, when all that he was in fact doing was expressing his feelings to others in a manipulative way. How might such a phenomenon come to occur? (*AV*, pp. 13–14, emphasis added)

How, indeed? Or, rather, we might ask: in accord with what conception of *language* could the occurrence of any such phenomenon come to be *imagined*?

The significant features of that conception become clear as MacIntyre develops his "philosophical/historical" narrative, which goes as follows. When all was well and there were still objective standards accepted by all the members of the polis (with a few exceptions about which nothing further need be said), moral discourse was such that there was always a dependable correspondence between (a) what moral expressions said and meant *in themselves,* and (b) what the people who *used* those expressions meant by them, and believed they were doing with them, and really did with them. In such a time, a listener could "safely infer" what someone was *doing* with a moral expression "merely by listening" to what that person *said*. And, in those good days gone, there was no confusion between expressions (or sentences) such as "I like it" and others such as "It is good."[3] The first, which *in itself* expresses some purely personal preference was then *used* only to express purely personal preferences; the second, which presupposes impersonal standards and *in itself* embodies an appeal to them, was *used* only to appeal to such standards.

Now, alas, the story continues, all is schism and confusion: that which was once one and united is now many and fractured, those things which once corresponded and matched are now "discrepant" and "at odds," and that which was once clear and dependable has become cloudy and shifting. Now, what passes for morality is an "unharmonious mélange" of "ill-assorted fragments," and there is no established way of deciding between conflicting claims (*AV*, p. 10). Now, " 'virtue' and 'justice' and 'piety' and 'duty' and even 'ought' have become other than they once were," so that "moral judgments lose any clear status and the sentences which express them . . . lose any undebatable meaning" (*AV*, pp. 10, 60). Now, people still *say* "It is good" and *think* they mean "It is good," but, without knowing it, they are really doing only what people used to do when they said "I like it" or "I want it," namely expressing their own feelings and trying to get other people to feel, do, or believe certain things. And everyone is deceived: listeners are deceived about what speakers are doing, speakers are deceived about what they themselves are doing, and moral philosophers are either deceived, complacent, or complicitous.[4]

MacIntyre wants to remind us what it was like before after-virtue, and what it is still like in a few places ("among . . . some Catholic Irish, some Orthodox Greeks and some Jews of an Orthodox persuasion, . . . in Scotland . . . [and in] Protestant communities in the United States, especially perhaps those in or from the South"—*AV*, p. 252), and what, in our heart of hearts, the rest of us really wish it would be like again. We reveal that we wish it by the very fact that we still *say* things such as "It is good," "It is right," and "Because it is your duty." For even though we are *using* those expressions only to disguise from each other and from ourselves what we are really *doing*—that is, expressing our merely personal preferences and desires in manipulative ways— nevertheless, because those expressions *in themselves* embody impersonal appeals to objective standards, our very *use* of them "expresses at least an aspiration to be or to become rational in this area of our lives" (*AV*, p. 10).

The question that must be asked of this as of any other account of the Fall is not merely whether, with respect to every posited *pre*lapsarian element, anything ever did or could happen that way but, no less importantly, whether, with respect to every deplored *post*lapsarian element, anything ever did or could happen otherwise. Thus, here, the significant questions would be whether expressions *ever* mean things "in themselves," whether anyone *ever* deduced motives directly from verbal forms, whether judgments could *ever* have undebatable meaning, and whether there is any use of language that does *not* try to get people to feel, do, and believe certain things.

The answer to all these questions is, of course, *no*. In particular, no verbal form has any meaning or force in itself or ever did have, even before the Fall. Nothing is "in" the form. Everything is "in" the verbal agents themselves, specifically in their tendencies to produce verbal forms under certain conditions and to respond to them in certain ways: tendencies that are themselves the corporeal traces of the differential consequences of those agents' using and responding to those forms in prior interactions with each other in particular verbal communities. The general dynamics through which a listener comes to respond in some way to a so-called impersonal and unconditional (or "context-independent" or "objective") judgment such as "Murder is wrong," "*Es ist schön,*" or "Business is business," is no different from the dynamics through which she comes to respond to any other type of statement, including such manifestly personal and otherwise conditional (or "context-bound" or "subjective") ones as "I want to kill now," "I just happen to find it appealing," or "For my money, business is business."

We are quite familiar by now with the idea that the "meaning," in the sense of force or effect, of any utterance can be "severed" from—or, rather, cannot be decisively attached to—the conditions of its production, including the intentions and identity or other characteristics of the speaker. There is no "type" of expression, however, whose force or effect is uniquely and characteristically so severed, and none, even the most Mosaic or otherwise oracular in form, and even where manifestly anonymous, that operates with the sort of autonomy that MacIntyre describes.[5] The degeneracy and homesickness of contemporary moral thought cannot be exhibited in the disparity between "*the* meaning" of moral expressions and "*our* use" of them because there is not and cannot be any such disparity. Expressions such as "It is right," "It is good," "Murder is wrong," and "Business is business" cannot embody objectivist appeals *in spite of* how they are being used because, *aside from* how they are being used, there is no way for them to embody anything

89

at all. To say that an expression has been "severed" from some "original" set of meanings is to say only that it has come to be *used* under a *different* set of conditions in relation to which it now "really means" something else.[6] Or, to put this another way, the notion of a disparity between the meaning and the use of a verbal form consists simply of privileging one set of conditions of usage—and more or less corresponding effects—over another. Commonly, as in MacIntyre's case, usages that were common at some earlier moment in the life of the community are privileged (as more authentic, inherent, or proper) over later ones—or perhaps it is here only earlier in the moral theorist's own life and, for that very reason, intuitively felt as more fundamental, more authentic, and embodied in the forms themselves.

The "meaning," in the sense of "force," "functions," and apparent "claims," of *all* judgments and justifications and, indeed, of *all statements or "expressions"* are conditional, contingent, and variable. To be sure, the ranges of variability tend to become relatively stabilized within some verbal community, but this is the emergent effect of the interactive practices of the members of the community themselves and not the product of some essential/residual semantic force inhering in verbal *forms*. Moreover, plausible situations can always be specified in which forms that *tend* to operate one way under *most* conditions would operate otherwise. Thus, ostensible "expressions of personal preference" such as "It's just my cup of tea" could, under readily imaginable circumstances, be replaced by ostensibly "impersonal and objective" forms such as "It's absolutely the greatest ever" with very little difference in function, force, apparent claim, or, in those senses, *meaning*. Indeed, the supposed binary distinctions between judgment "types" can always be observed to break down in verbal practice, for *any* verbal form can serve *any* discursive function—evaluative or other—under *certain* circumstances, and *each* of the two supposedly contrastive forms will, under *some* circumstances, serve the functions, operate with the force, make the claims, and have the meanings that, in classic axiological discourse-typology, are the distinguishing features of the *other* one.

As should be clear, the point of this analysis is not that there are *no* differences among the various verbal forms or discourse-types dichotomized in traditional value theory: it is, rather, that there are *many* differences, that they are not only and always contrastive, that they include many that are not commonly cited, and that those commonly cited must be described otherwise. A final point may be noted here by way of transition to the next section, which examines the relation between value judgments and other types of discourse with respect to their "validity" or "truth-value." Not only can one not tell from its form alone what the force of an evaluative judgment is; one cannot even tell whether an "expression" is evaluative at all. Virtually any verbal form ("How odd!"; "Is this the one you brought back from Rome?"; "It's ten o'clock already, let's go"; "Don't forget your umbrella") can, under some conditions, operate as a mark and sign of someone's "personal preferences," and there is a virtually unlimited range of forms ("cool," "the pits," "***," "XXX") through which someone can offer an ("objective," "impersonal") observation or estimate of the value of something for other people. Moreover, even such apparently simple and impoverished forms as appear in these examples may be expressively and informationally quite rich, subtle, and specific: as, for example, when the listener has prior knowledge of the speaker's tastes, interests, and, especially, his verbal habits or, as in published film ratings or travel guides, where the reader interprets the symbols in accord with some more or less elaborate "key" that she has already learned. These cases, however, are not very different from each other, and, in fact, represent the ways "expressions" of all "types" in all languages operate.

I suggested above that the syntactic and modal form of a judgment— whether it is "Gee, you could try Archie's, all the fellows at the office go there" as opposed to "It's the best restaurant in town"; or "I think it's horrible to hurt other people deliberately" as opposed to "Torture is wrong"; or, in the case of a justification, "Do it because I want you to" as opposed to "Do it because it is your duty"—may be responsive to, and indicate to a listener, quite subtle and specific matters. These are characteristically matters not about the objects or practices being evaluated but, rather, about the nature of the evaluator's *relationship* to those he addresses (*precisely,* to use MacIntyre's examples, whether he is the listener's superior officer *or* her lover, and whether he is afraid of the listener *or* wants something from her, and so forth) and also the evaluator's own *beliefs* concerning various relevant matters—for example, the extensiveness and stability of the conditions under which his judgment would be applicable, the extent to which relevant aspects of his personal economy, perspective, and assumptions are shared by his listeners, the nature of his listeners' interest in his judgment, and also the degree of his own confidence in his beliefs concerning all these matters. Although it is unlikely that any of these matters could be specifically articulated *as such* by the evaluator or his listeners, they are nevertheless what both (or all) of them will have learned in learning the _conditions of usage_ of the forms of evaluative language in their shared verbal community—which is, of course, why evaluations have any communicative force at all.

Because of other general aspects of communication to be discussed at length in the next section, particularly those involving inevitable disparities, differences, and asymmetries between what is "transmitted" by a speaker and "received" by a listener, a listener cannot (and never *could*, even before the Fall) "infer" any of these matters—or anything else—"safely" from the form of a judgment. To the extent, however, that certain verbal practices tend to occur with some regularity in our own verbal communities, we may observe that (a) the broader and more stable the range of conditions under which an evaluator believes the judgment she offers would be applicable, (b) the more extensive the set of people for whom she believes it would be appropriable, (c) the more closely she believes her personal economy and relevant assumptions coincide with those of her listeners, (d) the more she believes her listeners' interest in her judgment is in the object or practice evaluated rather than in her personal responses as such, and (e) the more confident she is in her own beliefs concerning all these matters, the *less* likely it is that her evaluation will take the form of a contextually qualified statement of personal preference and the *more* likely that it will tend to be "unconditioned" and "impersonal" in form and hence *appear to be* an "impersonal" judgment appealing to "objective standards."

Thus, and contrary to a crucial axiological supposition, when someone makes a formally unconditional and otherwise unqualified evaluative statement such as "It's nifty," "It's nauseating," "It's cheap," "It's bad manners," the fact that she does not name explicitly any limiting group of people need *not* imply that she is "claiming universal validity" for the judgment or that she takes the agreement of "everybody" to be its ideal limit. It may be and often is, rather, because she assumes that the defining features of the specific set of people for whom the judgment would be appropriable[7] can be *taken for granted* by her listeners: commonly as consisting of *herself*, plus *them*, plus all other people *like* them in the relevant respects (lovers of New Wave music, students of cinematic art, electronic engineers, communicants of the Catholic Church, professional people of means and leisure, etc.), but also quite often as inferable from the context of the judgment itself (for example, the book-review section of *The New Yorker* as distinguished from that of

Popular Mechanics, or the current *Michelin Guide to Italy* rather than a 1950 edition of *How to See Europe on $5 a Day,* or the policy recommendations of a sociological study of teenage pregnancy rather than a Vatican Encyclical). The evaluator's assumptions concerning what her audience knows or takes for granted may of course be mistaken, but the possibility of error of that kind is an ineradicable condition of all verbal transactions and does not undermine the appropriability of value judgments—or their "force" or interest of any other kind—any more than that of any other type of utterance.

A concluding word on the political implications of MacIntyre's analysis of value judgments may be added. It could be shown to follow from the account outlined above that the conditions for truly universally shared objective standards would be achieved insofar as the members of a community approached total homogeneity and the community itself approached the status of a closed and static system, both immured from external interactions and secured against internal sources of instability. Since in such a community the conditions of experience and judgment would always be the same, and the same for everybody, there would be, in effect, *no* contingencies and all judgments would be, in effect, "objective." Moreover, since everything would be presupposed by everyone in the same way, evaluative authority would be located in a truly universal consensus backed up by the combined power of the entire community except, perhaps, for a few unregenerately unassimilable malcontents.

It is doubtless the case that communal life requires shared goals or norms—or at least more or less congruous inclinations among the members of the community—and routines of action, reaction, and interaction that are, at least in the long run, mutually and generally beneficial (the two are not, of course, the same). It appears to be the characteristic belief of current social critics who pursue the nostalgic mode, however, that these are simple correlations or purely linear functions: that a community prospers, in other words, in proportion to the extent that its members have achieved consensus or that it prospers more as communal norms become more uniform, coherent, and stable.[8] But the well-being of any community is also a function of other and indeed opposed conditions, including the extent of the *diversity* of the beliefs and practices of its members and thus their communal resourcefulness, and the *flexibility* of its norms and patterns and thus their responsiveness to changing and emerging circumstances.

For, of course, with the exception of Paradise and some other transcendental polities, no community *can* be immured from interactions with a changing environment, nor can the heterogeneity of its members be altogether eradicated and their potential conflicts altogether prevented. Where *difference* continuously emerges, it must be either continuously negotiated or continuously suppressed, the latter always at somebody's cost and often enough, it appears, at, in the long run, considerable *communal* cost. Given such sublunary conditions, it is perhaps just as well for "our society" that its norms are a "mélange," that they constantly multiply, collide, and transform each other, that conflicts of judgment are negotiated ad hoc, and that normative authority itself is multiple and recurrently changes hands, variously strengthening and becoming diffuse. And, given such conditions, it is perhaps also just as well that malcontents continue to be engendered and Falls continuously enacted.

Value without Truth-Value

Two corollaries of the conception of value as radically contingent are of particular interest for classic and contemporary conceptions of "truth-value." The first is that a verbal judgment of "*the* value" of some entity—for example, an artwork, a work of literature, or any other kind of object, event, text, or *utterance*—cannot be a judgment of any independently determinate or, as we say, "objective" property of that entity. As seen above, however, what it can be (and typically is) is a judgment of that entity's *contingent* value: that is, the speaker's observation or estimate of how the entity will figure in the economy of some limited population of subjects under some limited set of conditions.

The second corollary is that no value judgment can have truth-value in the usual sense. The usual sense, however, is no longer all that usual. When interpreted in accord with some version of the traditional telegraphic model of discourse in which communication is seen as the *duplicative transmission* of a code-wrapped message from one consciousness to another, "truth-value" is seen as a measure of the extent to which such a message, when properly unwrapped, accurately and adequately reflects, represents, or corresponds with some independently determinate fact, reality, or state of affairs. As we know, that model of discourse, along with the entire structure of conceptions, epistemological and other, in which it is embedded, is now felt in many places to be theoretically unworkable. It has not, however, been replaced by any other widely appropriated model. There have been, of course, throughout the century, sophisticated demonstrations of precisely that unworkability; and there have also been attempts, some of them quite painstaking, to rehabilitate the key terms, concepts, and conceptual syntax of the traditional model.[9] What appears to be needed, and is perhaps emerging, is a total and appropriately elaborated reformulation, and, in particular, one in which the various fundamentally problematic explanatory structures involving duplicative transmission, correspondence, equivalence, and recovery are replaced by an account of the dynamics of various types of *consequential interaction*.

With respect to its epistemological component or what is traditionally referred to as "perception," "knowledge," "belief," and so forth, this would be an account of how the structures, mechanisms, and behaviors through which subjects interact with—and, accordingly, constitute—their environments are modified by those very interactions.[10] With respect to what we now call "communication," it would be an account of the dynamics of the differentially constrained behaviors of subjects who interact with, and thereby act *upon*, each other, for better and for worse. I shall return to this latter suggestion below, but for the moment it is enough to observe that, whatever its emergent shape (or, more likely, *shapes*), an alternate account of our commerce with the universe *and* our commerce with each other is not yet available.

In the meantime, the telegraphic model of communication, along with its associated conception of truth as correspondence to an independently determinate reality, continues to dominate theoretical discourse, and the theoretical interest of the term "truth" itself continues to be reinforced by its numerous—and, it must be emphasized here, irreducibly *various*—idiomatic and technical uses. Indeed, the term appears to be irreplaceable and, economically speaking, priceless: for its rhetorical power in political discourse alone—and there is perhaps no other kind of discourse—would seem to be too great to risk losing or even compromising. Nevertheless, as already indicated, the theoretical value of the concept of truth-value has already been compromised. Indeed, the value of truth and of truth-value seem to be as contingent—as historically and locally variable—as that of anything else.

The question of the truth-value of value judgments has, of course, been debated endlessly and unresolvably in formal axiology, and the continued preoccupation of disciplinary aesthetics with corresponding debates over the logical status and cognitive substance of aesthetic judgments, typically posited and examined as totally unsituated (or, at best, minimally situated) instances, has no doubt contributed to its reputation for dreariness and perhaps to its terminal sterility as well. Other, potentially more productive projects, however, may be undertaken more or less independently of such debates. One, which I have already outlined, is the exploration of the institutional and broader cultural and historical operation of literary and aesthetic evaluations, verbal *and otherwise*. Another, to be broached below, is the analysis of verbal value judgments considered not as a class of "propositions" identified through certain formal features but, rather, as a type of communicative behavior responding to and constrained by certain social conditions. The latter sort of analysis avoids but makes apparent the theoretical impoverishment as well as the fundamentally problematic dualism of more traditional "analytic" approaches. For, as will be seen, the classic dichotomies thereby produced (personal/impersonal, conditional/unconditioned, expressing subjective preferences versus making objective judgments, speaking for oneself alone versus claiming universal validity, trying to persuade and manipulate people versus indicating the true value of things, and so forth) have obscured not only the enormous range, variety, richness, and modulation of individual verbal judgments, but also the crucially relevant *continuities* between evaluative and other types of discourse, and, most significantly, the social dynamics through which *all* utterances, evaluative and otherwise, acquire value.

The Value of Value Judgments

"The work is physically small—18 by 13 inches—but massive and disturbingly expressive in impact."

"Brava, brava!"

"It's not up to his last one, but that's just my opinion."

"Yes, if you're looking for a teachable text; no, if you want the most current research."

"Absolutely beautiful, though not, of course, for all tastes."

"They gave it the Booker Prize in England, but I'll bet the Americans will pan it."

"XXX"

Value judgments appear to be among the most fundamental forms of social communication and also among the most primitive benefits of social interaction. It appears, for example, that insects and birds as well as mammals signal to other members of their group, by some form of specialized overt behavior, not only the location but also the "quality" of a food supply or territory. And, creatures such as we are, we too not only produce but also eagerly solicit from each other both, as it might be said, "expressions of personal sentiment" (*How do you like it?*) and "objective judgments of value" (*Is it any good?*). We solicit them because, although neither will (for nothing can) give us knowledge of any determinate value of an object, both may let us know, or—and this will be significant here—at least *appear* to let us know, other things that we could find interesting and useful.

It is evident, for example, that other people's reports of how well certain things have gratified them, though "mere expressions of their subjective likes and dislikes," will nevertheless be interesting to us if we ourselves—as artists, say, or manufacturers, or cooks—have produced those objects, or if—as parents, say, or potential associates—we have an independently motivated interest in the current states of *those people* or in the general structure of *their* tastes and preferences. Also, no matter how magisterially delivered and with what attendant claims or convictions of universality, unconditionality, impersonality, or objectivity, any assertion of "*the* value" of some object can always be unpacked as a judgment of its *contingent* value and appropriated accordingly: that is, as that speaker's observation and/or estimate of how well that object, compared to others of the same (even though only implicitly defined) type, has performed and/or is likely to perform some particular (even though unstated) desired/able functions[11] for some particular (even though only implicitly defined) subject or set of subjects under some particular (even though not specified) set or range of conditions.

Any evaluation, then, no matter what its manifest syntactic form, ostensible "validity claim," and putative propositional status, may have social value in the sense of being appropriable by other people. The actual value of a particular evaluation, however, will itself be highly contingent, depending on such variables as the specific social and institutional context in which it is produced, the specific social and institutional relation between the speaker and his listener(s), the specific structure of interests that motivates and constrains the entire social/verbal transaction in which the evaluation figures, a vast and not ultimately numerable or listable set of variables relating to, among other things, the social, cultural, and verbal histories of those involved, and of course the particular perspective from which that value is being figured.

In the case of someone's verbal evaluation of an artwork, for example, the value of that *evaluation* would obviously be figured differently by (a) *the evaluator* himself, who, we should note, could be anyone from the artist's teacher, student, brother, or agent to some casual gallery visitor, a Warburg Institute art historian, or a member of a Committee for the Preservation of Cultural Standards and Ideological Purity, (b) *the artist* herself, whose interest in the evaluation would be different from that of the evaluator but whose evaluation of it would still depend on the latter's identity and/or relationship to her and/or institutional role, (c) any of various *specifically addressed listeners* or some interested *bystander or eavesdropper:* for example, a potential patron, a gallery-going reader of *Art News*, a fellow art historian, or someone who just likes to know what's going on and what other people think is going on. For each of these, the evaluation would be "good" or "bad" in relation to a different configuration of heterogeneous interests: interests that might be unique but that might also be more or less shared by other—perhaps many other—people.

We may take note here of the recurrent anxiety/charge/claim—I shall refer to it as the Egalitarian Fallacy—that, unless one judgment can be said or shown to be more "valid" than another, then all judgments must be "equal" or "equally valid." Although the radical contingency of all value certainly does imply that no value judgment can be more "valid" than another *in the sense of* an objectively truer statement of the objective value of an object (for these latter concepts are then seen as vacuous), it does not follow that all value judgments are equally valid. On the contrary, what does follow is that the concept of "validity" *in that sense* is unavailable as a parameter by which to measure or compare judgments (or anything else). It is evident, however, that value judgments can still be evaluated, still compared, and still seen and said to be "better" or "worse" than others. The point, of course, is that their *value*— "goodness" or "badness"—must be understood, evaluated, and compared *otherwise*, that is, as something other than "truth-value" or "validity" in the objectivist, essentialist sense. I shall return to this point below.

The social value of value judgments is illustrated most concretely, perhaps, by the most obviously commercial of them, namely the sorts of assessments and recommendations issued by professional evaluators: film and book reviewers, commissioned art connoisseurs, and those who prepare consumer guides, travel guides, restaurant guides, race-track tipsheets, and so forth. Such evaluations are not only regularly produced but also regularly sought and bought by the citizens of late capitalist society who live in what is, in effect, a vast supermarket, open twenty-four hours a day, with an array of possible goods that is not only enormous but that constantly increases and changes and, moreover, does so at a pace that constantly outstrips our ability to obtain current information about them and thus to calculate how they might figure in our personal economies. Indeed, if we were the "rational consumers" so beloved by economists—that is, consumers who, given total information about market conditions, always buy the best for their money—we would have to spend so much of our time acquiring the necessary information that there would be little time left to buy, much less to consume, anything at all.[12]

The supermarket described here is, to be sure, a flagrant feature of contemporary Western society. It is not, however, as recent or as culturally unique as is sometimes suggested. For we always live in a market, always have limited resources—including limited time, energy, and occasion to locate and sample for ourselves the entire array of possible goods in it—and therefore always find it economical to pay others to locate and sample some of those goods for us. Professional evaluations—reviews, ratings, guides, tips, and so forth—are only highly specialized and commoditized versions of the sorts of observations and estimates of contingent value commonly exchanged more informally among associates in any culture; and though we do not always pay each other for them in hard coin, we do pay for them in coin of some sort, such as gratitude and good will, redeemable for return favors and future services.

It appears, then, that evaluations—of artworks along with anything else consumable, and what isn't?—are themselves commodities of considerable value, and this in spite of what is sometimes alleged to be their tenuous cognitive substance and suspect propositional status as compared with other kinds of utterances: "factual descriptions," for example, or "empirical scientific reports." Of course, the cognitive substance and propositional validity of aesthetic judgments have been strenuously defended. Indeed, the dominant tradition in post-Kantian aesthetic axiology has characteristically offered to demonstrate that such judgments *do* have truth-value, or at least that they can properly "claim" to have it under the right conditions—which, however, always turn out to be excruciating ones to meet and also rather difficult, or perhaps impossible, to certify as having *been* met. We are, however, approaching the issue from a different—in fact, reverse—direction, the procedure and objective here being not to demonstrate that value judgments have as much claim to truth-value as factual or descriptive state-

99

ments but, rather, to suggest that, just as value judgments do not have but also do not *need* truth-value in the traditional sense, neither, it seems, do any of those other forms of discourse.

There is, of course, no way for us to be certain that our associates' reports of their personal likes and dislikes are *sincere,* or that the ratings and rankings produced by professional connoisseurs and local men and women of taste are, as we might say, "honest" and "objective." Indeed, we may grant more generally that any evaluation, aesthetic or otherwise, will be shaped by the speaker's own interests, both as a party to the verbal transaction in which the evaluation figures and in other ways as well. It may also be granted that, since value is especially subject-variable for certain classes of objects, among them artworks, the appropriability of value *judgments* of such objects may be correspondingly highly subject-variable. For these reasons—that is, because we do tend to learn that there's no such thing as an honest opinion and that one man's meat is the other's poison—we typically *supplement* and *discount* the value judgments we are offered "in the light," as we say, of knowledge we have from other sources: knowledge, for example, of the reviewer's personal and perhaps idiosyncratic preferences, or the connoisseur's special interests or obligations and thus suspect or clearly compromised motives.

Or, rather, knowledge we *think* we have. For there is no way for us to be certain of the accuracy, adequacy, or validity of this supplementary knowledge either, and we may therefore seek yet further supplementary information from yet other sources: some trustworthy guide to travel guides, perhaps, or a reliable review of the reliability of film reviewers, or an inside tip on what tipsheet to buy. It is clear, however, that there can be no end to this theoretically infinite regress of supplementing the supplements and evaluating the evaluations, just as there is none to that of justifying the justifications of judgments, or grounding the grounds of knowledge of any kind—though, in practice, we do the best we can, all things considered . . . at least as far as we know those things, or think we know them. We need not linger over the epistemological regress here. What is more pertinent to observe is that *in all the respects mentioned,* value judgments are not essentially different from "descriptive" or "factual" statements, and that their reliability and objectivity are no more compromised by these possibilities—or, for that matter, any *less* compromised by them—than the reliability or objectivity of any other type of utterance, from a pathetic plea of a headache to the solemn communication of the measurement of a scientific instrument.[13]

100

Not *essentially* different: there are, however, *relative* differences of various kinds. That is, these types of discourse may be seen not as absolutely distinct by virtue of their radically opposed claims to "truth" or "objective validity," but as occupying different positions along a number of relevant continua. Thus, although the value of all objects is to some extent subject-variable, the value of some objects will be *relatively more uniform* than others among the members of some community—as will be, accordingly, the judgments concerning their value exchanged within that community. Similarly, although the conditions under which a particular judgment or report can be appropriated by other people are always to some extent limited, they will be *relatively broader* for some judgments and reports than for others. And, as I shall discuss below, although fraud, exploitation, and oppression are possibilities in any verbal interaction, their occurrence will be *relatively better controlled* by certain types of social and institutional constraints than others. Indeed, the familiar distinctions and contrasts among types of discourse that are at issue here—that is, between "merely subjective" and "truly objective" judgments, or between mere value judgments and genuine factual descriptions, or between statements that can and cannot claim truth-value—are no doubt continuously reinforced by the undeniability of just such relative differences which, however, in accord with certain conceptual operations perhaps endemic to human thought, are typically binarized, polarized, absolutized, and hierarchized.

We may return here briefly to the the Egalitarian Fallacy: the idea that a denial of objective value commits one to the view that all judgments are "equal," "equally good," or "equally valid." As noted above, this is a strict *non sequitur* since, if one finds "validity" in the objectivist, essentialist sense vacuous, one could hardly be committed to accepting it as a parameter by which to measure or compare judgments, whether as better or worse *or* as "equal." What feeds the fallacy is the objectivist's unshakable conviction that "validity" in *his* objectivist, essentialist sense is the only *possible* measure of the value of utterances. (The Egalitarian Fallacy is thus another illustration of the more general rule that, to the dualist, whatever is not dualistic is reductionist, or *If it's not distinguishable by my dualistic description of differences, then it's the same*.) What I am suggesting throughout this study is not only that there are other parameters by which the value—goodness or badness—of utterances can be measured,[14] but that there are other ways in which all value, including that of utterances, can be conceived.

As we have seen, value judgments may themselves be considered commodities. What may be added here, glancing at the issue of their

101

alleged "equality" under this account, is that some of them are evidently *worth more* than others *in the relevant markets*. Thus, the Michelin guides to Italian hotels, restaurants, and altar paintings have, we might say, a well-attested reputation for objectivity and reliability, at least among certain classes of travelers. This is not, however, because there is, after all, just a little bit of objective—or universal subjective—validity to which some judgments can properly lay claim. On the contrary, it may be seen as a consequence of precisely those compromising conditions described earlier and summed up in the lesson that there's no such thing as an honest opinion: no judgment, that is, totally unaffected by the particular social, institutional, and other conditions of its production or totally immune to the (assumed) interests and desires of its (assumed) audience—or, we could say, because it cuts both ways *and that is the point*, no judgment altogether *unresponsive to* those interests and desires. For, if we do not regard them as the regrettable effects of fallen human nature or as noise in the channels of communication or, in the terms of one account, as "distortions" of the ideal conditions "presupposed" by all genuine speech-acts,[15] then we may be better able to see them as the conditions under which all verbal transactions take place and which *give* them—or are, precisely, the *conditions of possibility* for—whatever value they do have for those actually involved in them.

The Economics of Verbal Transactions

That which we call "communication" is a historically conditioned social interaction, in many respects also an economic one and, like other or perhaps all economic transactions, a political one as well. It is historically conditioned in that the effectiveness of any particular interaction depends on the differential consequences of the agents' prior verbal acts and interactions with other members of a particular verbal community. It is an economic interaction—and thus, one could say, transaction—to the extent that its dynamics operate on, out of, and through disparities of resources (or "goods," such as material property, information, skills, influence, position, and so on) between/among the agents and involve risks, gains, and/or losses on either or all sides. Communication is also a political interaction, not only in that its dynamics may operate through differences of power between the agents but also in that the interaction may put those differences at stake, threatening or promising (again, it must cut both ways) either to confirm and maintain them or to subvert or otherwise change them.

Not all the implications of this conception of communication can be spelled out here.[16] What is significant for our present concerns is that *all* discourse—descriptive and factual as well as evaluative—operates by social economics and that, under *certain* conditions, speakers are constrained (so that it is, we would say, "in their own interest") to serve the interests of their assumed listeners in the ways we commonly characterize as "objectivity" and "reliability."

Thus, certain conditions relevant to the publishing industry (for example, the need for the Michelin guides or *Art News* to secure a minimum number of regular readers and subscribers plus the actual or potential competition from other such guides or individual evaluators) will make it more profitable for professional raters and reviewers to produce evaluations appropriable by a relatively large but still relatively specific set of people and, accordingly, less profitable for them to accept bribes for favorable ratings or to play out idiosyncratic or inappropriately specialized personal preferences. We recall the familiar disclaimer commonly attached to such judgments (here an obviously somewhat, but not *altogether*, disingenuous one): "Note that we have no ties to manufacturers or retailers, we accept no advertising, and we're not interested in selling products. The sole purpose of this book is to help you make intelligent purchases at the best prices."[17] To increase the likelihood that the review or rating of a particular object (such as a new play opening in Philadelphia or an altar painting to be seen in Palermo) will be appropriable by that group of readers, the evaluator will, of course, typically sample it for himself or herself, operating as a stand-in for those subjects or, we might say, as their metonymic representative, and, to that end, will typically be attentive to the particular contingencies of which the value of objects of that kind appear to be a function for people of that kind. To do this reliably over a period of time, the evaluator will also be attentive to the shifts and fluctuations of those contingencies: that is, to the current states of the personal economies of those readers, to what can be discovered or surmised concerning their relevant needs, interests, and resources, to the availability of comparable and competitive objects, and so forth.[18]

As this suggests, competent and effective evaluators—those who know their business and stay in business (and, of course, there are always many who don't do either)—operate in some ways very much like market analysts. But professional market analysis is itself only a highly specialized and commoditized version of the sorts of informal or intuitive research, sampling, and calculating necessarily performed by *any* evaluator, and if we are inclined to reserve particular loathing for professional market analysts as compared to professional critics, it is no doubt because the latter typically operate to serve our interests as consumers whereas the former typically operate to serve the interests of our marketplace adversaries: those who seek to predict, control, and thereby to profit from, our actions and choices, that is, producers and sellers. But it must be remembered that some of us—or, indeed, all of us, some of the time—are producers and sellers, too, a point to which I will return below.

Given the general conditions and dynamics described above, professional evaluators will typically seek to secure as large a group of clients as possible. The size of that group will always be *limited,* however, for, given also that one man's meat is the other's poison, the more responsive a judgment is to the needs, resources, desires, and tastes of one client, the less appropriable it will be by another. It is desirable all around, then, that verbal judgments, professional or amateur, be (as they usually, in fact, seem to be) more or less explicitly "tailored" and "targeted" to particular people or sets of people rather than offering or claiming to be appropriable by everybody or, in the terms of classic axiology, "universally valid."

Validity in Science and the Value of "Beauty"

The market conditions that constrain evaluators to produce what we call objective and reliable judgments have their counterpart in social and institutional conditions that characteristically constrain scientists' behavior to comparable ends. Western disciplinary science has been able to pursue so successfully its defining communal mission—which we might characterize here as the generation of verbal/conceptual structures appropriable by the members of some relevant community under the broadest possible range of conditions[19]—because it has developed institutional mechanisms and practices, including incentives or systems of reward and punishment, that effectively constrain the individual scientist to serve that particular mission in the conduct and reporting of his or her research.[20]

Physicists and other scientists often recall that, in the course of their pursuit, production, and testing of alternate models or theories, they were drawn to what turned out to be the "right" one by their sense of its "beauty" or "aesthetic" appeal. Attempts to account for this commonly focus either on what are seen as the formal and hence aesthetic properties of the model or theory itself (for example, its "simplicity" or "elegance") or on what is seen as its correspondence to or conformity with comparable aesthetic features in nature (for example, the latter's "order," "pattern," or "regularity").[21] What makes such explanations somewhat questionable, however—that is, their ignoring of the historical, social, and institutional conditions under which scientific constructs are produced and appropriated, and their assumption of a "nature" with independently determinate features—suggests an alternate explanation more pertinent to our present concerns.

No matter how insulated his laboratory or solitary his research, the scientist always operates as a *social* being in two fundamental respects. First, the language or symbolic mode of his conceptualizations—both its lexicon and syntax (that is, the tokens, chains, routes, and networks of his conceptual moves)—has necessarily been acquired and shaped, like any other language, through his social interactions in a particular verbal community, here the community of scientists in that discipline or field. Second, in the very process of exploring and assessing the "rightness" or "adequacy" of alternate models, the scientist too, like professional and other evaluators, characteristically operates as a metonymic representative of the community for whom his product is designed and whose possible appropriation of it is part of the motive and reward of his own activity. In this respect, the scientist also operates as does any other producer of consumer goods, including, significantly enough here, the *artist,* for, as mentioned earlier, a significant aspect of the "creative" process is the artist's pre-figuring of the shifting economies of her assumed and imagined audiences, whose emergent interests, variable conditions of encounter, and rival sources of gratification she will intuitively surmise and to which, among other things, her sense of the *fittingness* and *fitness* of her creative/productive decisions will be responsive.

The point here is that the process of testing the adequacy of a scientific model or theory is never only—and sometimes not at all—a measuring of its fit with what we call "the data," "the evidence," or "the facts," all of which are, themselves, the products of comparable conceptual and evaluative activities already appropriated to one degree or another by the relevant community; it is also a testing, sampling, and, in effect, *tasting* in advance of the ways in which the product will taste to other members of that community—which is to say also a calculating in advance of how it will "figure" for them in relation to their personal economies, including (though not necessarily confined to) those aspects

105

of those economies that we call "intellectual" or "cognitive." Thus, what is commonly called "elegance" in a theory or model is often a matter of how sparing it is in its introduction of novel conceptual structures (novel, that is, relative to conceptualizations current in the community), in which case its "beauty" would indeed be a matter of its "economy" for its consumers: in effect, minimum cognitive processing and hence expenditure would be required for its effective appropriation, application, or "consumption." The sense of "beauty" or aesthetic appeal that draws the scientist in one direction rather than another may indeed, then, be a proleptic glimpse of its "fit," "fittingness," or "rightness": not, however, in the sense of its correspondence with or conformity to an independently determinate reality but, rather, in the sense of its suitability for eventual communal appropriation.[22]

I have not specified any of the numerous and quite diverse ways in which a scientific construct *could* "figure" for the members of some relevant community. Consideration of such matters would be excessively digressive here, but one further point relating to the social economics of validity should be emphasized. Insofar as the development of a theory, model, or hypothesis has been directed toward the solution of some relatively specific set of technological and/or conceptual problems, its structure will have been produced and shaped in accord with the scientist's sense—perhaps largely intuitive—of its fitness or potential utility to that end, and its appropriability and hence social value will be largely a matter of the extent to which that surmised or intuited utility is actually realized. Or, it might be said, its validity will be tested by "how well it works" and consist, in effect, in its working well. Pragmatist conceptions of validity, however, are not much improvement over static essentialist or positivist ones if they obliterate the historically and otherwise complex processes that would be involved in the *multiple and inevitably diverse* appropriation of any verbal/conceptual construct (or, to appropriate Jacques Derrida's useful term and concept here, its "dissemination").

Pragmatist reconceptualizations of scientific validity, then, must give due recognition to the fact that theories and models that work very badly or not all—or no longer work—in the implementation of specific projects or the solution of specific problems may nevertheless "work" and acquire social value otherwise. They may, for example, come to figure as especially fertile metaphoric structures, evoking the production and elaboration of other verbal and conceptual structures in relation to a broad variety of interests and projects under quite diverse historical and intellectual conditions. One may think here of Marxist economics, psychoanalytic theory, and various ancient and modern cosmological models, including more or less "mystical," "metaphysical," and "primitive" ones—all of these, we might note, also classic examples of "nonfalsifiability" and/or nonscientificity in positivist philosophies of science.

The Other Side of the Coin

To remark, as we have been doing here, the ways in which verbal products and wares have value without truth-value is not to imply that that value is always high or positive, or positive for everyone. Indeed, what follows from the present analysis is that the value of any utterance—aesthetic judgment, factual statement, mathematical theorem, or any other type—may be quite minimal or negative, at least for someone and perhaps for a great many people. As has been stressed here, *value always cuts both, or all, ways.* An aesthetic judgment, for example, however earnestly offered, may—under readily imaginable social conditions—be excruciatingly uninteresting and worthless to some listener(s); or, conversely, though a factual report may be highly informative to its audience, it may—under readily imaginable political conditions—have been extorted from an unwilling speaker at considerable risk or cost to himself.

Such possibilities do not require us to posit any deficiencies of truth-value or breakdowns in the conditions that "normally" obtain in verbal transactions or are "presupposed" by them.[23] On the contrary, if anything *is* thus presupposed it is precisely such negative possibilities. Or, to put this somewhat differently, the possibility of cost or loss as well as of benefit or gain is a condition of any transaction in the linguistic market where, as in any other market, agents have diverse interests and perspectives, and what is gain for one may be, or may involve, loss for the other.[24]

We engage in verbal transactions because we learn that it is sometimes the only and often the best—most effective, least expensive—way to do certain things or gain certain goods. As speakers, it is often the best way to affect the beliefs and behavior of other people in ways that serve our interests, desires, or goals; as listeners, it is often the best way to learn things that may be useful for us to know and perhaps otherwise unknowable, including things about the people who speak to us.[25] And such transactions *may* be quite profitable for both parties. For listeners

107

do—not always, but often enough—respond to utterances in ways that serve their speakers' interests: sometimes because a listener is independently motivated to do so but also because she will have learned that, in so doing, she makes it at least minimally worthwhile for speakers to speak and thereby, possibly, to say something of interest to her. Similarly, speakers do—again, not always but often enough—tell listeners things they find interesting: typically because it is only through a listener's knowing or believing those things that the latter *can* serve the speaker's interests, but also because all speakers learn that, in so doing, they make it at least minimally worthwhile for people to listen and thereby to be affected in the ways they desire. It must be emphasized here—though the telegraphic and most other models of communication miss and obscure this crucial aspect of the reciprocality of verbal transactions—that *listeners*, like speakers, are verbal *agents*, and that their characteristic and even optimal re/actions are not confined to the relatively passive and altogether internal or mental ones suggested by such terms as "receiving," "interpreting," "decoding," and "understanding," but embrace the entire spectrum of responsive human actions, including acts that are quite energetic, overt, "material," and, what is most significant here, *consequential for the speaker*.

Verbal transactions are also risky, however, and in some ways structurally adversarial.[26] For, given the dynamics and constraints of reciprocality just described, it will tend to be in the *speaker's* interests to provide only as much "information" as is required to affect the listener's behavior in the ways he himself desires and *no* "information" that it may be to his general *dis*advantage that she know or believe;[27] at the same time, it will tend to be in the *listener's* interest to learn *whatever* it may be useful or interesting for her to know, whether or not her knowing it happens also to be required or desired by the speaker. Thus, to describe what is presupposed by all communication is to describe the conditions not only for mutually effective interactions but also *and simultaneously* for mutual mis-"understanding," deceit, and exploitation; and although the more extravagant reaches of these latter possibilities are no doubt commonly limited by their ultimately negative consequences for those who hazard them too often or indiscriminately, the converse possibilities remain radically excluded: specifically, the kinds of equivalences, symmetries, duplications, and gratuitous mutualities that are commonly posited as normally achieved in verbal transactions or as defining "communication."

108

Indeed, by the account outlined here, there is *no* "communication" in the sense either of a *making common* of something (for example, "knowledge") that was previously the possession of only one party or in the sense of a *transferral or transmission of the same* (information, feelings, beliefs, and so on) from one to the other. What there is, rather, is a *differentially consequential interaction:* that is, an interaction in which each party acts in relation to the other differently—in different, asymmetric ways and in accord with different specific motives—and also with different consequences for each. It is inevitable that there will be disparities between what is "transmitted" and what is "received" in any exchange simply by virtue of the different states and circumstances of the "sender" and "receiver," including what will always be the differences—sometimes quite significant ones—produced by their inevitably different life-histories as verbal creatures. In addition, the structure of interests that motivates and governs all verbal interactions makes it inevitable that there will also be differences—sometimes very great ones—between the particular goods offered for purchase and those that the customer/thief actually makes off with, and also between the price apparently asked for those goods and what the customer/gull ends up paying. *Caveat emptor, caveat vendor.*

It appears, then, that the same economic dynamics that make it worthwhile or potentially profitable for both parties to enter into a verbal transaction in the first place operate simultaneously to generate conditions of risk for each. It also appears that the various normative or regulative mechanisms (ethical imperatives, maxims, discourse rules, social conventions, and so forth) invoked by speech-act theorists and others to account for the fact that speakers *are* ever honest, and that listeners *do* ever understand their "intentions" and behave accordingly, must be seen as descriptions of a system of constraints that emerges not in opposition to but *by virtue of* the interests (or, which seems to be the same, "self-interests") of the agents involved. To be sure, as already indicated, the motivating interests of the speaker or listener may consist largely of an independently motivated concern for the other's welfare or for some more general social welfare.[28] Also, both parties may very well have interests in common (which is to say coincident interests and/or goals) that could be better, or only, implemented by their reciprocal and, in effect, cooperative exchanges. It must be emphasized, however, that any of these possibilities, which perhaps occur quite frequently, nevertheless occur *within* the general structure of motives that energize

109

and sustain verbal interactions, not outside of or in contrast to their economic dynamics.

Habermas and the Escape from Economy

The preceding point requires emphasis in view of the current but dubious attractiveness of accounts of communication that produce exclusions and draw contrasts of that kind. Thus, Habermas regards genuine communication as occurring only when and insofar as the participants' actions are "oriented" toward an "agreement" that presupposes the mutual recognition by both parties of "corresponding validity claims of comprehensibility, truth, truthfulness [in the sense of 'sincerity'], and rightness [in the sense of 'moral justness']" and, moreover, that "terminates in the intersubjective mutuality of [their] reciprocal understanding, shared knowledge, mutual trust, and accord with one another."[29]

"Genuine communication" so defined must, according to Habermas, be strictly distinguished from what he refers to as "strategic" or "instrumental" actions, which he defines as those "oriented to the actor's success" and glosses as "modes of action that correspond to the utilitarian model of purposive-rational action."[30] In terms of the analysis outlined here, it is clear that, in defining genuine communication as something altogether uncontaminated by strategic or instrumental action, Habermas has secured a category that is quite sublime (and, as such, apparently necessary to ground his views of the alternate possibilities of human society) but also quite empty: for, having thus disqualified and bracketed out what is, in effect, the entire motivational structure of verbal transactions, he is left with an altogether bootstrap operation or magic reciprocality, in which the only thing that generates, sustains, and controls the actions of speakers and listeners is the gratuitous mutuality of their presuppositions.

It is significant in this connection that Habermas does not recognize that *listeners*—as such, and not only in their alternate role as speakers—perform any *acts* relevant to the dynamics of communication; or, rather, he conceives of their relevant actions as consisting only of such altogether passive, covert, and internal ones as "understanding" and "presupposing." What is thereby omitted is, of course, the whole range—one might say arsenal or warehouse—of acts, including quite overt and physically efficient or materially substantial ones, by which a listener can serve a speaker's interests in *all* that might be meant by her "response" to the speaker. It should be noted, in addition, that a listener's or reader's responses, including here what might be meant by her "interpretation" or "understanding," always extend beyond the moment of hearing or reading—a unit of time that could, in any case, be only arbitrarily specified. Indeed, it may be questioned whether the boundaries of a "speech act" can be, as Habermas and many other communications-theorists evidently assume, readily or sharply demarcated from the speaker's and listener's other—prior, ongoing, and subsequent—activities.

In connection with the more or less utopian theories of communication mentioned above, a final point may be emphasized here. The linguistic market can no more be a "free" one than any other market, for verbal agents do not characteristically enter it from positions of equal advantage or conduct their transactions on an equal footing. On the contrary, not only can and will that market, like any other, be rigged by those with the power and interest to do so, but, no less significantly, it always interacts with *other* economies, including social and political ones. Individual verbal transactions are always constrained, therefore, by the nature of the social and political relationships that *otherwise* obtain between the parties involved, including their nonsymmetrical obligations to and claims upon one another by virtue of their nonequivalent roles in those relationships, *as well as* by their inevitably unequal resources and nonsymmetrical power relations *within* the transaction itself. (The latter inequalities and nonsymmetries are inevitable because they are a function of *all* the differences among us.) To imagine speech situations in which all such differences have been eradicated or equalized and which are thus "free" of all so-called distortions of communication is to imagine a superlunary universe—and even there, it seems, the conditions of perfection will always call forth someone, an archangel perhaps, who will introduce difference into the company.[31]

Some of the inequalities and nonsymmetries indicated above are no doubt often negotiated or adjusted under conditions of partnership, paternalism, or mutual good will, and a case could certainly be made for the desirability of more extensive negotiations and adjustments of that kind and/or for more extensive good will generally. It is unclear, however, how—or, indeed, by what kinds of "strategic actions"—any more radical social engineering along these lines would be pursued, and unclear also how (since equalization does not have equal consequences for everyone) the costs and benefits would fall out. Even more fundamentally, however, especially in view of the supposed political implications of Habermas's program for the reconstruction of the presuppositions of all speech acts, one must wonder what those implications could actually be for a *sublunary* universe. For, of course, the closer one moved to the ideal speech situation of Habermas's fantasy, the less motive there would be for any verbal transactions to occur at all and the more redundant any speech act would become.

The image of a type of communication that excludes all strategy, instrumentality, (self-)interest, and, above all, the profit motive, reflects what appears to be a more general recurrent impulse to dream an escape from economy, to imagine some special type, realm, or mode of value that is beyond economic accounting, to create by invocation some place apart from the marketplace—a kingdom, garden, or island, perhaps, or a plane of consciousness, form of social relationship, or stage of human development—where the dynamics of economy are, or once were, or some day will be, altogether suspended, abolished, or reversed: where no winds blow ill and there need be no tallies of cost and benefit, where there are no exchanges but only gifts, where all debts are paid by unrepayable acts of forgiveness, all conflicts of interest resolved, harmonized, or subsumed by a comprehensive communal good, and exemplary acts of self-sacrifice are continuously performed and commemorated. Given what seems to be the inexorability of economic accounting in and throughout every aspect of human—and not only human—existence, from the base of the base to the tip of the superstructure, and given also that its operations implicate each of us in loss, cost, debt, death, and other continuous or ultimate reckonings, it is understandable that the dream of an escape from economy should be so sweet and the longing for it so pervasive and recurrent. Since it does appear to be inescapable, however, the better (that is, more effective, more profitable) alternatives would seem to be not to seek to go beyond economy but to do the best we can going *through*—in the midst of and perhaps also by means of—it: "the best," that is, all things considered, at least as far as we know those things, or think we know them.

"Self-Refutation"

I anticipate here two questions—or, rather, two versions of the same question/objection—that the foregoing account frequently elicits. The first asks: If there is no truth-value to what anyone says, then why are you bothering to tell us all this and why should anyone listen? The second, a quite classic taunt, goes as follows: But are you not making truth-claims in the very act of presenting these views, and isn't your account, then, self-refuting?

By way of reply I would point out first that, since these questions and objections appeal to *the very network of concepts that are at issue*, they simply beg the question. Thus, when someone (an objectivist, for example) insists that I make truth-claims when I speak, he merely reasserts his inability to entertain any alternate structure of conceptions of what he calls "truth." It is equivalent to his saying that I can exist only under his description of me and, specifically, that I can *speak* only under *his* (objectivist) description of language.[32] According to the analysis of language that maintains that I make truth-claims in the very act of opening my mouth ("to communicate" or "to assert" as distinguished from just yawning), my dog likewise makes truth-claims in the very act of opening his. Indeed, in accord with a transcendental analysis of language, our mutual interactions (that is, mine with my dog) flourish only because of our mutual presuppositions of truth and sincerity: my dog assumes that when I call "Here, Fido, dinner!" his dinner is really there, and I assume that when he barks at my arrival home, he is sincerely happy to see me. (Of course, we could just be trying to manipulate each other.) My point here is not to ridicule such an account per se, but to emphasize that what neo-Kantian transcendental analysis describes as the "presuppositions" of speech are *redescribable* as the recurrent tendencies of verbal agents, human or otherwise, as the products of the differentially effective consequences of their prior interactions.[33]

What I am offering here is neither an "assertion" of some *p* nor a "denial" of assertion-in-itself or truth-in-itself, but an *alternate description* of what is *otherwise described* as "assertion," "denial," and "truth." Moreover, this alternate description of what the other fellow (Platonist, objectivist, neo-Kantian speech-act theorist, and so on) describes otherwise is, under *its own* rather than *his* description, not self-refuting but *self-exemplifying*. Thus, my reply to the charge of self-refutation consists of everything I have already said here, from which my own *saying* of it is, of course, *not* exempt. Having designed this verbal/conceptual construct to be of value—interest, use, and perhaps even beauty—to the members of a certain community, I exhibit it here for sale, hoping that some of its readers will, as we say, "buy it," but by no means expecting all of them to do so. For, as the account itself indicates and as I very well recognize, each reader enters such a transaction with only so much coin and with other investments to secure: most significantly, prior cognitive investments, but also, perhaps, other (for example, professional or specifically religious) ones. My hope and expectation is that this account, or a piece of it, will find some buyers and, among those who cannot afford any of it, at least some admirers and, among those who do not admire it, at least some who are nevertheless affected by it. For it is thus—in part anyway, and in this respect like both the scientist and artist—that I am paid. As the account indicates, however, and as I also recognize, I cannot, in spite of my efforts to do so, predict or control either the fact or the manner of its consumption, now or henceforth, for both are as radically contingent as the value of the account itself. These conditions apply, it appears, to all those doing business in a market of this kind: such are the constraints, such are the risks, such are the possible rewards.

Economic Metaphorics *(not just capitalist societies)*

Of course, objections to the foregoing analysis of verbal transactions could also be made to the economic analogies *as such*. Such objections commonly take one of three lines and sometimes all three together. One of them, already mentioned, is that an analysis of communication as reciprocal exchange projects the Western liberal's idealized conception of economic behavior and ignores the differences of power in actual verbal interactions.[34] As noted above, however, since the present account *stresses* those differences (along with other inequalities and asymmetries among the parties in verbal exchanges), this objection has no force here. A second, related objection is that the analysis I develop in this book adopts an ethnocentric and historically limited model that characterizes only the behavior of and relations among parties in the markets of capitalist societies—the assumption being, it appears, that reciprocal exchanges, the possibility of profit and loss, exploitation, and perhaps even economy itself are features only of capitalism. This objection, however, begs the question of just what the historical and cultural limits of those features *are*. Although the answer to that question is to some extent an empirical matter and thus cannot be taken for granted in advance (and there is also no reason to suppose that the alternatives must be either some human universal—*homo economicus*—or what I describe further on as a putative Fall into Commerce), it must be added that even where archeological and ethnographic data are available, the possibility of circularity in their *interpretation* is very strong. That is, the discovery of apparent market-like exchanges in archaic or otherwise simple tribal societies could be taken either as a refutation of the belief

114

that their features are characteristic only of late capitalism or as evidence that the serpent had entered Eden earlier than was previously thought.[35]

Among anthropologists, it was apparently Karl Polanyi who first raised the question of the theoretical propriety and methodological desirability of extending the concepts and techniques of postindustrial Western economics to the description and analysis of other (for example, archaic, tribal, primitive, or peasant) socioeconomic systems, and it remains a central issue in economic anthropology. Although these controversies are relevant to the present discussion, a number of different issues should be distinguished. One is whether the extension of Western economics to the analysis of other economies is good anthropology. Although aspects of the issue fall beyond my competence, I find the more skeptical, anti-universalist views of Polanyi, Dalton, and Sahlins more congenial and persuasive here.[36] A quite different issue, whether the terms and concepts of Western economics can be extended to other forms of *social interaction* (in the West or elsewhere), has been decided affirmatively by the development of social-exchange theory, decision science, and game theory, each of which consists of precisely such extensions (or, from another perspective, "reductions").[37] The latter developments do not, of course, resolve the further issue of whether such extensions, however *possible,* are altogether *legitimate* or, to put it differently, altogether to be welcomed. This, however, is clearly another *kind* of question and, as it happens, one deeply implicated in what I will describe later as "the double discourse of value": that is, the emergence of, and effort to maintain, a strict separation between two different and perhaps fundamentally antagonistic—sacred versus profane or, in contemporary terms, humanistic versus economistic—articulations of economy.

It is here also that we find the third line of objections raised against the present account, namely that, in describing the motives and processes of verbal communication and other social interactions in terms drawn from the marketplace, I express and encourage a cynical (or, alternately, "pessimistic") conception of human beings as inevitably self-serving and incurably calculating and adversarial. One way to reply to such objections is by recalling that, in spite of the segregating efforts mentioned just above, metaphors of economy—of the gain, loss, circulation, and exchange of goods; of price, coin, purchase, and payment; and of debt and redemption—are ancient and pervasive in our language, occurring both in formal discourses (including, as suggested above, theological ones) and in songs, poems, games, and proverbs. This reply will not, however, answer all such objections, for they—and the sense of unease produced by the particular economic metaphorics developed here—often reflect the radical diversity of conceptual styles that can exist between, on the one hand, certain aspects of traditional humanistic thought and, on the other, alternative conceptualizations (of "man," "social relations," "communication," and so forth) that diverge from or challenge it, the names of which are not confined to those usually invoked here (utilitarianism, economism, biologism, sociological reductionism, and so forth) but are, so to speak, legion. The analysis of the dynamics of verbal transactions outlined above is not, I think, cynical. Nor is it "pessimistic" except in the question-begging sense that any analysis must be so if it does not underwrite a particular script for the salvation or emancipation of mankind. The diversity and resulting conflict of conceptual styles just mentioned are, however, certainly crucial for this study; for, as I will discuss further in Chapter 6, insofar as such a metaphorics flagrantly transgresses the borders that segregate the two discourses of value, it threatens not only the security of those borders but the entire—dualistic—conception of the universe that defines humanistic redemptionism and that grounds its belief in, and promise of, an ultimate deliverance from *all* economy.

Changing Places: Truth, Error, and Deconstruction

The implications for intellectual history of Jacques Derrida's and other, related critiques of traditional conceptions of "truth"[38] have been developed within deconstruction itself and are also exemplified by it. Thus, Samuel Weber suggests that there has been a transformation of the genre by which deconstruction thinks of Western thought: that is, the genre in which Derrida's texts describe Western intellectual history and inscribe his own project within it—or, if not quite within, then not altogether outside it either.[39] Specifically, Weber suggests that there has been a shift from drama, where that history is presented as a scene of *opposition* played out upon a *single* stage, to narrative, the telling of what is seen as an endless tale in which there is "alteration without opposition," where time is reversible so that anticipation is also repetition, and where the single stage, scene, or "unity of place" is replaced by "places that are constantly in movement or on the move."[40]

This transformation of genre is illustrated, in Weber's account of it, by "the distance traversed" from Derrida's *La Voix et le phénomène* (1967) to *La Carte postale* (1980). Although the earlier text anticipates the "motifs of repetition, iteration and reversible circulation" that are foregrounded and played out more consistently in the later one, "the dynamics of difference is [in *La Voix et le phénomène*] still . . . contained and confined within the space of an opposition." Thus, for example, Derrida's text could still "assume an argumentative stance," could still offer to demonstrate or "show" how Husserl, conceived as an integral sublect, moves "against himself," and could still describe the metaphysics of presence as a stubborn self-delusion, "a desire that obstinately seeks to save presence" and seeks also to efface or repress the processes of iteration. As deconstruction becomes a narrative, however (as in *La Carte postale*, particularly the section entitled *"Spéculer—sur 'Freud'"*), that recurrent desire is reinscribed not as *psychomachia*, not as a tragicomic drama in which the same battle is repeatedly fought and repeatedly lost, but as an economically motivated activity, pursued "in the hopes of reaping a profitable return."

Weber suggests that the fulfillment of this reinscribed desire may now be seen not so much as fatally doomed and self-contradictory, but as inescapably constrained. The desire for presence is, at heart, a desire for profit and power. One puts one's text or coin (or indeed *self*) in circulation, sometimes or typically claiming to offer it gratis but counting on its earning one some interest when it arrives at its destination. Since, however, one cannot fully control the system of circulation (the economy or, as in *La Carte postale*, the postal system), one cannot determine—predict or control—how one's coin, in changing hands, will be spent, how one's text, in being multiply read, will be multiply rewritten, how one's self will be appropriated by others to their own profit. And whereas, in an oppositional drama, deconstruction could inscribe its own role, or the role of its writing, as the tripping up of logocentrism (the hapless antihero of Western metaphysics), in a narrative of alteration without opposition, where every *telos* becomes a *tele*, a distance traversed but also a "gap never closed," it is seen that the desire in question—that is, the desire not only to be read but to control the reading—is unavoidable, that all writing, "even the most self-consciously deconstructive," cannot help repeating it. Deconstruction, then, inscribes itself as but one more thing that comes and goes, its place among the places that are constantly in movement being, perhaps, to articulate the very inevitability of that desire, as in *La Carte postale*, in which the desire is no longer demonstrated *elsewhere* but conspicuously self-enacted.

The transformation of which Weber speaks is, I think, significant and, as he suggests, seems to have been inevitable given the defining perspective and project of deconstruction. I should like to pursue here some of its implications for the conceptualization of truth and error and will begin by considering the *scope* of that project: what is sometimes called the dismantling or, as in Weber's essay, "the unraveling" of the metaphysics of Western thought.

When the tale of deconstruction is told or dramatized in accord with the familiar masterplot of intellectual historiography (that is, the *oppositional* plot from which deconstruction itself has shifted), it is seen to have overthrown or undermined certain errors, follies, and delusions in past and prevailing thought: certain *pseudodoxia*. The root folly, if one adopts the related metaphor of root and branch, is identified as "logocentrism" or "the metaphysics of presence."[41] It is seen, however, not merely as a deeply rooted and highly ramified folly, but as a constitutive one: that is, Western thought is not simply implicated in the metaphysics of presence, but consists of it; logocentrism is not merely a loose or discolored strand that can be plucked from the fabric, but the very thread of which it is woven, so that to begin to pluck at it is to unravel the whole of it.

The *extent* of the whole of it can hardly be overestimated. For it is clear that what deconstruction describes as the metaphysics of Western thought is not confined to the conceptual operations and structures that happen—by an unlucky accident, as it were—to have developed in Western philosophy: the classic philosophic texts are merely its most systematic and self-reflexive articulation. Neither is it distinct from some other type of Western *non*metaphysical thought—scientific thought, for example, or poetic or everyday thought; for these, too, can be seen to articulate the metaphysics of presence and to be thoroughly implicated in it. Neither is it—or need it be—confined to *Western* thought; for although the recurrent insertion of the qualifier "Western" may be taken as a mark of scholarly caution, modesty, or responsibility, there is no reason to believe that the metaphysics of Western thought is distinct from that of Eastern thought, or tribal thought, or the thought of illiterates or of preverbal or as yet unacculturated children. On the contrary, I would suggest here that what deconstruction names "the metaphysics of Western thought" *is* thought, all of it, root and branch, everywhere and always: that is, the operations and structures of all human—and, I think, not only human—intelligence, and thus, insofar as it is seen as the producer and product of error and delusion, the ultimate, universal *pseudodoxia epidemica*.

In that connection, we may note that certain characteristic ontological formulations produced by deconstruction—that is, formulations of what *is* and *isn't* or, in its kinetic phase, what *goes on* and *doesn't go on*—pose an anthropological and more broadly epistemological question. For example, when Derrida writes "Nothing is, anywhere, simply present or absent. There are only, everywhere, differences and traces of traces,"[42] the question is *why*, if there are only, everywhere, differences and traces of traces, we should ever have come to think that anything was, anywhere, simply present or absent. Similarly, when Weber writes, "What goes on . . . , what has never ceased to go on, is that the being-named, the being of the name, comes and goes, be-comes without ever arriving at its proper destination,"[43] the question is why we should ever, as appears to be the case, have come to think otherwise.

These are not rhetorical questions: they are not self-answering, nor do the answers go without saying. Weber suggests one way to put the answer—in effect, the will to power and the profit motive: "The key to presence is power"; "Presence is something that must be gained." Another way to put the answer—though not another answer—follows from the identification, proposed above, of "the metaphysics of presence" or "Western thought" with *all* thought; for we may then say that we could never have thought otherwise because that is the way thought works. That being so, however, the anthropological question reverses itself: If that is how thought works, how is it possible for us to escape its working, to escape the metaphysics of presence and to think in some other way?

This, too, is not a rhetorical question. The answer that Weber suggests, and which I mean to endorse here, is that we cannot think otherwise but that escape, like opposition, is an inappropriate move or desire. We cannot escape the workings of thought—we can only repeat them; but we always repeat differently. It was appropriate, then, for deconstruction to move from the familiar oppositional drama of overturning and undermining to the narration of an endless tale in which its own role is that of inevitable repetition—which, however, like all repetition, is always different and may always have, in Weber's words, "transformative, alterative force" and "disruptive power." I shall turn to the transformative force below, but focus first on the repetition.

It is possible to see the ontological formulations of deconstruction as taking their place among (that is, repeating and no doubt anticipating) other attempts by Western metaphysics to think what *is*, or what *goes on*, independent of our thinking. It is also possible to see the project of deconstruction as another in the array of projects that have sought to identify what it is in our thinking that prevents us from thinking what *is* or what *goes on*. For example, it seems that many of the conceptual operations and structures upon which deconstruction has focused attention and which it has identified as root or branch of logocentrism have, by other names, been repeatedly identified *in* the classic logocentric texts of Western metaphysics as sources and consequences of error, distortion, or blindness—or, in the language of the metaphysics of presence, as veiling the truth, obscuring reality, preventing us from seeing nature as it really is.

A rather engaging classic text of this sort was produced in the year 1620 by Francis Bacon, who spoke of the *pseudodoxia*, "the false notions which are deeply rooted [in men's minds]," as *Idols* and described them in four categories: first, "The Idols of the Tribe," which are inherent in human nature and thus the very race or tribe of man—for example, our natural tendency to suppose that our senses give us direct knowledge of reality and to forget that the coherence and regularity that we find in it have been imposed on it by our desire for coherence and regularity; second, "The Idols of the Cave," which arise from the fact that each of us inhabits the private cave of our individual temperaments and personal histories, in whose discolored light we interpret the whole of nature by that part of it which we know (Bacon acknowledges the repetition of Plato here); third, "The Idols of the Marketplace," which arise from the commerce among men, particularly language, and which lead us, among other things, to treat those words which name fictions as if they were the names of real entities; and fourth, "The Idols of the Theatre," or "those errors which have crept into men's minds from the various dogmas and systems of philosophy"—systems which, like stage plays, are merely charming inventions that do not give us a picture of nature as it actually is.[44]

Bacon also describes at some length a set of strategies by which, he thought, thought could escape its captivity to the idols. I will not rehearse them here but will recall that they amount, more or less, to what was later elaborated and codified as "the scientific method" (the title of Bacon's own text is *Novum Organum*, that is, "the new method"). We may also note here, however, that that liberation, which was certainly a disruptive and transformative one *in its place*, became in due course another form of captivity—indeed, another Idol of the Theatre—from which it is presently the purpose of another project of Western thought to liberate thought: a project still, as it happens, pursued in oppositional terms, as "against method."[45]

I do not mean to suggest here that the project of deconstruction is simply a renaming of various classically named idols and errors (though it may be noted that, just as repetition in intellectual history is never *only* repetition, so also even renaming is never *simply* renaming either). For, to focus now on differences, not only have all the other projects that named Error done so in a manner that articulated or were implicated in what deconstruction exposes as the root error of logocentrism but, if it is rigorously pursued, the logic of deconstruction must identify the very opposition of Truth and Error, Reason and Folly, as ramifications of that root, as oppositions to be unraveled along with the rest. Accordingly, deconstruction is not truth and does not expose error; neither (also accordingly) was the attempted exposure of error in the classic texts itself folly or error.

To unravel the opposition of Truth and Error, we must reconceptualize the structure of error and rename, in nonoppositional terms, the classic idols whose names are legion, including what deconstruction has named "logocentrism" or "the metaphysics of presence." It will be useful here to return to the observation that the metaphysics of Western thought *is* thought, or what we may think of not as specifically conceptual, theoretical, cerebral, or, in the narrow sense, intellectual activity but, rather, as the epistemic activities of all organic systems: that is, the processes by which an organism's structure is continuously modified through its interactions with its environment—an environment (or "universe" or "manifold") whose *specific features* are themselves produced *in their specificity* by those very interactions.

The processes in question are something like Bacon's Idols in being always both "of the tribe" and "of the cave," and sometimes of the marketplace and the theater as well. That is, they are to some extent innate, which is to say conditioned by structures and mechanisms produced in the course and as the consequence of evolutionary history, but also to some extent conditioned by the organism's interactions (always constrained as well as energized by those very structures and mechanisms) with its particular environment, including other creatures of its own kind and what they have produced—or, as we sometimes say, conditioned by "culture." What sustains these epistemic processes, and not only sustains but strengthens them, is that they are profitable: that is, they work to the organism's benefit—not absolutely optimally, and that, as will be seen, is very much to the point—but well enough to keep him/her (the organism) and thus them (the processes) going. Or, to put this in other terms, they have evolved and developed phylogenetically and ontogenetically as competitively cost-efficient ways for the organism to process information, to link, in an economical feedback loop, that which we sometimes call "perception" and "action" but which we now see as not really distinguishable.[46]

As just mentioned, the processes in question, though competitively economical, nevertheless do not work absolutely optimally. If there had ever been an organic system that worked truly optimally, there would have been no evolution: that system would have cornered all markets; it would still be here and there would be no others.[47] This does not mean that evolution moves toward overall optimality: rather, it moves toward increased competitive efficiency in some respects under current conditions, and thus toward the production of new structures and often more complex processes—which, however, *also* do not work optimally. Organic evolution is thus like the evolution of technology: the more mechanisms we add to make the machine work better in some respects under current conditions, the more that can go wrong in those and other respects under those and emergent conditions, and thus the more that can be made better and go wrong, and so forth.[48] It is an endless tale without *telos*.

To return, however, to the nonoptimality of thought, let me give an example here—drastically simplified and somewhat speculative, but designed to suggest how it seems to happen. It appears that the cheapest way for any system to process an array of information is by binary classification, which is, of course, the minimal classification. Moreover, because, in an organic system, the process of classification, like any other activity, is itself economically energized—energized, that is, by self-interest, or, if you like, the profit motive—any classification that is produced is also likely to be an *evaluative hierarchy*. It is clear that, to the extent that the organism's environment is stable and recurrent, it will be profitable or at least cost-efficient for any category and its evaluative hierarchy to survive beyond the occasion of its originating functionality; for energy need not, then, be expended on the process of classification and evaluation each time a similar array is produced. Thus, the categories and their evaluations will become fixed—sometimes, through evolutionary mechanisms, fixed in the DNA. Or, to glance at the other extreme of complexity, we may note that *language* (that is, verbal or symbolic behavior, which is not discontinuous with the other activities described here but which could also be described as a product of cultural/technological evolution) apparently facilitates both the subtlety of the processes of categorization but also the fixity of its products, and thus does everything better and makes everything worse. For it is also clear that fixity (and I speak here not of language but of classification

fixity
as
unprofitable

generally) will be unprofitable to the extent that the organism's environment is *not* recurrent or stable (and, of course, the more complex the organism's own structure, the more complex and less stable and recurrent will be the environment it can produce and interact with); the fixity will be *un*profitable, in other words, to the extent that it prevents the organism from responding appropriately—that is, in a way that sustains the organism itself—to novel and emergent conditions.

The general rule illustrated by this example—and there are comparable rules for other processes—is that stability and flexibility are both profitable, but that one is always bought at the cost of the other so that neither can be maximized at the same time or all the time.[49] Or, to return to Western thought (which we have never left), it appears that it has its good and bad points *and that they are the same.* Thus also, to return us to the Idols, it appears that when Western thought reflects upon itself, it identifies its own *less* profitable operations as Folly and fallacy and their less profitable products as Error, and its own *more* profitable operations as logic and Reason and their more profitable products as Truth—thus repeating its own characteristic processes of binary classification and polarized evaluation.

If, reflecting on the less profitable aspects of oppositional logic, Western thought strives to do otherwise, it may redescribe any of the specific categories, hierarchies, and binary oppositions produced by Western thought—including such oppositions as Truth and Error and such metaphysical and ontological structures as Reality and Being—as structures which, *while* they are working, have a working integrity, coherence, distinctness, and stability but which can always be *alternately produced* as arbitrary, unbounded, indeterminate, unstable, otherwise configurable, and more minutely differentiable. Moreover, because Western thought has not only some good points but some quite remarkable points, it can, in a strenuous exercise of its own flexibility and capacity for disruption and alteration, also foreground and focus on that very aspect of all the structures it produces: that is, on the arbitrariness of their production, their unboundedness, fluidity, indeterminacy, multiple configurability, infinite regressibility, and infinitely minute differentiability. In which case, it may produce texts that say things like "Nothing is, anywhere, simply present or absent; there are only, everywhere, differences and traces of traces," or "What goes on, what has never ceased to go on, is that the being-named, the being of the name, comes and goes, be-comes without ever arriving at its proper destination."

The *articulation* of what thought produces as radical and ramified inarticulateness will necessarily sound like paradox, circumlocution, violent metaphor, and nihilistic negation *relative to* the structures and syntax of *prevailing* thought and the discourse that articulates *it*. However, that inarticulateness will have been produced precisely because— and when, and by those for whom—the structure and syntax of prevailing thought and discourse have themselves become *inoperative:* often because the latter have been interfered with and disrupted—that is, both knotted and unraveled—by other more competitively effective or profitable structures and syntax: perhaps richer, more subtle, more comprehensive and connectible ones, or more elegant and parsimonious or, as it is said, "economical" ones. Thus, such discursive and conceptual structures (words and concepts) as "meaning," "reality," "truth," and "intrinsic value," and also the syntax of their traditional indication and predication, may *in some places* simply stop working, draw a blank. When and where this happens, it is not by virtue of some special perverseness, stubbornness, or incapacity (or, for that matter, transcendence), but through the operation of the *same processes* that produced and sustained those structures when they did work—or, indeed *where they still do work;* for, we recall, not only are the places constantly in motion, but there is no unity of place.

It appears, then, that thought begins to unravel itself utterly when and where it, and its products, are already pretty unraveled. But because thought seems to work that way, the very process of its disintegration produces new thought. Thus, the deconstruction of ontology is appropriated as new ontology; that which was "neither a word nor a concept"[50] begins to function as, and becomes, both word and concept; and as figure and ground change places, the unraveling of Western thought, marking another moment in its history, weaves another figure in the fabric of Western thought.

6

The Critiques of Utility

Poor soul, the center of my sinful earth,
[Thrall to] these rebel powers that thee array,
Why dost thou pine within and suffer dearth,
Painting thy outward walls so costly gay?
Why so large cost, having so short a lease,
Dost thou upon thy fading mansion spend?
Shall worms, inheritors of this excess,
Eat up thy charge? Is this thy body's end?
Then, soul, live thou upon thy servant's loss,
And let that pine to aggravate thy store;
Buy terms divine in selling hours of dross;
Within be fed, without be rich no more:
    So shalt thou feed on Death, that feeds on men,
    And Death once dead, there's no more dying then.

Shakespeare, Sonnet 146

Humanism, Anti-Utilitarianism, and the Double Discourse of Value

In company with a cluster of related terms including "efficiency," "instrumentality," and "practicality," "utility" figures as a distinctly demoted, grudged ("mere"), and profane good in the discourse of the contemporary humanistic disciplines (for example, literary studies, aesthetics, and ethics), especially as distinguished from that of disciplinary economics and such related fields as political science and economic psychology. In these latter fields, "utility" figures as a technical term: central to some accounts or models, useful enough in others and valued accordingly, but by no means regarded everywhere as, in any sense, a pure good.[1] Indeed, an active critique and substantial modification of the traditional utility-maximizing or "rational-choice" model of economic (and political) behavior is currently being generated within these fields[2] as well as in sociology, anthropology, and philosophy. Anti-utilitarianism, however, whether as more or less casual aspersions and demotions or as specific critiques of "utilitarianism" or "utility theory," seems to operate as a qualifying mark of the contemporary professional humanist and also as his or her perhaps most centrally self-defining ideological stance.

The particular traits of contemporary anti-utilitarianism (its rhetorical modes and moods, argumentative strategies, textual allusions, historical and hypothetical examples *ad horrendum,* and so on) are the product of a long and complex ideological and institutional history that cannot be traced here. For the concerns of this study, however, what is notable about that history is that it involves, among other things, the continuous mutually reinforcing interactions between both classical and modern philosophic ethics and various forms of religious and secular redemptionism, in all of which certain kinds of good or gain are *opposed to* but also seen as *exchangeable for* some other kind of good or gain. The first (bad) kind of good or gain is characteristically identified with material enlargement and individual welfare and associated with usury, greed, commerce, Mammon, the bourgeoisie, and capitalism. The second kind of (good) good or gain, for which the first is seen as well worth paying, losing, or sacrificing, is identified with spiritual enlargement and collective welfare and associated with charity, love, God, the aristocracy, the poor, and pre- and/or post-capitalism. Although the language of the literal marketplace often invades—or is pointedly invoked in—the articulation of this opposition/exchange of goods, it is always ultimately rejected as inadequate. Indeed, the distinctive feature of this economy (system of distribution and exchange of goods) is its effort to escape or transcend economy altogether, and the distinctive feature of its attendant discourse is the claim to have done so already or at least to know how to do so. Thus, as in the epigraph to this chapter, spiritual meditation or *contemptus mundi* readily takes the form of prudential and, indeed, rational economic calculation (*Why so large cost, having so short a lease? Buy terms divine in selling hours of dross,* etc.), but, at the end, moves toward and counts on an ultimate transcendence of all economy, all change and exchange, all transformation, and all possibility of loss: "And Death once dead, there's no more dying then."

Although its specifically theological or religious content is not always as evident as here, the dualistic structure of the economy just described continues to dominate the discourses of humanistic studies. It recurs in the familiar distinctions drawn between lower and higher—or, alternately, "superficial" and more "profound"—types of value or modes of valuing: between, for example, valuing things "instrumentally" or "as a means to some end" and valuing them "for their own sake" or "as ends in themselves." It also recurs wherever the value produced through

126

certain forms of production and consumption is conceived and defined in pointed contradistinction to the value produced through other forms of production and consumption, and, more generally, in the carefully monitored boundaries between two discursive domains each of which is centrally concerned with questions of value. On the one hand there is the discourse of economic theory: money, commerce, technology, industry, production and consumption, workers and consumers; on the other hand, there is the discourse of aesthetic axiology: culture, art, genius, creation and appreciation, artists and connoisseurs.[3] In the first discourse, events are explained in terms of calculation, preferences, costs, benefits, profits, prices, and utility. In the second, events are explained—or, rather (and this distinction/opposition is as crucial as any of the others), "justified"—in terms of inspiration, discrimination, taste (good taste, bad taste, no taste), the test of time, intrinsic value, and transcendent value.

The decisive moves in the generation and maintenance of this double discourse of value are commonly made under the quasi-logical cover of *We must distinguish between:* for example, we must distinguish between mere price and intrinsic value, between mere consumers and discriminating critics, between true artistic creativity and mere technological skill, and so forth. The question posed here and throughout this study is *must* we and, indeed, *can* we? (The attendant question "Who *are* 'we'?" is of course as relevant here as everywhere else.)

Specific definitions and other kinds of elaborated usage indicate that the conception of *utility* operating in the definitively humanistic anti-utilitarianism is thoroughly dualistic, which is to say deeply implicated in such familiar problematic dichotomies as mind-body, spirit-matter and, especially in some anthropological versions, culture-nature. It is also, both thereby and otherwise, arbitrarily limited. The arbitrariness becomes evident if the utility of an object is conceived in a way that does not already build in the dualism at issue: in accord, for example, with the usage in one branch of contemporary economic theory, where the utility of something for some subject is operationally defined as his or her "revealed preference" for it[4] or, alternately, in accord with much informal idiomatic usage, where the utility of a thing seems to be thought of as any positivity or positive effect that could be produced through some subject's engagement with it at any time (its handiness or suitability, for example, or its profitableness in some way, or the fact that it contributes to the satisfaction of some kind of need or desire, and so forth). Given either of these nondualistic conceptions of utility, what

127

is otherwise referred to as the "nonutilitarian" value of something or, in explicit opposition to utility or use value, as its "symbolic" or "aesthetic" (etc.) value, could readily be redescribed as *itself a utility*, though perhaps, in the case of things such as art, play, gifts, souvenirs, friendship, or wilderness preservation, one that happens to be especially diffuse, deferred, remote, subtle, complex, multiple, heterogeneous, and/or, for these or other reasons, difficult to measure or specify.

Whatever their limits and other inadequacies, neither of the two conceptions of utility outlined above "reduces all value to utility" in the dualistically conceived senses of either "value" or "utility"; nor do they identify utility either with such specifically "utilitarian" concepts as overall ratios of pleasure to pain or with such literally economic benefits as more coins in the pocket.[5] Both points are worth emphasizing in view of the fact that such reductions and identifications are commonly thought to be *necessarily* entailed by any conception of value that does not exhibit and explicitly affirm the kind of dualistic conception being questioned here. Such a conviction is, of course, itself a repetition and playing out of precisely that dualism: in other words, to the dualist, whatever is not dualistic is reductionist.

The charge of "reductionism" here has more than logical or intellectual force, however, for, as suggested above, the dualistic conception of utility is deeply implicated in the redemptionist and other religious as well as ethical commitments of contemporary humanistic discourse. Consequently, the location of use value where it was previously invisible, like the identification of elements of self-interest in apparently charitable acts, is not only an intellectually thankless achievement in humanist circles but likely to be regarded as a self-excommunicating— and, indeed, a specifically Mephistophelean—one. Quite conversely, of course, the economic theorist who can demonstrate the operation of utility-maximization in even the most apparently irrational economic behavior will be considered as having made a significant contribution to the coherence of his discipline.[6]

In certain respects, the oppositions here are no longer quite so stark as they were even twenty-five years ago. We might note, for example, that as research in decision science and social psychology indicates increasingly subtle psychological, social, and symbolic constraints on choice— and, accordingly, as economic theorists' efforts to retain the classical concept of rationality as utility-maximization oblige them to take into account increasingly subtle utilities (such as, in one set of studies, the relative anticipated emotional costs of *regretting* different choices)[7]—the *[handwritten margin note: double discourse (econ + humanistic) begin to collapse into one]*

terms of the economist's analysis will begin to look increasingly like those of the humanist and the double discourse of value begins to collapse into one. ("Utility" and "rationality" certainly begin to lose their specifically marketplace associations.) Moreover, the traditional segregation of these discourses is being eroded from the other direction as well, as literary critics, art historians, and others working in the humanistic disciplines explore with increasing subtlety the complex ways in which *economic* dynamics, at every level of analysis, condition the production and reception of artworks and, more generally, condition the value of all cultural objects and practices.[8] It may appear, then, that a deconstruction of the double domain of value is at hand. Perhaps it is. Since, however, the distinction between humanistic studies and disciplinary economics is implicated in more fundamental conceptual and ideological oppositions and is clearly a highly charged and to some extent self-defining distinction on one side, there is no reason to think this will happen easily or soon.

Also, we must recall that the double discourse of value is itself sustained by and participates in other more fundamental—general, ancient, and perhaps ineradicable—conflicts. In accord with a familiar difficulty, however, the appropriate (most accurate, adequate, valid, revealing, etc.) *description* of those conflicts is part of what is at stake in them. Following Durkheim, for example, a number of sociological and anthropological theorists maintain that there is a fundamental distinction between "sacred" and "profane" spheres of value in any society or, in a more recent formulation, at least a recurrent opposition between, on the one side, the symbolizing and classifying practices of "culture" and, on the other side, the "natural" forces of economy itself, particularly the otherwise omnivorous and indiscriminately commoditizing appetites of the market.[9] In accord with such an account, those currently called and calling themselves "humanists" could readily be seen as the counterparts of the priestly agents of any society who preside over the demarcation of spheres of value, establish the classification of certain objects as sacred, and protect them from the forces of "nature"—from "the jungle," as we sometimes say, speaking of the operations of the market itself, or from certain unregenerate aspects of "human nature" as exemplified in the market's most egregious and distinctive agents, the merchant, trader, and banker. Such an account would imply, among other things, that the value of certain entities *must* be framed as *absolutely* different in order for that value to be effectively maintained, or, in other words, that mystification is necessary for the very operation of

129

culture or for the survival of civilization in the jungle clearing. It would
follow, of course, that any exposure of the continuities between the
calculable and incalculable, the marketable and priceless, must be vigor-
ously opposed or at least carefully confined lest one risk eroding the
protective barriers that constitute the only or most effective way to make
sure that everything is not sooner or later put up for cash sale.

Some version of this anthropological account seems, in fact, to figure
in the dominant self-conception of contemporary humanistic studies,
and the vigorous opposition just mentioned—that is, to any exposure of
the continuities between traditionally segregated spheres of value—is a
central feature of anti-utilitarianism. Among the various forms it takes
in the literary academy are such familiar ones as the revulsion at merchant and banker (or "middleman," "shopkeeper," and "usurer"),[10]
the fear of the "collapse of standards" and "return to the jungle," and
the charges of relativism, barbarism, vulgarity, and reductionism
("confusing" one kind of value with another, "flattening out" distinctions, and so on) that are regularly leveled at any theoretical critique of
its dualistic structure and, as well, at any practical transgression of the
spheres of value thus segregated.[11]

Even aside from its dubious transhistoricism and static dualism, however, this anthropological account presents serious theoretical and empirical difficulties. It is not clear, for example, why mercantile practices
should be seen as any less cultural (or conversely, any more natural)
than those of classification or priestcraft; and, indeed, the associated
Christian-Marxist-humanist-redemptionist effort to draw a clear line
between societies before and after the Fall into Commerce is made increasingly questionable by recent research and analysis in economic
history and sociology as well as in contemporary anthropology.[12] Indeed, a number of such studies suggest an *alternate* account of the pre/
trans-history of the culture-versus-economics struggle that does not require myths of the Fall, gratuitous culture/nature oppositions, or an
elaborated intellectual Manichaeism.

In accord with such an account, the double discourse of value would
be seen not as the reflection of an eternal *psychomachia* but, rather, as an
instance of the more general tendency to dualistic thinking—with its
characteristic assemblage of hypostasization, binarization, polarization,
and hierarchization—that, as discussed earlier, seems endemic to at
least Western thought. This tendency, when played out in conceptualizations of the multiple, heterogeneously interactive relations between
and among diverse social practices (which are, it should be observed,
never *inherently* divided into "cultural," "natural," "symbolic," "aes-

130

thetic, "economic," and so forth), yields the binarized reifications of "culture" and "economy," their polarized opposition-segregation into separate discourses of value, and their separate physical and metaphoric sites: the temple and the marketplace. Insofar as these opposition-segregations are also reproduced in the academy as separate disciplines (say, departments of English and of Economics), each could be expected to attract practitioners with rather different personal, social, and educational histories and also different arrays of skills, tastes, temperaments, political identities, and ideological allegiances, all of which both perpetuate and sharpen their mutual opposition.

It may be suggested, as well, that this institutional-ideological opposition tends to be exacerbated historically whenever, and to the extent that, there is a sharp or acutely sharpening conflict between, on the one hand, the more or less conservative (normative, standardizing, controlling, classifying, supervising, maintaining, regulating) practices of the relevant community and, on the other hand, its destabilizing and transformative practices, mercantile or otherwise, including the more or less innovative, entrepreneurial, and diversionary activities of those who stand to gain from a reclassification, circulation, and redistribution of commodities and cultural goods and, thereby, of social power—including the profit and power to be had just from *mediating* their circulation. While it is clear that any community requires—and, as a whole, stands to gain from—both types of practice and the dialectic between them (that is, between continuity and coherence on the one hand and responsive innovation on the other), it is also the case that particular individuals and groups stand to gain or lose *differentially* from any *particular* redistribution of goods.[13]

In accord with this account, the market does not characteristically operate as the site of desecration but, rather, as the arena for the negotiation, transformation, and redistribution of value, including social-symbolic-cultural value; and the traditionally despised trader, banker, and merchant ("panderer," "usurer," "shopkeeper") are seen, accordingly, as the most visible mediators of *change* as well as the most most obvious profiteers of *exchange*.[14] Also accordingly, the priest/humanist's struggle to chase the money changers from the temple, to preserve the sacred objects from the merchant, and to name and isolate their value as absolutely different from and transcendent of exchange value and use value, would be seen here as participating in the broader and more continuous struggle between those with something to *lose* from a reclassification and circulation of goods and those with something to *gain* from them.

131

This account, it should be noted, does not make any general identification between "those with something to lose" and "those with something to gain" and any specific class grouping, such as the wealthy versus the poor or the socially established and powerful versus the deprived, oppressed, or marginalized. For one could not say in advance, or without specifying the particular economic, social, cultural, and other conditions very carefully, which class of person stands to gain or lose— and gain or lose *what*—by the mere fact that certain items or even types of items go on the market and change hands. (The difficulties become clear if one thinks of how differently the gains and losses might be distributed, under different conditions, in the case of the commodification of, say, a Byzantine altarpiece and the ivory from a herd of slaughtered elephants.) Nevertheless, since possession of certain sorts of good(s)—for example, money, social dominance, and what Bourdieu calls "cultural capital"—implies possession of or access to many others, one would expect a general preference on the part of those who already have those sorts of goods for practices that conserve the present distribution of *all* goods. And one might accordingly also expect a certain degree of complicity between the latter, that is, members of what we call the established classes, and those whose characteristic role in the society is to monitor and preserve established cultural classifications: that is, in our own society, professional humanists.

Folded into the present account, Bourdieu's analysis of the economics of cultural capital illuminates the professional humanist's characteristic insistence that what *matters* with respect to the value of cultural goods is neither their marketplace price nor their utility in the sense of their satisfaction of some obvious—for instance, bodily—need or desire.[15] The humanist would be right inasmuch as these are *not* what matters in marking and maintaining the value of cultural goods, but he would, in Bourdieu's term, "mis-recognize" as their "intrinsic" or "nonutilitarian" value that which *does* matter, namely control over their classification as such—that is, *as* cultural goods (as "works of art" or "literature," for example)—and of the academic institutions that transmit the culturally appropriate manner of their consumption (or, as we say, their "true appreciation"). One could add, of course, that it is the exercise of precisely this control that, in contemporary Western societies, defines the role of the professional humanist.[16]

In the concluding section of this chapter I will suggest an alternative to both classic utilitarianism and its humanist/redemptionist critiques. I

would like to add a brief word here, however, concerning the antago-
nisms at issue and the double bookkeeping that reflects them. Outside
the academy, the force of the opposition/segregation of the discourses of
value is most evident, perhaps, in the recurrent struggles between two
kinds of calculation or cost-benefit analysis: on the one hand, the kind,
so named, that frames its objective as the efficient arrival at a specific
and readily specifiable (often, though not necessarily, monetary) "bottom line" and, accordingly, ignores or downplays less readily measurable and less comparable costs, risks, and benefits, or acknowledges
them but precisely as "incalculable"; and, on the other hand, and typically in agonistic relation to the first kind, *another* calculation, *not named
as such*, that characteristically foregrounds and promotes exactly what
was ignored by the first and counts exactly what was discounted: that is,
all those (relatively more) subtle, diffuse, deferred, remote, heterogeneous, etc. costs, risks, and benefits which may or may not themselves be
named as such. Although they operate agonistically in political arenas
(conservationists versus land developers, antinuclear activists versus energy companies, animal-rights activists versus researchers in both commercial and "nonprofit" laboratories, and so on) and are certainly antagonistic in some more fundamental temperamental and ideological
respects, nevertheless, as the description just given indicates, these two
kinds of cost-benefit analysis could also be seen as parallel and com-
plementary, the categories and considerations with which they deal and
the operations they perform being only *relatively* and *locally* distinguishable from one another. Viewed merely as calculative processes, in
other words, the two kinds are not absolutely or essentially distinguishable from each other except from the perspectives that produce
them and in the discourses that inscribe them.

This being so, the question may arise as to whether it might not be
worthwhile—to someone's benefit and perhaps the benefit of many—to
integrate these two evidently not fundamentally discontinuous kinds of
cost-benefit analysis: not only theoretically and discursively, as in the
alternate conceptualization of value developed in this study, but also in
practice, which is to say in the practice of calculating. Indeed, it might be
claimed that this—that is, "counting" or "taking into account" not
merely economic (in the sense of short-range, monetary) considerations
but the entire range of costs, risks, and benefits (in effect, *everything*)—is
precisely what the anti-utilitarian humanist does and asks be done by
others. No doubt that is often the motive of the calculations accordingly
performed and certainly how they are publically articulated and de-

fended or, as we say, "justified." Moreover, their consequences are unquestionably often of considerable benefit to many. But is it really the case that the entire range of costs, risks, and benefits has been taken into account? Is it not, rather, that the professional humanist, in her role as such, is asking not for a consideration of *everything* but, rather, for a *specific arrangement* of values or *hierarchization* of goods and benefits and, in particular, for the promotion of those that she, by virtue of her specific identity as a humanist (temperament, training, institutional interests, ideological allegiances) calculates as *preferable* to whatever it is that her adversary in the particular struggle has, in his role as industrialist, land developer, animal researcher, politician, or publisher, calculated *otherwise*? The question here may also be framed as whether the humanist per se or, indeed, anyone at all could speak for the general long-range benefit of any community (not to mention "mankind" or "humanity") or, to put it the other way around, whether the concept of "the benefit of the community," along with any other social-aggregate or totalizing concept of value, is not only fundamentally questionable but one of the most characteristic and dubious features of, precisely, Benthamite utilitarianism.

Bataille's Expenditure

> Every time the meaning of a discussion depends on the fundamental value of the word *useful*—in other words, every time the essential question touching on the life of human societies is raised, no matter who intervenes and what opinions are represented—it is possible to affirm that the debate is necessarily warped and that the fundamental question is eluded. In fact, given the more or less divergent collection of present ideas, there is nothing that permits one to define what is useful to man.[17]   —Georges Bataille

To be sure. Indeed, precisely: there is nothing that permits one to define it, to specify it, to name its limits; nothing, in fact, that permits one to suppose that "what is useful to man" is anything in particular— or any particular "principle"—that answers the "essential" or "fundamental" question with something essential or fundamental. There is nothing, moreover, that permits one to assume in advance what is "man."

Bataille's writings have evidently figured centrally (whether specifically acknowledged or not) for, among others, Jean Baudrillard, Pierre Bourdieu, Jacques Derrida, Gilles Deleuze, and Félix Guattari (and, thereby, for many of those for whom the work of each of the latter has figured) and are themselves marked deeply by the thought of Marx, Nietzsche, Durkheim, and Mauss. They operate, therefore, as a virtual thoroughfare of continental anthropology and sociology and of twentieth-century political and cultural theory more generally.[18] Although "the notion of expenditure" is elaborated more fully in his later work, all of it of considerable importance in twentieth-century French social thought, the essay so-titled is, in the words of its current translator, "crucial": in it, the latter writes, "Bataille lays his cards on the table" (p. xvi). In its sophisticated exemplification of many of the problems as well as themes I have been discussing, the essay also repays close attention here.

The initial and centrally motivating observation of Bataille's essay is that classic utility theory privileges the acquisition, production, and conservation of material goods and the reproduction and conservation of life. He cites no specific theoretical formulation, but one may supply here any positing, explicitly "utilitarian" or other, of material aggrandizement and the survival of the individual-as-bodily-organism as the inevitable, fundamental, and/or ultimate "goods" to which all human activity is subordinated.[19] What he will offer in opposition to this—and implicitly in opposition to every rational/economic account of human action or to what he sees as the definitively bourgeois "reasoning that balances accounts"—is the evidence of a fundamental human need for "nonproductive *expenditure*" and interest in "absolute *loss*": that is, a loss that is not otherwise compensated or reciprocated and thus does not operate as a means to some gainful end.[20]

The question here is the extent to which Bataille's effort to produce a counter-utilitarian principle of human motivation is successful, and the answer I shall develop below is that its success is distinctly *limited:* that is, however rhetorically powerful and intellectually fertile his critique of utility theory (so defined) may have been, it appears that Bataille managed only to reverse certain of its most familiar terms while duplicating many of its most dubious features, including its implication in classic dichotomies and dualisms, its sharp means-ends disjunctions, its assumption of a clearly bounded subject or agent, and its positing of a specific fundamental and universal human nature. As we shall see, other less specular alternatives are available.

Human activity is not entirely reducible to processes of production and conservation, and consumption must be divided into two distinct parts. The first, reducible part is represented by the use of the minimum necessary

135

for the conservation of life and the continuation of individuals' productive activity in a given society . . . The second part is represented by so-called unproductive expenditures: luxury, mourning, war, cults, the construction of sumptuary monuments, games, spectacles, arts, perverse sexual activity (i.e., deflected from genital finality)—all these represent activities which, at least in primitive circumstances, have no end beyond themselves . . . [These forms of expenditure] constitute a group characterized by the fact that in each case the accent is placed on a *loss* that must be as great as possible in order for that activity to take on its true meaning. (p. 118)

The initial exemplifications of the operation of "the principle of loss" in "irreducibly" unproductive forms of activity include the expenditure of money, time, or energy on such things as expensive jewels, ritual sacrifice, gambling, and artistic activities and/or the risk or loss of bodily comfort or survival in relation to such activities. It is immediately apparent, however, that the unproductivity of these various activities is not at all irreducible for, in each case, Bataille himself gives—while denying its possibility—a cost-benefit analysis of the expenditure at issue. That is, it is as if, in his very description of these activities, he cannot avoid pointing out what is gained by the loss or what other value is, in his own words, "produced" by the material expenditure or mortal risk involved. Thus, he speaks of the enhancement of the "symbolic value" of jewels, of the "production of sacred things" in the "bloody wasting of men and animals," of the production of a "feeling of stupefaction" (evidently in some way desirable) through the energy "squandered" in competitive games, and of the provocation of laughter or "dread and horror" (again, evidently in some way desirable) by literature and theater. In every case, Bataille indicates that there is a gain in the economy of the individual or the community: either an arithmetically summative (plus-over-minus, "net," or, in effect, "bottom-line") gain, or an exchange of one kind of "good" for some other kind which, in some respect, acquires a commanding priority either from the perspective of the individual subjects or community involved and/or from Bataille's own perspective. In either case, it is a gain or exchange that makes the particular expenditures and risks "rational" in an economistic/utilitarian sense: that is, they have some more or less proportional relation to a desired/able outcome. These activities do not, then, represent the pursuit of "*absolute loss.*" Whether or not one finds Bataille's specific analysis of each of these practices persuasive, "the reasoning that balances accounts" can always be discerned in that very analysis.[21]

The benefits or gains in these examples are not, to be sure, what are usually spoken of or counted as material goods, nor can they readily be seen to yield any enhanced preservation of the individual-as-organism's life. In this respect, Bataille's critique of crude *economism* is quite telling. It does not follow, however, that *economy*—that is, an apportionment and circulation of goods—is not operating in the activities he describes or that some new *principle* of economic psychology, specifically a fundamental interest in "absolute loss," must be invoked or created to account for them. What such examples demonstrate, rather, is that certain—perhaps "classic"—identifications of "good(s)" or "utility" are indeed "restricted," but (as suggested above) in the sense of being arbitrarily confined in accord with such familiar problematic dualisms as matter/spirit, body/mind, and real/symbolic.[22] Although Bataille is explicitly concerned to undo these dualisms,[23] the apparent paradox that he produces here—namely, that *loss* can itself be fundamentally desired/able—nevertheless participates in them, only reversing their valence. Thus, most egregiously here in his division of consumption into "two distinct parts" but also elsewhere throughout the essay, he continues the familiar opposition between, on the one hand, activities that yield presumably "distinct" material and bodily gains and, on the other hand, those that have "no end beyond themselves." Indeed, it may be noticed that while Bataille *valorizes* the latter "nonutilitarian" forms of activity, he simultaneously hedges the question of their use and value by assigning them quite specific individual *ends* and/or social "functions." In this respect, his account duplicates structurally the classic problems of valorizations of play or artistic creativity in opposition to work or material productivity, where the value of certain practices or their products, while pointedly characterized as "nonutilitarian" or as "ends-in-themselves" and thus, presumably, as yielding no benefit to the individual or community, is nevertheless defended through some demonstration of, precisely, how those practices or products benefit the individual or community. The general principle here is that no valorization of anything, even of "loss" itself, can escape the idea of some sort of positivity—that is, gain, benefit, or advantage—in relation to some economy. I shall return to this point below.

The difficulties of Bataille's account are especially evident in his Romantic characterization of poetry, which he sees as a "sacrifice" *par excellence*, and of the poet, whose performance of that sacrifice "condemns him to the most disappointing forms of activity, to misery, to despair, to the pursuit of inconsistent shadows that provide nothing but vertigo or rage, . . . [who] is often forced to choose between the destiny of a reprobate . . . and a renunciation whose price is a mediocre activity, subordinated to vulgar and superficial needs" (p. 120). Is this not, however, once again a balancing of accounts? The misery, despair, and disappointment entailed by devotion to artistic creation are, in Bataille's words, the "price" of the poet's not having to endure another kind of misery, despair, and disappointment which the poet and/or Bataille evidently experience or calculate as *more* unendurable;[24] and they are also the price of his gaining at least the possibility and occasional actuality of a reward that is doubly "priceless"—one for which he would sacrifice everything and one for which others, perhaps, would not pay anything. The poet who will not pay that price, who is "forced to choose" to *renounce* poetry, may thus be seen to have sacrificed his sacrifice, and although from Bataille's perspective he thereby gets the worst of the bargain, it is still, and in either case, precisely a bargain and "in conformity with the balancing of accounts."

As Bataille would no doubt have agreed, the poet who does pay the price is no different in this respect from any other classic renouncer of "vulgar and superficial needs," including the monk, scientist, computer hacker, or drug addict, all of whom participate in a *contemptus mundi* for the sake of (which is to say, *in exchange for*) what Bataille characterizes later in the essay as "glory." But what distinguishes any of these from the bourgeois, any prodigal son from his prudent father, Satan from what Bataille calls elsewhere "the God of work," is not that one engages in economic calculation while the other does not do so or that one seeks absolute loss while the other seeks bottom-line gain, but the quite banal fact that what counts as gain for one counts as loss for the other. The arithmetic is the same: only, in relation to different personal economies, the figures or their *valence* are different. What would require a truly revolutionary economic principle would be evidence not merely of the value (plus) by one measure of that which is loss (minus) by another measure, but of value utterly *without positivity:* value without valence. Given the traditional conceptual syntax of the very notion of *value*, however,[25] the question is not whether such evidence exists but whether it could ever be identified and articulated as such.

Elaborating the central paradox of the essay, Bataille flagrantly reverses the classic utilitarian means-end analysis. It is not that we *ever* expend "in order to" produce but that production and acquisition are "still only means subordinated to expenditure" (p. 120). In short, expenditure itself is always the "end," the motivating and terminal goal and, in his words, the "true meaning" of productive activity. *Loss* thus becomes the ultimate object of desire, the highest good. Although later in the essay this "end" is itself seen as subordinated to—and thus becomes an instrumental "means" toward—another even more ultimate and higher end, the arithmetic is still arithmetic, and one good is replaced with another good or, indeed, exchanged for it *with a net gain.*

The central paradigmatic example of expenditure is potlatch, the reversal of means and ends being said to appear "most clearly in primitive economic institutions" (p. 121).

> It is the constitution of a positive property of loss—from which spring nobility, honor, and rank in a hierarchy—that gives the institution [of potlatch] its significant value . . . [The] archaic principle of wealth is displayed with none of the attenuations that result from the avarice developed at later stages; wealth appears as an acquisition to the extent that power is acquired by a rich man, but it is entirely directed toward loss in the sense that this power is characterized as power to lose. It is only through loss that glory and honor are linked to wealth. (p. 122)

One might demonstrate yet again the operation of cost-benefit ratios in potlatch, where "glory and honor"—if not power—are what are purchased by the expenditure of material goods and what are at risk in the failure to expend. Several further points, however, may be made. First, there is good reason to question whether "the power to lose" is in fact the only or, as Bataille suggests, *terminal* power involved in potlatch or in any other of the conspicuous expenditures documented by anthropologists. An alternate reading of the anthropological (and historical) data is certainly possible. Bourdieu, for example, writes as follows:

> Economic power is first and foremost a power to keep economic necessity at arm's length. This is why it universally asserts itself by the destruction of riches, conspicuous consumption, squandering, and every form of *gratuitous* luxury. Thus, whereas the court aristocracy made the whole of life a continuous spectacle, the bourgeoisie has established the opposition between what is paid for and what is free, the interested and the disinterested, in the form of the opposition . . . [between] business and sentiment, industry and art, the world of economic necessity and the word of artistic freedom that is snatched, by economic power, from that necessity.[26]

Sumptuary expenditure is, moreover, sometimes *inversely* related to prestige and social power. Thus, describing a village in Narayanpur, Alfred Gell considers at length the complex economies—psychological,

139

intrafamilial, societal, and so forth—governing the behavior of a powerful and honored local chieftain who owns five excellent houses and a fortune in land and buffaloes but "chooses to sleep—year in, year out, winter and summer—on an open threshing field in the midst of his fields. He is, to all appearances, a man of the most abject poverty. He wears a cotton g-string and an old woolen pullover, filthy and full of holes."[27] The fact that this account could be read as an instance *either* of conspicuous miserliness—and thus the ultimate extension of the utilitarian's privileging of "conservation" and "acquisition"—*or* of "the principle of loss" illustrates both the self-canceling paradox of that principle and also the theoretical reversibility of all means/ends distinctions.[28]

Bataille's retelling of Mauss's account of potlatch[29] produces a Romantic myth of the Fall: a cruel and horrible but also noble, glorious, and courageous "primitive economy" is succeeded (the intervening historical steps being glided over without comment) by "capitalist economy," the latter seen as a degeneration into various practices characterized in demoting terms drawn not only from Marxist economics ("exploitative," "oppressive," and so on) but also from two other perhaps not altogether surprising realms, namely the aristocratic/aesthetic ("vulgar," "superficial," "petty," "depressing," "boring," "tiresome") and the Christian/ethical ("hypocrisy," "trickery," "avarice"). Bataille writes:

> It is important to know that exchange, at its origin, was *immediately* subordinated to a human *end;* nevertheless it is evident that its development . . . only started at the stage at which this subordination ceased to be immediate . . . In the market economy, the processes of exchange have an acquisitive sense . . .
>
> Today the great and free forms of unproductive social expenditure have disappeared . . .
>
> A certain evolution of wealth, whose symptoms indicate sickness and exhaustion, leads to shame in oneself accompanied by petty hypocrisy. Everything that was generous, orgiastic, and excessive has disappeared. (pp. 123–124)

It is, I think, hardly necessary to point out here all that goes with the positing of original immediacies and subsequent degenerative mediations.[30] It may be noted, as well, that while Bataille accounts for the noble savage in terms of putatively natural, universal ("fundamental" and "endemic") economic psychology, he speaks of the ugly bourgeois in terms of a local and historically emergent pathology. As was discussed earlier, this kind of explanatory asymmetry and its particular terms—that is, natural/universal/normal/ideal versus special/local/pathological/deviant—is a characteristic feature of the questionable logic of all classic axiologies.

Mauss's discussion of the operation of nonmaterial needs, goods, and capital in tribal economies apparently operated for Bataille (as it has for others since) as an empirical refutation of classical economics that justified his no doubt quite variously motivated loathing of certain elements of contemporary economic, political, and cultural life, all under the names "capitalism" and "bourgeois," while simultaneously permitting him to retain elements of a traditional moral ideology and discourse.[31] It is clear, however, that no dent has actually been made by this anthropological discovery in the tendency to repeat the classic ("utilitarian" and other) means-end analysis in which all expenditure of energy or goods is inscribed as a means directed toward and subordinated to a specific profitable end, either other kinds of goods or goods in exchange for energy. Though the *ends* are now seen to be *other*, they are not problematized as such but strictly reversed. And, as the essay develops, the anthropological analysis of tribal practices is increasingly pressed to serve the justification of Bataille's revulsion at (= "critique of") the bourgeois and his promotion of a redemptive apocalyptic revolution.

The succeeding section of Bataille's essay, titled "Class Struggle," opens as follows:

> In trying to maintain sterility in regard to expenditure, in conformity with a reasoning that balances *accounts*, bourgeois society has only managed to develop a universal meanness . . . What remains of the traditional modes of expenditure has become atrophied, and living sumptuary tumult has been lost in the unprecedented explosion of *class struggle* . . .
>
> Without a doubt bourgeois society, which pretends to govern according to rational principles, and which, through its own actions, moreover, tends to realize a certain human homogeneity, does not accept without protest a division that seems destructive to man himself; it is incapable, however, of pushing this resistance further than theoretical negation. (p. 125)[32]

Given the posited fundamental human need for absolute loss and expenditure without reserve, the various "losses" and "disappearances" cited here and elsewhere throughout the essay are hardly surprising. Indeed, they could be seen as the inevitable working out of that very need in what Bataille later speaks of (in strictly Hegelian terms) as "the qualitative change constantly realized by the movement of history" (p. 129). That is, a degenerative entropic history—successive disappearances and losses, expanding failure, and increased homogeneity—or, in effect, an endless "fall," is precisely what one would expect.

Bataille continues with a brief analysis of the "agonistic social expenditure" that, in "bourgeois society," functions to maintain a disjunction between "the masters" and "the workers" and specifically to "engender [the latter's] abjection."[33] *"The end of the workers' activity is to produce in order to live, but the bosses' activity is to produce in order to condemn the working producers to a hideous degradation"* (pp. 125–126). Certain "subterfuges" are said to mask this agon: for example, the fact that bourgeois society "announces . . . *equality* by inscribing that word on the walls" (p. 125) and that "in the Anglo-Saxon countries, and in particular in the United States of America, the primary process takes place at the expense of only a relatively small portion of the population . . . [while] to a certain extent, the working class itself has been led to participate in it" (p. 126).[34] But, he adds,

> these subterfuges . . . do not modify in any way the fundamental division between noble and ignoble men. The cruel game of social life does not vary among the different civilized countries, where the insulting splendor of the rich loses and degrades the human nature of the lower class.
> It must be added that the attenuation of the masters' brutality—which in any case has less to do with destruction itself than with the psychological tendencies to destroy—corresponds to the general atrophy of the ancient sumptuary processes that characterizes the modern era. (p. 126)

Thus, equality is the opiate of the people, drugging them into a complicitous participation in the degenerate system that denies them both the ultimate gain of absolute loss and also the glory of brutal as well as absolute degradation.

In a section titled "Christianity and Revolution," Bataille suggests that although Christianity made it possible "for the provoked poor to refuse all moral participation in a system in which men oppress men" (p. 126), "only the word Revolution . . . carries with it the promise that answers the unlimited demands of the masses" (p. 127) so that "class struggle . . . becomes the grandest form of social expenditure" (p. 126): "Class struggle has only one possible end: the loss of those who have worked to lose 'human nature'" (p. 128). The familiar and indeed paradigmatically Christian form of this apocalyptic paradox is notable,[35] and, of course, one might ask why the economy of loss should stop here: that is, wouldn't the most glorious social expenditure of all be not the loss, but the *loss of the loss*, of those who cause "human nature" to be lost?[36]

> Human life . . . cannot in any way be limited to the closed systems assigned to it by reasonable conceptions . . . Life starts only with the deficit in these systems [cf. Shakespeare's "Then soul, live thou upon thy servant's loss, / And let that pine to aggravate thy store"]; at least what it allows in the way of order and reserve has meaning only from the moment when the ordered and reserved forces liberate and lose themselves for ends that cannot be subordinated to anything one can account for. It is only by such insubordination—even if it is impoverished—that the human race ceases to be isolated in the unconditional splendor of material things. (p. 128)

Bataille's rejection of accounts of human action in terms of closed systems or narrowly economistic conceptions of rationality is, to be sure, admirable as such. At the same time, however, one cannot but acknowledge that this invocation of nonmaterialistic nonsubordinatable ends hardly differs from the more commonplace invocations of higher or transcendent goals, goods, interests, and values discussed in the previous section. He continues:

> In fact, in the most universal way, isolated or in groups, men find themselves constantly engaged in processes of expenditure . . . whose principle is loss . . . [These processes are animated by] *states of excitation*, which . . . can be defined as the illogical and irresistible impulse to reject material or moral goods that it would have been possible to utilize rationally (in conformity with the balancing of accounts). Connected to the losses that are realized in this way . . . is the creation of unproductive values; the most absurd of these values . . . is *glory*. Made complete through degradation, glory . . . has never ceased to dominate social existence; it is impossible to do anything without it when it is dependent on the blind practice of personal or social loss. (pp. 128–129)

"Blind" is evidently inserted here not to question the implicit teleology of classic utility theory but, rather, to secure these practices of transcendent loss from any accounting in terms of vulgar utilitarian/rational *calculation*.[37] But the question remains: Have they really escaped *all* economic accounting?

Apparently not. The essay concludes as follows:

> If on the other hand one demonstrates the interest, concurrent with glory (as well as with degradation), which the human community necessarily sees in the qualitative change constantly realized by the movement of history, and if, finally, one demonstrates that this movement is impossible

to contain or direct toward a limited end, it becomes possible, having abandoned all reserves, to assign a *relative* value to utility. Men assure their own subsistence or avoid suffering, not because these functions themselves lead to a sufficient result, but in order to accede to the insubordinate function of free expenditure. (p. 129)

This final equation summarizes and encloses all the previously elaborated reversals in a sanctified utilitarianism: *the ultimate value, end, and true meaning* of "utility," of that which man produces in order to preserve life and avoid suffering, consists in its making possible the unlimited exhibition of his irreducibly sovereign free will, his insubordinate subordination of matter to spirit, and thereby his uniquely and definitively human transcendence. Bataille's critique of classical utilitarian logic is thus of a piece not only with that logic but also with the strictly classical transcendental logic of its own equally classical forebears.

Endless (Ex)Change

While the difficulties of Bataille's critique of utility theory do not redeem the latter, they do indicate directions for alternative critiques. The one that I outline below follows from the present reconceptualization of value as discussed in earlier chapters and from a corollary conception of economic activity as having *no* "end," neither *telos* nor *terminus*. That is, there is no overall, underlying, or ultimate governing outcome toward which each instance of human productive-acquisitive *or* consummatory-expenditive activity (all making, getting, and spending, we might say) is directed, and also no conclusion to the continuous exchange and circulation of goods. Indeed, in accord with such an alternate conceptualization, there is no "economic" activity per se. There is simply activity, variously motivated or, in Bataille's terms, "animated," with various outcomes, all of which may be viewed under various aspects, including none at all (in which case it could be seen as Brownian motion, Heraclitean flux, or Nietzsche's pure "play of forces"),[38] but also including the "economic" aspect of the apportionment, circulation, and exchange of goods. Viewed in the latter aspect, all human (and not only human) activity could be seen to consist of a continuous exchange or expenditure (whether as payment, donation, sacrifice, loss, or destruction) of goods of some (but any) kind, whereby goods of some other (but, again, any) kind are secured, enhanced, or produced. Thus, money or material provisions are expended whereby power is enlarged and status confirmed, sumptuary goods are donated or destroyed whereby social or symbolic value is marked and maintained, bodily comfort and life are sacrificed whereby exhilaration and glory are gained, "hours of dross" are sold to buy "terms divine," and so forth— and also, for *any* of these exchanges, vice versa: money is hoarded whereby status is risked, glory is forgone whereby comfort is secured, terms divine are sacrificed whereby hours of dross are gilded— everywhere, in every archaic tribe and "modern era," *endlessly*.[39]

"Whereby" in the formulation just outlined is not to say "in order that." For one thing, the very nature of the causality operating in human activity is part of what is at issue here. Secondly and relatedly, there is no "end" whatsoever required here, including the *telos* of "purpose." To be sure, human agents can and often do produce verbally (or otherwise) articulated calculations as part of their ongoing activities; but purposiveness in the sense of a "conscious" or "deliberate" matching of activities to specifically foreseen and desired outcomes is hardly the rule and need not be invoked at all. In a general formulation of the economics of activity (and, in this form, not confined to human or verbal agents), teleological accounts of motivation and behavior would be replaced by accounts of the ways that activities are sustained and transformed by their own past and current consequences for the agent. Activities are only arbitrarily describable as segmented into individual "acts" or "choices," and what we refer to as "motivation"—the energizing and shaping or "animating" of human behavior—is no more a matter of linear pushes (by "forces"—such as biological, cultural, or ideological) than of linear pulls (by "ends," "goals," "objects of desire"). It is, rather, a matter of the continuous mutually modifying interactions between and among ongoing activities and current traces of past activities—structures, mechanisms, tendencies, impulses, desires, concepts, images, memories, plans, hungers, habits, and so forth—that operate at every level of the agent's organization and are continuously modified by their differential consequences under different sets of conditions.[40]

It must be emphasized that the "goods" in question in the formulation outlined above may be of *any kind* whatsoever: none are privileged by reference to any presumed fundamental or essential human necessity or universal human nature. Indeed, they are *constituted* as "goods" (that is, as profits, satisfactions, gains, benefits, etc.) only in relation to a particular state of a particular agent's personal economy—that is, the nature, distribution, and trajectory of her desires and resources at some

145

moment: "desires" and "resources" that, in accord with the present analysis, must be understood as themselves the product of the continuous interaction between, and thus mutual production by, the agent and an environment that is itself *always* socially and culturally constituted.

Goods, either one by one or collectively (as in "the good"), are not reducible to anything else *in particular*, such as pleasure, the enhancement of survival, or the promotion of communal welfare. This is not, as some modern ethical theory suggests, because goodness is an essential, intuitively apprehended primary quality of things.[41] The irreducibility is a function not of objective qualities but, rather, of Western (perhaps human) thought and language within which "good" or some counterpart term or set of terms operates conceptually and discursively as *a generalized positivity* that can be locally specified but not further analyzed: in other words, (one) "good" can only be exchanged for (an)other good, in discourse and otherwise. This seems to be a principle of the most general economy or the most general principle of economy.[42] As the recurrent tautologies, circularities, and infinite regresses that mark the discourses of value suggest, the concept of "good" operates axiomatically within them: its radical positivity cannot be dispensed with nor can it be defined, explained, or analyzed without recursion to another concept of radical positivity, whether by the name of "good" or one of its virtual equivalents, such as "benefit," "profit," "gain," "payoff," "reward," "positive reinforcement," or, of course, "value" itself used as a valenced (positive) term.[43] Indeed, it appears that "good" operates within the discourse of value as does money in a cash economy: *good* is the universal value-form of value and its standard "measure"; it is that "in terms of which" all forms of value must be "expressed" for their commensurability to be calculated; and *good* is that *for* which and *into* which any other name or form of value can—"on demand," we might say—be (ex)changed. Bataille's effort to turn the utilitarian model of economy upside down by privileging the classic contrary cases (resource-destruction, individual or communal sacrifice, self-annihilation, and so forth) as themselves constituting the fundamental good or as the necessary route to the ultimate good fails for that very reason: that is, at the very moment that "absolute loss" is constituted as a good or a means to a good, it ceases to be absolute loss.

Like Baudrillard and others who seek to produce a discourse of value that escapes or transcends an economic conceptualization,[44] Bataille sought to constitute and articulate a good that would successfully resist being interpreted as (or exchanged for) gain, benefit, advantage, or positivity: that is, a good without "good." It appears from the present analysis, however, that just as the classic "value-form," money, operates within a market economy to commoditize (that is, to "put a price on" or assign a cash equivalence to) *everything*, so also, within the economy of the discourse of economy, *anything* that is indicated, predicated, or otherwise constituted either as a positivity within some economy or as the object of a need, desire, or interest (individual or collective) is measured, in the very moment that it is put forward as such, as so much "good"; and this *anything* includes expenditure, consumption, sacrifice, self-annihilation, death, universal destruction, and even "absolute loss."

We may return now to the initial flourish of Bataille's essay and to what is indeed, from the perspective of the present study, one of the major "insufficiencies of the principle of classical utility."[45] Not only is it impossible to say "what is useful to man" in general, but it is also impossible to say it for any individual subject. The question will always be *What is "man"*? That is, what kind of entity is postulated in the anthropological-economic accounts at issue here? What, for example, is the nature of the "self" in relation to which the agent pursues (or, for that matter, renounces) "self-interest"? By what mode of boundary can we or should we delimit the "person" whose personal economy we would describe? And by what kind of unit can we or should we indicate the individual subject in adding her up with other "individuals" (or "men" or "selves" or "persons") in the aggregate?

It is not that there are *no* answers to such questions but that there are many answers and no obviously or fundamentally compelling (or otherwise noncontingent) reason for adopting one rather than another. Thus, we may stress again that the personal economy of the subject (or "agent" or "organism"—the range of names here indicates the possibility of alternate accounts) may always be conceived as a system of *multiple* economies, each of which interacts with a shifting environment and all of which not only continuously interact but also may at any point come into more or less radical conflict.[46] What this suggests here is that the organization of our activities—the relation between, on the one side, our actions and, on the other side, our knowledge, beliefs, interests, and goals (however any of these are ascertained)—is not "rational" in either the economist's or ethical philosopher's sense: i.e., our actions, choices, beliefs, desires, interests are neither in smooth mutual coordination nor in perfect mutual adjustment in relation to higher ends or more comprehensive goals. Neither are they, instead, specifically irrational in either the psychoanalyst's or cultural anthropologist's sense: that is, ultimately controlled either by libidinal energies or by "social meanings." Neither are we (or our beliefs, actions, and the relation between them) therefore either divinely "free" in the theological sense or, what is sometimes suggested as the only alternative, utterly chaotic, purely whimsical, and/or totally incoherent.

What I am suggesting here, rather, is that what all such terms and accounts (*homo economicus, homo ludens,* man as rational creature, cultural creature, biological creature, and so forth) offer to conceptualize is something that might just as well be thought of as our irreducible *scrappiness.* I wish to suggest with this term not only that the elements that interact to constitute our motives and behavior are incomplete and heterogeneous, like scraps of things, but also ("scrap" being a slang term for fight) that they are mutually conflicting or at least always potentially at odds. That is, the relations among what we call our "actions," "knowledge," "beliefs," "goals," and "interests" consist of continuous interactions among various structures, mechanisms, traces, impulses, and tendencies that are not necessarily ("naturally" or otherwise) consistent, coordinated, or synchronized and are therefore always *more or less* inconsistent, out-of-phase, discordant, and conflictual. It must be added, however, that although these interactions obey no "rule" and have no "reason," they do *nevertheless* operate reliably enough under recurrent conditions to permit their more or less coherent description through various modes of reflexive (that is, self-descriptive) analysis and also yield local resolutions and provisional stabilities that, for longer or shorter periods of time, are good enough to keep us—and thus *them,* the interactions—going.[47] It is out of these scrappy (heterogenous) elements and the local resolutions and provisional stabilities yielded by their continous scrappy (more or less conflictual) interactions that we (and, from various perspectives, others) construct our various versions of our various "selves" and, as necessary, explain or justify our actions, goals, and beliefs. It is also out of the scrappy interactions of these scrappy elements—though on a more general scale—that theorists in the different disciplinary traditions cited above construct, from their accordingly different perspectives, their accordingly different general accounts of human behavior.

There is no single, particular, nonarbitrarily specifiable domain that encloses all the interactions indicated above. There is also no nonarbitrarily definable arena within which all the conflicts are played out, within which the ever-shifting priorities are ever "*finally*" assigned and settled. (As Bataille saw, but not steadily, there is no "closed system.") There is thus no particular single dimension or global parameter, whether "biological"/"material" *or* "cultural"/"spiritual"/"psychological," with respect to which entities can be tagged or tallied as, "in the last analysis," good or bad—profit or cost, reward or punishment, pleasure or pain—for any subject or set of subjects, much less for man in general. There is thus also no way for individual or collective choices, practices, activities, or acts, "economic" or otherwise, to be ultimately summed-up, compared, and evaluated: neither by the single-parameter hedonic calculus of classic utilitarianism, nor by the most elaborate multiple-parameter formulas of contemporary mathematical economics, nor by any mere inversion or presumptive transcendence of either. There is no way to give a reckoning that is simultaneously total and final. There is no Judgment Day. There is no *bottom* bottom line anywhere, for anyone or for "man."

7

Matters of Consequence

It's insofar as there's been an awakening to a whole series of
problems that the difficulty of doing anything comes to be
felt. Not that this effect is an end in itself. But it seems to me
that "what is to be done" ought . . . to be determined . . . by a
long work of comings and goings, of exchanges, reflections,
trials, different analyses . . . The necessity of reform musn't be
allowed to become a form of blackmail serving to limit, reduce, or halt the exercise of criticism.   *Michel Foucault*

Critiques and Charges: The Objectivist Generation of "Relativism"

It is recurrently said that the present analysis, specifically its questionings of absolute value and of the idea of objective standards, is "quietistic," or, as the latter term and associated objection are usually explained, that the positions that such questionings entail prevent one
from opposing bad things and promoting good ones. Allegedly, the
author of this study must look on bad things benignly as simply what
the other fellow prefers and on all things, good and bad, with passive
"egalitarian tolerance."[1] As a "relativist," she must, it is said, face the
choice of being either morally and politically nerveless or logically inconsistent. Someone might develop such views in theory, it is said, but
no one can hold them in practice; no one, she is told, can *live* that way.

   The currency and repetition of these observations make the quietist
objection almost as common and casual in contemporary axiological
debates as the self-refutationist argument and Egalitarian Fallacy have
been in eras past. Indeed, it echoes both of them and can readily be seen
as their combined current versions, the major difference being the
sharpness of its ethical/political—as distinct from logical/epistemolog-
ical—edge. Although these charges must and will be given attention
here, they cannot, for reasons that touch on the heart of the matter, be
quite "refuted." For part of what is at issue here is the viability of the
terms in which the charges themselves are framed and of the entire
system of conceptualizations and attendent conceptual syntax by which
they are generated and through which they are articulated. Objections

150

registered by orthodox objectivists to this study and to its author's presumed political and moral life do indeed hinge on inconsistencies of theory and practice: what is inconsistent with her theory is *their theory;* what is inconsistent with her practice is *their description of her theory.* To explain why this is so and also to broaden the scope of the discussion, it will be useful to approach the quietist objection in relation to the more general charge of "relativism."

There are, of course, many relativisms. Two will concern us here. One is any more or less extensively theorized questioning—analysis, problematizing, critique—of the key elements of traditional objectivist thought and its attendant axiological machinery. In that sense, this study is relativistic. The other is *such questioning as perceived and interpreted by that which it questions:* a phantom heresy dreamt by anxious orthodoxy under siege or, in other words, a "relativism" created by traditional objectivism itself. In this second sense, the present study is not and *could not be* relativistic.

At the most general theoretical level, the relativism exhibited by this study is not a "position," not a "conviction," and not a set of "claims" about how certain things—reality, truth, meaning, reason, value, and so forth—really are. It is, rather, a general conceptual style or taste, specifically played out here as (a) a conceptualization of the world as continuously changing, irreducibly various, and multiply configurable, (b) a corresponding tendency to find cognitively distasteful, unsatisfying, or counterintuitive any conception of the world as fixed and integral and/or as having objectively determinate properties,[2] and (c) a corresponding disinclination or inability to use terms such as "reality," "truth," "meaning," "reason," or "value" as glossed by the latter objectivist conceptions.[3] What is *not* exhibited in this study is the set of foolish "positions," "convictions," and "claims" produced by objectivist thought when, confronted by such alternative conceptualizations of the world, it imagines itself turned upside down. This is not to say that no one either makes the foolish claims in question or believes the *allegedly* entailed quietistic dispositions are appropriate ones to display. There certainly are such people, including some more or less boisterous sophomoric ones who may refer to themselves as "relativists" and who are, it appears, objectivists standing on their heads. It is to say, rather, that those positions and dispositions cannot be *derived from* the analyses and formulations developed in this study (or in the works by Feyerabend, Goodman, Barnes, and Bloor cited in the note above) except by the exercise of the very objectivist logic that they question and reject.

It is just these latter products of generation by self-inversion, however, that must be dealt with in responding to the charges I mentioned earlier. The most central, classic, and perhaps enduring of them—that is, objectivist characterizations of and simultaneous objections to "relativism"—are:

a) its *alleged* claim/assertion that all truth is relative, said to be self-refuting in that it dissolves its own truth-claims and/or grants the truth of the assertion that it is false;

b) the Egalitarian Fallacy: that is, its *alleged* belief/claim that all judgments are equally valid, all objects equally good, all practices equally justifiable; and

c) "anything goes"—that is, its *alleged* belief/claim that reality is totally subjective, that there are no constraints on belief or behavior, that one can think and do anything one likes.

As I indicated in an earlier chapter and will discuss further below, the first two of these are repetitions-in-reverse of the fundamental *objectivist* conceptions of "truth" and "validity."[4] The third is the joint product of the traditional subjective/objective dichotomy, its attendant all-or-nothing logic, and a related set of assumptions about the dynamics and constraints of individual and social behavior that, as we shall see, are crucial to objectivist thought.[5]

In addition to these alleged claims and positions, certain attitudes or behavioral dispositions are seen to follow from the questioning or critique of orthodox objectivism, and are routinely associated with "relativism." These include:

d) limp, lax, and indiscriminate aesthetic and intellectual tolerance; fatuous forbearance; the inability to exert evaluative authority; the disinclination or refusal to recommend or criticize objects, enforce or oppose practices, or promote or argue against ideas; and

e) political and moral paralysis, torpor, and despair; Panglossism and status-quoism; an inability, disinclination, or refusal to take a stand or to work for change.

Here, of course, is where the quietist objection finds its place. Before examining any of them more specifically, we may add to this list of alleged positions and dispositions the set of intellectual, social, and political *calamities* seen, again by self-inversion, to be the inevitable consequence of the critique or abandonment of objectivist axiology—or, as it is said, to which relativism "opens the gate":

- f) the loss of the authority of truth, facts, logic, universal principles, and natural rights;
- g) the disappearance of genuine science, moral reasoning, and rational discourse;
- h) the collapse of aesthetic standards;
- i) the breakdown of law and morality, the takeover of democratic institutions by totalitarianism, the eruption of social chaos and anarchy, the return to the jungle;
- j) the Gulag, the Nazi death camps.

It will be noticed that a number of these calamities—for example, (f), (g), and (h)—amount simply to a description of the world in the absence of the conceptual/discursive idiom of traditional axiology. These dread occurrences consist, in other words, of the "loss," "breakdown," "collapse," and "disappearance" *not* of various moral, aesthetic, and scientific practices, phenomena, and institutions, but, rather, of the possibility of describing and accounting for various practices, phenomena, and institutions in familiar objectivist ways. Given the tendency of objectivist thought to reify theoretical constructs, it is not surprising that it regards the articulation of alternative *conceptualizations* as an attack on fundamental *entities*. Unable to accommodate the idea of a world conceived otherwise, objectivist thought concludes that, in the absence of its own conceptualizations, there could not *be* a world, or any *thought* at all. Thus, Hilary Putnam remarks: "If one abandons the notions of justification, rational acceptability, warranted assertibility, right assertibility, and the like, completely, then 'true' goes as well . . . But if all notions of rightness, both epistemic and (metaphysically) realist, are eliminated, then what are our statements but noise-makings? The elimination of the normative is attempted mental suicide."[6] Of course, if one *defines* "the normative" as the orthodox axiological machinery of "justification, rational acceptability, warranted assertibility, right assertibility, and the like," then, *by definition*, the rejection of those notions in their traditional conceptualization is the "elimination of the normative." If, however, "the normative" is taken in the *non-question-begging* sense of either (a) the operations of sociocultural institutions of value marking, value maintaining, value transforming, and value transmitting, or, in relation to "true," (b) the self-regulating mechanisms of verbal interaction, its dynamics can be quite otherwise described. The question is whether, so described, they would still *count* as "the normative" from Putnam's perspective, and the answer is that they probably would *not*, which is to say we are at the sort of impasse that seems characteristic of these debates.[7] One could, of course, ask Putnam how he accounts for the apparent fact that some people *do* "abandon" those notions and manage both to think and to live to tell the tale. If all goes true to form, however, he would reply to the effect that, if such people have lived to tell the tale and do continue to think, it proves they have not really abandoned those notions, for no one could live or think that way.

Not all the calamities listed above are, of course, merely alarmed descriptions of a world without orthodox descriptions of the world. In certain cases, notably (i) and (j), what sustains the idea that they are engendered by the questioning and critique of objectivist thought—which is to say by "relativism"—is the intractably self-privileging logic of objectivist thought itself, here the conviction that only its own theoretical (logical, epistemological, theological, etc.) security and widespread affirmation bar the gate to the polis and keep the night, the jungle, and the jackals at bay. That conviction obviously requires a specific and highly dubious sociopolitical theory and, with it, a more general and equally dubious theory of the mechanisms—psychological, political, and other—by which individual and social behavior are motivated and constrained: dubious because, among other reasons, it is evident that the jackals, the Gulag, and the death camps have *not* been kept from the polis in spite of what has been, up to now, the theoretical dominance and widespread affirmation of objectivist thought.[8]

The question is often put: "But how would you answer the Nazi?" The reply has two parts. The first part is, *it depends:* it depends on where the Nazi and I—given, of course, my particular identity—each are, and what resources and power, institutional and other, are available to each of us. Under some conditions, I would not say anything at all to him or do anything else in particular (there are self-styled Nazis to whom I am not now saying anything, and about whom I am not now doing anything in particular either); under other conditions, I would look for the fastest and surest way to escape his power; under yet other conditions, I would do what I could, no doubt with others, to destroy him. The question to be asked in turn is whether, given a similar identity and under comparable conditions, anyone else, including an objectivist, could do or ever did otherwise. Second, I would suggest that "answering" the Nazi, in the sense of getting one's ethical/epistemological arguments in good axiological order, is not, in any case, what is wanted. What is wanted, I think, is a theoretically subtle and powerful analysis of the conditions and, even more important, *dynamics* of the Nazi's emergence and access to power and, accordingly, a specification of political and other actions that might make that emergence and access less likely, both in one's own neighborhood and elsewhere. It must be added, however, that any such analysis must expect to compete with *others* and, accordingly, with the specification of other political efforts, including—as we must never forget—those mounted by Nazis as well. The point is that, whereas "answering" the Nazi with axiologically grounded arguments will do nothing at all to prevent or destroy his power, developing theoretical analyses and political programs will not do *everything*. The latter will not be decisive; nothing can guarantee that the jackals will be kept at bay, neither axiology nor any specific alternative that replaces it.

Richard Rorty's recent efforts to deal with the assignment of "the traditional epithet" of relativism to views he has elaborated and endorsed under the name pragmatism are instructive here. Referring to his view "that there is nothing to be said about either truth or rationality apart from the familiar procedures of justification which a given society—*ours*—uses in one or another area of inquiry," Rorty remarks: "It is not clear why 'relativist' should be thought an appropriate term for [this—'ethnocentric,' as he calls it] view."[9] After all, he goes on to explain: "the pragmatist is not holding a positive theory which says that something is relative to something else. He is, instead, making . . . [a] purely *negative* point" (p. 6). That negative point, in Rorty's restatement of it, is that "there is nothing to be said about truth save that each of us will commend as true those beliefs which he or she finds good to believe." This is not, Rorty insists, a positive theory about the nature of truth. "If it were," he remarks in passing, "such a theory would, of course, be self-refuting." "But," he continues, "the pragmatist does not have a theory of truth, much less a relativistic one. As a partisan of solidarity, his account of the value of cooperative human inquiry has only an ethical base, not an epistemological or metaphysical one. Not having *any* epistemology, *a fortiori* he does not have a relativistic one" (p. 6).

Rorty's more general difficulties—and, as he sees them, *dilemmas*—in regard to charges of relativism will be discussed in some detail later. What is important to note here is how difficult it is for him to unfix the label with the sort of disclaimer just presented; for, as he recognizes, even if the pragmatist does not have an epistemological/metaphysical account of truth, he still appears to his realist adversary to be saying things about *it*, "truth"; and even though he himself hears what he is saying as an altogether negative point, the realist will hear it as equivalent to a positive and positively appalling point, namely that just someone's finding something good to believe is enough to *make* it "true" *in the realist/objectivist sense.*[10]

Thus the relativism/anti-relativism match is recurrently constructed and enacted: a game of pure nonengagement, ending in a draw by default. Disclaimers of the label and refutations of its alleged entailments are difficult at best and, in many companies and under most informal conditions and constraints of time, impossible. The various positions, dispositions, and calamities that are typically alleged to follow from a denial of objectivism and which give any point to the *charge* of relativism as such, will, despite all denials and indications of evidence to the contrary, continue to be generated unavoidably and unwittingly through the self-inversion of objectivist thought.

We could observe here that all the terms of the standard objectivist objections to relativism, as listed above, are implicated in a radically contingent—that is, historically, culturally, linguistically, and institutionally *local and particular*—conceptualization and discourse of "reality," "validity," "justification," "reason," "truth," "facts," and so forth. We could also observe, accordingly, that the objectivist's elaborations of his charges *and* the pragmatist/relativist's attempts to refute them or to dissociate himself from the beliefs he is alleged to hold, both become, perforce, only more or less emphatic restatements of the radically divergent views of each side: divergences of conceptual style, conceptual temperament, conceptual taste, and conceptual idiom that sooner or later exhibit themselves as intractable conceptual/discursive impasses. Observations such as these, however, can neither transcend the argument nor break the circle for, of course, the idea that conceptualizations are radically contingent and that conceptual/discursive impasses may be intractable will be, to the objectivist, a mark of relativism.

Quietism and the Active Relativist

In accord with the quietist objection, the situation just described would be expected to produce in the relativist a condition of genial, torpid philosophical che-serà-seràism. "Well," she might be expected to say, "it takes all kinds. Some like objectivism, some don't—it's like chocolate and vanilla. Let's all go out and sit on the porch swing." As we shall see, however, although that *could* happen and, under some conditions, is pretty much what *does* happen, there are specific reasons why, and conditions under which, the relativist will become quite energetic, both as a social and political agent and as a promoter and defender of her conceptual tastes *as such*.

We may observe, first, that someone's critique of objectivist thought and axiology and, accordingly, denial of "absolute value," "universal standards," and "objective truth," could hardly be thought to produce her *total* paralysis—to prevent her, in other words, from acting at all, or from acting, generally, more or less in accord with her particular beliefs, perceptions, desires, interests, tastes, preferences, judgments, and so forth. The question, then, is why it is thought she would be given to such deep pause or immobility upon discovering that these (her perceptions, desires, etc.) are not merely contingent "in theory" but are, in practice and *in vivo*, at odds with other people's.

The answer, and an idea crucial to all versions of the quietist objection, seems to be that, although a nonobjectivist might undertake to *do* things, nevertheless because she must believe that everybody "has a right" to his own perceptions, beliefs, interests, and preferences, or that all the latter are "equally valid," she could not *justify* doing them or do them and *be consistent*. As I have repeatedly indicated here, however, what the nonobjectivist allegedly *must* believe is something that she not only *need* not, but *cannot*, believe. Contrary to the self-refutationist argument, an abandonment of objectivist conceptualizations of "truth" does not (and hardly could) oblige one to acknowledge that objectivism itself may be *true* in the objectivist sense. Nor, contrary to the Egalitarian Fallacy, could a denial of traditional conceptions of objective "validity" oblige one to regard other people's opinions, beliefs, tastes, etc., as equally *valid*. Since a nonobjectivist, by definition, does not conceptualize "truth" and "validity" the way an objectivist does, she cannot give to "true" or "valid" the meanings those terms have for him, which are also the meanings that are required either for her position to be self-refuting or for her to be committed to that form of egalitarianism which, to the objectivist, defines relativism and entails quietism. In short, a nonobjectivist *by definition* cannot be "committed to" what the objectivist objects to in what he names "relativism," nor is she, then, behaving inconsistently when she *acts* in a way inconsistent with those alleged commitments.

Various versions and key variants of the quietist objection can be handled accordingly.

(1) The first concerns what the relativist can and cannot "say," the way her *verbal behavior* is constrained by her alleged commitments. It is sometimes objected, for example, that one cannot live as a nonobjectivist because, in the real world of real peasants, politicians, and police, one must deal with people for whom only objectivist-type considerations and justifications—appeals to "fundamental rights" and "objective facts," not just to contingent conditions—will be acceptable and effective. Two replies may be made here. One is that it would be no more logically inconsistent for a nonobjectivist to speak, under *some* conditions, of fundamental rights and objective facts than for a Hungarian ordering his lunch in Paris to speak French. Under *some* conditions: what I refer to here as objectivism and nonobjectivism are, of course, formally articulated conceptualizations and critiques which, as such, are most commonly played out not in interactions with police, peasants, and politicians but, rather, in arenas of theoretical discourse and exchange. This is not to say that they have no implications for action in other domains: far from it, as I have indicated throughout this study and explicitly just above. The actions that follow from them, however, are not necessarily *verbal* actions, and specifically neither the formal recitation of formal theories or, in the name of some altogether irrelevant "consistency," the earnest substitution of technical terms for idiomatic ones. For the lexicon, syntax, and register of *all* discourses are *always* constrained by, and accommodated to, the particular features of a communicative situation. The other and equally important reply, however, is that the power, richness, subtlety, flexibility, and communicative effectiveness of *a nonobjectivist idiom*—for example, forceful recommendations that do *not* cite intrinsic value, or justifications, accepted as such, that *do* cite contingent conditions and likely outcomes rather than fundamental rights and objective facts—are characteristically underestimated by those who have never learned to speak it or tried to use it in interactions with, among others, real policemen, peasants, and politicians.

(2) In relation to various forms of *pedagogy* or *instruction,* including institutional teaching, academic literary criticism, domestic child rearing, and missionary work, the quietist objection maintains that a nonobjectivist conception of value, especially the idea that value is always seen

158

and measured from some perspective, commits one to the view that people cannot or should not evaluate for other people: that it would be wrong, for example, to remark, with regard to some object or practice such as Seneca's *Medea,* or the concealment of the genitals in public, or the study of Old Norse, a value that they had not remarked for themselves or evidently considered quite differently. It also maintains that nonobjectivist conceptions of value commit one to the view that parents, teachers, and missionaries cannot or should not *urge* and, as necessary, *impose* that unremarked value or unappreciated practice on children, students, and various other persons understood to be immature, benighted, or misled as to their true interests and desires by their upbringing, their cultures, or the mass media. For, such objections typically go on to argue, even though the object or practice in question may appear undesirable, disagreeable, or outlandish from the perspective of the latter persons, it might nevertheless be the case that it was really (essentially, intrinsically, objectively) good, and/or that, even though they did not (yet) realize it, the object or practice would perform fundamentally beneficial and ultimately desirable functions for them—for example, edifying, economic, therapeutic, or salvational ones.

It is clear that this version of the quietist objection presupposes the entire axiological machinery that the nonobjectivist problematizes and thus begs all the crucial questions at issue. Those questions are: first, whether something's being really good (or really bad)[11] could be determined from *no* perspective whatsoever or whether we don't have, in such cases, a *particular, other perspective* masking itself as no perspective, which is to say tacitly privileging itself or the perspective of some dominant group; second, whether it could be from *no* perspective or only from some *particular, other perspective* that the alleged benefits would be counted as fundamentally beneficial and ultimately desirable; and third, whether the pedagogic version of the quietist objection doesn't, therefore, back up toward and slip irrevocably into the familiar infinite regress of all axiological claims. For the real goodness seen by the parent, teacher, or missionary could not be self-evident or it would have already been evident to the children, students, or benighted natives who have failed to see it, and any attempt to justify those *alternate judgments* would also have to justify the privilege accorded to the *alternate perspective* from which they were made.[12] *None of this is to say that the observation of an otherwise unnoticed contingent goodness cannot be made or should not be urged on other people, or that the privilege involved could not be defended and granted by some and perhaps all concerned.* It is to say, rather, that, since

159

the contingency of all value cannot be evaded, whoever does the *urging* cannot ultimately suppress, or ultimately evade taking responsibility for, the *particularity* of the perspective from which he does so.

The rejoinder typically entered at this point is that if a judgment is particular and partial, it cannot be *justified,* a conclusion that follows naturally and logically from the *objectivist* conception of "justification" as a structure of objective/impersonal argumentation built on objective/ empirical (or transcendental) foundations. As I have suggested through- out this study, however, the social, political, and communicative dy- namics of verbal or other overt *judgments* and, accordingly, the structure and operation of their *justification* can be reconceived along other lines. Specifically, and within the particular domain of instruction and peda- gogy, justifying a particular judgment to those whose welfare is one's responsibility and over whom one has social, political, and/or institu- tional power (the latter an aspect of the situation rarely mentioned) may be conceived as *making as explicit as necessary to them the various considerations that produced that judgment* (and consequent recommen- dation, prohibition, or requirement), stopping not when the expli- cation hits "objective" rock bottom but when it turns the trick, that is, *secures their acquiescence.* Of course, it could happen that it doesn't turn the trick and seems never likely to do so, in which case some other form of enlightenment and persuasion might seem called for: bribes or threats, for example, or, of course, physical force. If and when one has recourse to these alternatives, especially the last, *might* will not "make *right,*" but it will certainly have been exercised; and it may be granted that the quietist objection has some substance in its suggestion that someone who conceived of all value as radically contingent would, in dealing with those in her charge, be edged toward this last alternative less readily than the absolutist/objectivist, and would be, under these conditions, more reluctant to exercise that force.

There seems, however, to be a further subsidiary anxiety in the pedagogic variant of the quietist objection. Though not usually given in such terms, it is the fear that someone's acknowledging the fact and partiality of her perspective would make her authority—that is, pre- cisely the *privilege* of her perspective—vulnerable. And indeed, while such acknowledgment would not necessarily or in itself undermine someone's authority over her students, children, or native parishioners, it might make it more subject to their interrogation; and, if her authority was not otherwise and ultimately sustained for them by, for example, what they acknowledged as her wider experience, shrewder calculating

160

ability, access to better sources of knowledge, or demonstrable—for whatever reason—concern for their welfare, it would put it at risk. But the securing of authority from interrogation and risk could hardly be thought an unqualified or intrinsic good. On the contrary, it might be thought there was some communal value to ensuring that all authority was *always* subject to interrogation and *always* at risk. *All* authority: which must mean that of parent, teacher, and missionary as well as that of tyrant, pope, and state flunky.[13]

(3) I have spoken of what does not follow, of alleged claims the non-objectivist does not make, alleged positions she does not occupy, alleged convictions she does not hold. What *does* follow? What, in particular, may one expect a relativist to *do* as a sociopolitical or, as it is said, moral or ethical agent? The answer, in the first instance, must continue to be negative or at least undramatic; for it must be insisted that, given only that denial of objectivism which is sufficient to evoke the quietist objection, *no particular moral positions or types or modes of moral action follow from it at all,* neither those typically attributed to "relativism," such as liberalism, egalitarian tolerance, and passivity, or any others. The answer to the question of "what follows," then, cannot be a description and celebration of what relativists per se characteristically do as moral agents, but only the observation that various forms and modes of action are altogether consistent with the denial or questioning of objectivism, including those forms and modes commonly said to be logically excluded or psychologically disabled by it.

Someone's distaste for or inability to grasp notions such as "absolute value" and "objective truth" does not in itself deprive her of such other human characteristics, relevant to moral action, as memory, imagination, early training and example, conditioned loyalties, instinctive sympathies and antipathies, and so forth. Nor does it deprive her of all interest in the subtler, more diffuse, and longer-range consequences of her actions and the actions of others, or oblige her, more than anyone else, to be motivated only by immediate self-interest. What sustains common views to the contrary is, of course, the traditional idea that the only thing that prevents people from behaving like beasts or automatons is their being leashed by/to some transcendental or otherwise absolute authority. Accordingly, what could refute such views would not be a roll-call of selfless and visionary relativists, for such a list would only be re-cited by the objectivist as proof that no one can *live* that way, but the development and widespread appropriation of *alternative, nonobjectivist accounts of the dynamics of human choice and action*. I do not undertake that project here, but my conception of its most profitable directions is visible in what follows and elsewhere in this study.

Someone's abandonment of the notion of absolute value does not per se deprive her of morally relevant human characteristics, but neither does it *endow* her with any. Indeed, a relativist in that sense could very well be a moral monster: a resentful, self-absorbed, vengeful, stupid, lazy, and, in all technical and idiomatic senses, "irrational" creature— as, of course, all other people are from time to time, including, it seems, objectivists. To ask what could prevent such a person from wreaking social havoc—since, by definition, her actions are not governed by ab- solute moral constraints—is, of course, another version of "if God is dead, everything is permitted," and the reply to both is the same. Before considering that reply, however, we must grant here that perhaps noth- ing could, would, or will prevent it: individual relativists may very well behave like the careless, cynical, vicious amoralists of history and litera- ture, and secular society (or any chunk of it you like: post-Reformation society, American consumer society, late capitalist postindustrial soci- ety, and so on) may very well be caught up in sociopathological patterns of action that will conclude with some total apocalypse or universal extinction. There is nothing in the postaxiological views of human judg- ment and action presented in this study that can exclude such pos- sibilities. To the extent that anything could prevent such individual amoralism or social havoc, however, it would be the same things that have always made some actions and patterns of action if not impermis- sible, then at least *unlikely*—and that, I think, is as good as we can get.

Among the most important of those things—"constraints," if you like, though the term is misleading in this connection—are the innu- merable, subtle, continuously operating, nonformalized, usually un- recognized, but nonetheless strong *behavioral tendencies* that emerge from individual and social practices themselves. These are *not*, as terms such as "rules," "norms," "standards," and "contraints" suggest, *external forces* that operate upon agents to direct or control their actions but are, rather, *the recurrent inclinations of the agents themselves:* inclinations, to act in certain ways rather than others, that are the corporeally inscribed traces of the differential consequences of their own prior and ongoing actions and interactions.

In addition to these more or less recurrent and, among the members of some community, more or less similar and congruent patterns and inclinations (which could also, therefore, be called behavioral "tastes"), what prevents individual relativists and whole societies of pagans from running amok is the tendency and power of social groups to channel the practices of individual members through various more or less formal and more or less institutionalized "sanctions," or rewards and punishments—all of which, it may be noted, *also* operate on agents as differential consequences of their own actions. This tendency is never annihilated and power never altogether crippled—if diminished at all—by the failure or refusal of some, or indeed many, of the members of the group to grasp the intrinsic value of those practices or to grant the objectively grounded legitimacy of those sanctions.[14]

The feedback loop of differential consequences—that is, the mechanism whereby the different consequences of different actions (whether, for example, more effective or less so, and to what extents, and with what variations under what varying conditions) produce in agents a tendency to repeat, modify, or avoid those actions in the future—operates to adjust actions to the conditions in which they are practiced. Or, bearing in mind (a) the earlier discussions of how constraints operate both on speakers and listeners in verbal communication and also on the activities of scientists and artists in the process of evaluation/production that characterizes both (that process being, as I have pointed out, a loop of just this kind), and also (b) the model of Darwinian natural selection invoked earlier at several points, we might say that the feedback mechanism thus described tends to make practices and activities more effective by making them "fit better" and thus "more fit." While that process or mechanism does not *correct* our actions in the sense of making them increasingly "right" or "better" from some transcendent perspective, it certainly does keep them—that is, all our individual acts and moral practices, and also the characteristic activities of speakers, interpreters, artists, critics, and scientists—from being, as in "anything goes," *anything*.

(4) The relativist finds that other people's perceptions, beliefs, interests, desires, preferences, and judgments are more or less *different* from hers. This does not paralyze her will, however, or leave her frozen in quandaries, since she also continuously finds, just as she expects and assumes, *other* differences that are crucial for her social/political choices and actions, the most significant of which are the various, different *stakes* involved and the various, different *resources* available to her to change things—or, for that matter, to preserve them. The relativist's social and political choices and actions are "compelled," then (and, in effect, her

163

"stands" are "given a base"), by the specific, contingent *conditions* in which she operates as an agent, as she perceives, interprets, and considers those conditions—or, in short, *evaluates* them.

Certain aspects of the dynamics and limits of "considering" must be recalled here from the earlier discussions of *the evaluative process*, especially to distinguish it from the deduction of Right Action from Universal Principles through Moral Reasoning. While "the best" the active relativist could *do* can never be better than the-best-all-things-considered, *all* things can never, in fact, *be* considered. She cannot (nor can any other agent) know *how many* things there are, or which are *the most important*, or which should *go first;* and, because time is always a constraint, some things must always be considered at the expense of the consideration of other things. In her inability to conceive of an objective basis for determining or choosing even which things to *consider*, however, the relativist acknowledges and takes responsibility for the fact that, for better or worse, it's a judgment call all the way down.

The relativist's actions are differentially "compelled" or "constrained" by different contingent combinations of conditions. It may happen, for example, that the disparity between her perceptions, desires, or judgments and those of some other fellow appeared to have virtually no consequences, now or in any imaginable future, for her or for anyone or anything that mattered to her in any imaginable way; or it could happen that she had virtually no interactions with the other fellow and/or virtually no power to affect him. Under these extreme but by no means uncommon conditions, she might very well behave exactly like the torpid relativist of popular and philosophic fancy, and *do* virtually nothing. Where the disparity was altogether theoretical or, as Bernard Williams puts it, "notional"[15] (as, for example, the difference between her cosmology and that of the members of some hypothetical society on the other side of the moon), there would be no reason and, of course, also no *way* for the relativist to take any substantial *action*. But, then, there would be no way for anyone else to take any action either, though, given an objectivist's missionary feelings about One Objective Truth, he may think and also think it very important that he *say* that the benighted Moonmen *should* be told how the universe really is.

Moonmen are sometimes not hypothetical and not especially far away, but the relativist's inability to grasp the idea of "objectively wrong" would not oblige her, when she heard of their practices, to suppress her horror—if it was horror—and *do* nothing but murmur *"De gustibus"* or "Live and let live." To be sure, whatever her reaction was, she would not think of it as having any "objective grounds." Indeed, she might think of it as having no other basis than her "personal feelings"; and while she may have organized and elevated some of the latter into relatively general and verbally articulated "principles," she might also continue to conceive of them as a more or less scrappy assortment of memories, habits, unconscious associations and identifications, instinctive sympathies and antipathies, cognitive consonances and dissonances, aesthetic attractions and revulsions, and so forth. Still, nothing in any of this would prevent her from *acting*, under various conditions, in various ways, even in some way that an objectivist moral theorist might consider the *right* way. The question, as always, is whether *just* her thinking about her actions in these nonobjectivist ways would differentially determine the actual dynamics of her motivation and the particular choices and actions she actually pursued and, specifically, whether she would *therefore* act significantly differently from anyone else, including some morally reasoning moral theorist. The answer being suggested here is, of course, negative on all counts.

When the other fellows (or Moonmen) are real and close enough, the stakes more or less substantial, and the relativist has at least minimal resources, she may be expected to act, accordingly, quite actively and energetically.[16] Depending, as always, on various relevant conditions as she saw and evaluated them, she might attempt to modify the other fellow's different perceptions, beliefs, or desires by converting, educating, or enlightening him (either superficially or substantially, transiently or permanently, and more or less violently), or by bribing, threatening, fining, or shaming him, or by issuing stirring appeals, including, possibly, some framed in absolutist terms.[17] Where her resources, compared to his, were relatively limited, she might offer to negotiate the difference with the other fellow, or attempt to minimize her interactions and thus conflicts with him: she might, for example, end the conversation, leave the party (or the Party), change jobs, or emigrate. And, of course, she might attempt to secure the assistance of other people in limiting the other fellow's ability to *act out* his differing—and, for her and them, disagreeably consequential—interests, desires, and preferences, perhaps by voting him out of office, perhaps by paralyzing, imprisoning, or exiling him, and perhaps by killing him.[18]

Insofar as the cooperation, assistance, or noninterference of other people was necessary for these or any other of her actions, nothing would prevent the relativist from "justifying" her actions along the lines indicated above: that is, from setting forth, in greater or less detail, how

165

she saw and evaluated the relevant conditions, what she believed the stakes were for all involved, what resources she thought were available to them as a group, her own interest in the outcome, and also—since nothing in her "position" would deprive her of access to such considerations—what she saw as the desirable consequences, now or at some time in the future, for those other people themselves and/or for some collectivity she shared with them. All this considering and explicating could be *hard work,* of course, but the idea that relativism makes one's moral or political life *easy* is an especially absurd fantasy of objectivist thought.

Nor, finally, would anything in her cognitive and theoretical tastes bar the relativist, either logically or temperamentally, from conceiving of and working for a collective good, or from proposing and participating in a transcendent or transpersonal project. For she could, quite consistently with her gagging at such notions as "objective truth" and her inability to grasp the idea of "intrinsic value," perform actions that she saw as part of a longer-range pattern of acts that appeared to have, as their likely outcome, a state of affairs that she, along with other people, saw and evaluated as desirable.

There is nothing remarkable or even interesting about any of this. That is the point. The actions of the relativist per se—repeat, per se—are not special in any way, not different from those of other agents with other conceptual tastes, including objectivist moral theorists per se. A final twist of the quietist objection may, however, be anticipated here— namely that, however decent, appropriate, and effective the relativist's modes of action, as described above, might appear, her acts would still be "only instrumentally rational" and could not be described as exhibiting "genuine moral reasoning." But it is, of course, only a twist; for, like the other objections to "relativism" listed earlier, this withholding of legitimating labels from actions *otherwise described* is either one more instance of the inability of objectivist thought to imagine any alternative to itself or a repetition of its refusal to yield a monopoly over the terms of theoretical discourse.

Community, Solidarity, and the Pragmatist's Dilemma

Richard Rorty's essay "Solidarity or Objectivity?" was examined briefly above as an example of the difficulties of "refuting" the charge of relativism. It is worth considering further, however, for, while Rorty's general predicament is shared by all who question orthodox objectivism and still wish to dwell among their fellow men and women, his framing and attempted resolution of that predicament create their own problems. Specifically, in an effort to produce an alternative both to objectivism and *also* to the objectivist-generated phantom heresy of "relativism"—including its alleged self-refutation, egalitarianism, and quietism, all of which Rorty is unfortunately content to accept as descriptions of *something*—he develops a complex of ideas involving "community" and "solidarity" that are not only, from the perspective of this study, unsatisfactory but also, to judge from other aspects of his thought and work, at odds with Rorty's own more general conceptual tastes and political bents. Indeed, although, in line with his other works, the essay itself offers many bold, powerful, and important formulations, it fashions and occupies positions that are not only, in Rorty's words, "provincial" (p. 12) but, it appears, determinedly naïve.

Difficulties appear in the title itself and in the explication of those alternatives—that is, solidarity *or* objectivity—with which the essay opens: "There are two principal ways in which reflective human beings try, by placing their lives in a larger context, to give sense to those lives" (p. 3). These two ways or, as Rorty also calls them, "stories" are, first, those in which people "describe themselves as standing in immediate relation to a nonhuman reality," which, he says, reflect their desire for *objectivity* or, second (this being the pragmatist's recommended alternative), those that "tell the story of their contribution to a community" and thus, he says, reflect their desire for *solidarity*. What is needed as a productive alternative to "objectivity," however, is not *another monolithic principle* but the development of an altogether different *type* of conceptualization. It is not merely that there are more than two kinds of stories that people tell about themselves and that Rorty's oversimplification here must be questioned as such; it is also that, given the multiple, heterogeneous, shifting, and more or less mutually inconsistent and conflictual (or, as the term was discussed above, "scrappy") nature both of our desires, beliefs, and actions and also of the relations among them, we must ask whether—and at the cost of what else— any of us ever does or *could* "give sense to our lives" in some *single, particular* way.

Nor can "solidarity" or "community" serve as a replacement for "objectivity" in the sense of another monolithic principle by which the pragmatist or anyone else can get around the continuous task of figuring out and working out sociopolitical choices and actions. Indeed, to the extent that the concept of communal solidarity denies or obscures both *difference* and *dynamics,* including *internal* difference and dynamics, it can only encourage the illusion, undesirable for political theory and dangerous for political practice, that there is some mode of thought or set of principles that would ultimately eliminate all difficult and disagreeable encounters with other people.

Like others who currently and increasingly invoke "community" as a solution to the problems revealed by contemporary nonobjectivist thought (problems, especially, in traditional conceptualizations of "authority," "validity," "truth," and "legitimacy"), Rorty ignores the mobility, multiple forms of contact, and numerous levels and modes of interconnectedness of contemporary life and forgets, accordingly, that contemporary communities are not only internally complex and highly differentiated but also continuously and rapidly reconfigured. Clifford Geertz's description of the "enormous collage" in which we are now living is apt and vivid:

> It is not just the evening news where assassinations in India, bombings in Lebanon, coups in Africa, and shootings in central America are set amid local disasters hardly more legible . . . It is also an enormous explosion of translations . . . from and to languages—Tamil, Indonesian, Hebrew, and Urdu—previously regarded as marginal and recondite; the migration of cuisines, costumes, furnishings and decor . . . ; the appearance of gamelin themes in avant garde jazz, Indio myths in Latino novels, magazine images in African paintings. But most of all it is that the person we encounter in the greengrocery is as likely, or nearly, to come from Korea as Iowa . . . Even rural settings, where alikeness is likely to be more entrenched, are not immune: Mexican farmers in the Southwest, Vietnamese fishermen along the Gulf Coast, Iranian physicians in the Midwest.[19]

What Rorty's (and other current) invocations of community miss and obscure, is that at any given time as well as over the course of anyone's life history, *each of us* is a member of many, shifting communities, each of which establishes, for *each* of its members, multiple social identities, multiple principles of identification with other people, and, accordingly, a collage or grab-bag of allegiances, beliefs, and sets of motives. Recognition of this situation requires a conception of "community" and an image of individual social life and mental life that is considerably richer, more subtly differentiated, and more dynamic than that articulated by contemporary communitarians. Indeed, the current invocation of "community" as a replacement for "objective reality" is not only a

168

problematic gesture but an empty one. Where it is not (as it seems to be in Rorty's case) a conceptual retreat and apparent move toward socio-political isolationism, it is usually a form of neo-objectivism.

This brings us to the pragmatist's dilemma—or, rather, to what he thinks is his dilemma. As Rorty sees it, since the pragmatist knows he has no ahistorical standpoint from which to endorse, as he wishes to, the habits of modern democracies, he is faced with the choice of either "attach[ing] a special privilege to [his] own community or pretend[ing] an impossible tolerance for every other group." What Rorty recommends is that the pragmatist firmly grasp the former horn, which he calls "ethnocentrism," and *thus* both resolve the dilemma and exculpate himself from the charge of "relativism": "The pragmatist, dominated by the desire for solidarity, can only be criticized for taking his own community *too* seriously. He can only be criticized for ethnocentrism, not for relativism" (p. 13). The sort of dilemma that could, at the end of the twentieth century, be thought to require a reflective human being to embrace any kind of ethnocentrism must, I think, be examined closely, as must also the nature of that ethnocentrism itself.

To be ethnocentric in a pragmatist way is, Rorty explains, "to divide the human race into those to whom one must justify one's beliefs and the others"—the former (one's *ethnos,* as he calls it) being further glossed as "those who share enough of one's beliefs to make fruitful conversation possible" (p. 13). Given almost any contemporary understanding of social dynamics, and given also the pragmatist's own *other* commitments, this seems to be wrong in every way. First, an *ethnos* or tribe—in the sense evidently intended and needed here of a social grouping that commands its members' loyalties, produces their sense of solidarity, and reinforces their beliefs—would not be constituted, at least not in the first instance, of those who share *beliefs* but, rather, of those who share situations or conditions and, therefore, also share histories and economies and, accordingly, have developed, over time, more or less congruent routines and patterns of behavior, and, therefore, engage in mutually consequential interactive practices. Shared beliefs and the possibility of fruitful conversations neither establish nor sustain tribes but are, rather, the emergent by-products of these other, more significant and determinative aspects of cohesive social relations. Moreover, what will matter with regard to *justifying* our beliefs are not those people whose beliefs we already share but, rather, those whose attitudes and actions in relation to our beliefs (which perhaps they do not share) have *consequences* for us.

169

Further problems are created by Rorty's specific—and, with minor variations, repeated—naming of "the liberal intellectuals of the secular modern West" (p. 12) as the pragmatist's own *ethnos*. Most obviously, perhaps, it raises the question of what attitude the pragmatist means to take to the damage done by, and sometimes in the name of, the secular modern West not only to the common physical environment but to various other people, including some who are, perhaps, the pragmatist's or liberal intellectual's *own tribesmen* in other *ethnē*—the latter a possibility that, as we have seen, Rorty's formulation does not accommodate. The more significant problem, however, is that, in defining his *ethnos* in terms that do not engage with and effectively obscure the issues of contemporary political life, the pragmatist virtually bows out of both political analysis and political action; for, of course, the differential tribal features in relation to which the most strenuous intertribal conflicts occur are not, in our time, primarily matters of West per se versus East per se, or of secular societies per se versus theocratic ones per se, or of liberals per se versus anything else in particular, but, rather, the multiple clashings of subhemispheric state powers and transnational social classes, and, irrespective of the degree of reflectiveness of those involved, clashings of racial *ethnē* and of gender.

After remarking the self-privileging circularity of all sociopolitical self-recommendations, Rorty reflects on the pragmatist's desire to justify his belief that the liberal habits of modern democracies are superior to the ways of "primitive, theocratic or totalitarian societies." This justification, he concludes, can ultimately take the form only of "a comparison between societies which exemplify these habits and those which do not, leading up to the suggestion that *nobody who has experienced both would prefer the latter* . . . Such justification is not by reference to a criterion, but by reference to various detailed practical advantages" (pp. 11–12, emphasis added). Although the latter part of this formulation is, to my mind, just what is wanted, the italicized clause cannot but recall I. A. Richards's commonsense justification, examined earlier, of the superiority of Keats's sonnets to those of Ella Wheeler Wilcox. A comparison by "qualified" persons who had experienced both was said by Richards to show that the former were "more efficient," and "that's the same as saying that [Keats's] works are more valuable."[20] Like Richards's justification, Rorty's, so phrased, is open to the same sorts of questions and leads to the same infinite regresses as any alleged *empirical* validation of value, including Hume's attempted validation of standards of taste, as examined in Chapter 4. On the basis of what presumed human universals could it ever be declared that "*nobody* who has experienced both" would prefer otherwise? And if it is not literally "no-body," then whose preferences are being tacitly privileged here and whose omitted or discounted? Are there not, in fact, people who have experienced as much of modern democracies as Rorty has probably experienced of primitive, theocratic, or totalitarian societies and who have, in fact, chosen one or the other of *the latter*? And, finally, is the identity of the societies that exemplify the virtues of contemporary civilization (which Rorty specifically indicates as "toleration, free inquiry, and the quest for undistorted communication") altogether self-evident? And so forth.

In a significant passage toward the end of the essay, where Rorty is discussing the remnants of positivism in the thought of a few contemporary analytic philosophers, he observes: "If we could ever be moved solely by the desire for solidarity, setting aside the desire for objectivity altogether, then we should think of human progress as making it possible for human beings to do more interesting things and be more interesting people, not as heading toward a place which has somehow been prepared for humanity in advance" (p. 10). What he pictures here, and subsequently elaborates as the *telos* of the pragmatist's own theoretical practices, appears to be an ultimate universal embrace of that "philosophy of solidarity" which he sees as "prepar[ed] for" by, among other things, "Socrates' turn away from the gods [and] Christianity's turn from an Omnipotent Creator to the man who suffered on the Cross" (p. 15). One must note here not only the exceptional force and special sense of "interesting" this formulation requires, but also that, although Rorty rejects the prepared-in-advance features of a fully teleologic conception of *progress*, he retains the classic ideas of a general gradient and directionality. Both of the latter are equally expendable, however, and would themselves be rejected in an "anarchist" conception of intellectual history, such as that of Paul Feyerabend in *Against Method*, or in the comparable conception of "changing places" outlined here in Chapter 5. As the pragmatist perhaps would have said himself if he were not so gun-shy of charges of relativism, gradients and directionality are, to be sure, perceptible, but only on a local/historical scale, in relation to confined sets of problems, and from the perspective of specific populations of observers.

The passage just cited continues: "So the pragmatist suggestion that we . . . think of our sense of community as having no foundation except shared hope and the trust created by such sharing . . . is put forth on practical grounds . . . It is a suggestion about how we might think of ourselves in order to avoid the kind of resentful belatedness—

characteristic of the bad side of Nietzsche [what Rorty had just referred to as the latter's 'idiosyncratic idealizations of silence, solitude, and violence']—which now characterizes much of high culture" (p. 15). The vague but strongly demoting characterization of contemporary high culture here (what does "resentful belatedness" mean? which specific cultural practices exemplify it?) recalls the more or less reactionary nostalgia of various other current social critics, such as Charles Taylor and Alisdair MacIntyre, who also invoke a (lost) sense of "community." What, one must ask, is the relation between the pragmatist's views and that of such theorists? One may also ask, finally, whether it is not that Nietzsche, rather than *idealizing* "silence, solitude, and violence," *recognized,* as Rorty perhaps resists doing, the practical necessity of the first two of these for anyone who, in relation to the solid solidarity of his tribe, is in some way "idiosyncratic," and a certain general inevitability of the third.

Rorty's resolution of the pragmatist's dilemma in favor of ethnocentrism is altogether dubious. But so also was his delineation of that dilemma to begin with. For the pragmatist, having *abandoned* epistemological objectivism, is *not* then obliged to choose between the *objectivist's* "relativism" and "ethnocentrism," between "pretend[ing] an impossible tolerance for everyone" and "attach[ing] a special privilege to his own community." What he could always do instead is issue a *prompt, sharp, total,* and, as necessary, *repeated* dismissal of the first "horn"—which is, of course, the Egalitarian Fallacy—as a straw herring, succeeded by the equally prompt, sharp, and total rejection of the other as a regressive and self-deluded gesture, succeeded by the strenuous and wary pursuit, as appropriate, of the following:

(a) insofar as the pragmatist operates as a *theorist, not* the construction either of new forms of self-privilege (grounded on alleged ethical bases or otherwise) or of newly polarized and politically naïve descriptions of human action and interaction, but the continuous development and refinement of more richly articulated, broadly responsive, and subtly differentiated nonobjectivist accounts of, among other things, "truth," "belief," "choice," "justification," and "community";

(b) insofar as he operates as a social and political *agent, not* the premature and categorial embrace of some totally cerebral *patria,* but the continuous effort to recognize and implement, situation by situation, the practical implications of his own nonobjectivist accounts, which would mean also his choosing courses of action in view of various conditions and consequences and his own various, sometimes conflicting, beliefs, allegiances, and desires, plus as necessary, his arguing or indeed battling for those courses of action in opposition to other people, including those who *don't* already share his beliefs; and, finally,

(c) insofar as he has also rejected axiological *universalism*, maintaining a state of acute skepticism with respect to all utopian-redemptionist invocations of "solidarity" and "community,"[21] coupled with, as among the most significant practical implications of the idea of the irreducible diversity of one's fellow creatures, the recognition of the possibility or indeed inevitability of their conflict with each other and his own conflict with them.[22]

Politics and Justification

Among the audiences of a study such as this, there are two major areas of practice in relation to which its critique of traditional axiology elicits anxious questions concerning *justification*. One, of course, is the domain of academic criticism and pedagogy, which I have already discussed. The other, the domain of politics, I have touched on at many points but would like to examine in more detail here in relation to what is currently called, in the sense indicated below, "critical theory."

In his instructive introduction to Jean Baudrillard's *For a Critique of the Political Economy of the Sign*, Charles Levin notes the tautologies and other logical difficulties of the Marxist account of exploitation and surplus value. Like others, however, who continue to find Marxist economics the most viable comprehensive grounding of oppositional political action, he rescues Marxism from his own critique of it. Thus, citing and endorsing Herbert Marcuse's observation that "there are no 'transcendental guarantees,' " Levin writes: "And so we have the autonomous subject, making free choices, independently. This is an indispensable idea, so fundamental that if we do away with it completely, we explode any recognizable version of 'emancipation,' as Habermas calls it—not to mention 'revolution'—and implicitly, we abandon the possibility of critical theory."[23] What is evidently not to be thought of here is that perhaps "the possibility of critical theory" <u>*must be*</u> abandoned: that is, that insofar as "critical theory" is understood as any analysis that strives and claims to expose ideology or false consciousness and thereby to reveal the true, underlying, actual workings of the present state of affairs or "system" (capitalism, postmodern industrial society, patriarchy, and so forth), it is problematic in itself. It is most obviously problematic in that it presupposes an asymmetric epistemology and posits a sharply stratified and polarized collectivity with, on the one hand, those who already know the objective truth and, on the other, those so captivated by the system in question that they cannot recognize their own interests or desires, including what must be posited as their hidden, distorted, or perverted but still fundamental and ineradicable underlying desire for what the critical theorist sees as the necessarily desirable alternative to the present state of affairs: for example, a classless society, sexual equality, or human emancipation. Since the existence of this underlying desire is not self-evident, it must be posited as there in spite of all evidence to the contrary, and the critical theorist, in his effort to explain how *we*, the enlightened, know that *they*, the unenlightened, really do desire the radical transformations for which they seem disinclined to agitate, will always move, in strict accord with axiological logic, to the creation-by-invocation of just the necessary human universals.

Levin himself is bitterly sharp in his parody of these various delineations of "the shadow of a hidden human substance waiting in the wings to be liberated whole when the mask of alienation has ended":

> Man is an animal who makes himself. He defines himself through his work—give him back some real work. Man is a talking animal, a tool-making animal, a desiring animal, an unconscious animal, etc. And so the critical critics dance their way nimbly through a kind of essentializing evasion of the practical consequences implicit in their own vocabulary: some kind of compulsory therapy, or social engineering on a massive scale. Man at last becomes what he already was anyway by recovering in pristine form the activity that defines his nature; the social infrastructure is thus cleansed (or the other way around), and all the mucky confusion that normally froths atop is automatically eliminated.[24]

Although he is skeptical of efforts to explain how an underlying human nature has been distorted or perverted by a benighting system, and also alert to the evasion of the coercive implications of such conceptions, Levin cannot formulate an alternative (and remains, accordingly, rather captivated by Baudrillard's sensational account of these matters). As I have suggested, however, there *are* alternative, nonobjectivist ways to conceive of the relation between sociopolitical analysis and political action: ways that would not be incompatible with other key aspects of, for example, Marxist and feminist theory, and that might be more effective than efforts such as Baudrillard's or Habermas's in helping to produce—not everywhere and finally, but in some places and to some extent—states of affairs accordingly seen as desirable.

There are no transcendental guarantees, and also no objective truths of History, Experience, Science, or Logic, and also no theoretical analyses, whether economic, anthropological, historical, political, or other, that can expose any state of affairs as objectively (that is, empirically, mathematically, or transcendentally) unjust or wrong and, thereby, justify objectively (that is, independent of our particular identities and perspectives) our desire that it be otherwise.[25] Rather, there are various continuously developing analyses that account for, in the sense of *make sense of and imply ways of changing,* particular current states of affairs that we, *given and in relation to our identities and consequent perspectives,* see as undesirable.

The "autonomous subject freely choosing" is not the only alternative to "transcendental guarantees." To be sure, since neither a Marxist, feminist, or any other analysis can be developed as a transcendental account of the objective wrongness of the current state of affairs, anyone who desires a change must assert her desire and exert her will for it independent of any such presumptively objective justificatory analysis. The crucial point, however, is that, if the theoretical analysis is not transcendental, then it must be historical, and if the justification is not universal and unconditioned, then it must be restricted, partial, and local, which is *not* to say, it must be heavily emphasized, "subjective" in the usual limited objectivist senses of the latter, or "privatized" or "individualistic" in *their* current polemical senses.

"The subject"—that is, *any* subject, and there are clearly *many* subjects, and they clearly cannot be considered identical except by being question-beggingly posited as so in some essential, underlying way— has a *particular,* that is, individuated though not in all respects unique, identity/economy/perspective in relation to which the present state of affairs is undesirable or not and, accordingly, also in relation to which she "makes her choice" that it be otherwise or that it remain the same. Two points should be noted immediately. First, to anticipate a common question or objection, it makes no difference in this formulation and others below whether the state of affairs is undesirable (or not) in the subject's view of it or, as might be said, "in fact": that is, whether by her own calculations or by the calculations, perhaps subtler, that someone else performs on her behalf (and by which her choices may be, at some time, informed and transformed). Second, to emphasize the central point here, it must always be recognized that the state of affairs that is *undesirable* for "the subject" may be, and perhaps inevitably will be, quite *desirable* for at least some of those many other subjects who also exist; and, for yet other subjects, it may be at least not *so* undesirable

175

that they will want to risk a change or will find it profitable, on balance, to put their limited resources of time, energy, capital, and so forth into working for its change.

The choices that the subject makes with respect to some state of affairs are free only in the sense that they must be made in the radical absence of, and therefore independent of, any theoretical underwriting of those choices, and, in particular, in the radical absence of any account of that state of affairs that would objectively justify *just* and *precisely* her own choices and no other subject's choices. But they are *not* free in the sense of being altogether independent of anything and everything, for they must be made in relation to the subject's identity/economy and her consequent perspective on that state of affairs. Someone may, of course, make her choices altruistically, perversely, or otherwise "irrationally," that is, in more or less willful disregard of what appear, to her and/or others, to be her personal interests. The possibility of such willed and therefore chosen disregard, however, does not eradicate the dependence of the subject's choices on her identity/economy/perspective, for it must be in relation to some set of yet *other* of her interests, that is, other aspects or *configurations* of her identity/economy/perspective, that that willful disregard of *certain* of her interests has been made.[26]

The justification of more or less radical political action may be seen, accordingly, not as the production of a theoretical underwriting of the objective wrongness of some state of affairs and the objective desirability or necessity of some particular alternative or particular corrective action but, rather, as a rhetorical account: specifically, as some political agent's description and analysis of the state of affairs in question that coordinates and stabilizes her own interests, attitudes, and actions and/or affects the attitudes and actions of some set of other people in some relevantly desirable way. To explain this further: the agent who desires change in the present state of affairs and chooses to promote such change "freely," without transcendental guarantees, may *justify* her choices and consequent actions by (a) verbally (though not necessarily overtly) articulating her more or less heterogeneous and vagrant "reasons for" them, thus giving coherence and stability to those reasons, choices, and actions; and/or (b) producing an overt account or, indeed, a full-blown "critical theory" of the present state of affairs that makes sense of it to some set of other people such that their actions are motivated as she would wish them. "Political justification" in this sense is, of course, a form of "manipulation"—but, by now, that can be no surprise or objection.

176

In the sense described above, political justification can have only limited success. The latter, however, should not, as such, be scorned. On the contrary, and contrary also to the quietist objection, it appears that doctrinaire absolutists have, historically, been more prone to despair and paralysis than "technocrat" relativists; for the latter characteristically do *not* scorn limited successes or forgo *any* success in order to hold out only for *total* ones. The point here, in any case, is that, since the political agent's identity/economy/interests and consequent perspective will always be *changing* in relation to changing conditions, the power of a justificatory theoretical account to organize and stabilize her perceptions and choices can never be altogether secure. (Indeed, just in proportion to the degree of external shift and internal conflict, she may become increasingly rigid and doctrinaire and, to that extent, unresponsive and ineffective.) Moreover, since her interests and perspective will always be *partial* (that is, though perhaps shared by many others, still not shared by *everyone*), her analysis, choices, and proposed actions always may and often will come into conflict—which may be more or less intractable—with the analyses, interests, and perpectives of some other people, and she cannot expect to secure either a universal acceptance of the unique propriety (historical, theoretical, etc.) of her account of the present state of affairs, or a universal acknowledgment of the propriety or necessity (rational, logical, etc.) of her proposed actions to change them. Although she may be able to make her perspective recognizable *as such* to others, and even make coherent to others how her actions follow from her analysis, she will always and necessarily fail if she sets her goal as having either her analysis or actions make such compelling sense to *everyone* that there will be no opposition to them and everyone will eventually take up arms to join her effort to change the present state of affairs in just that way. In other words, it remains the case that there is no *account,* no matter how coherent, intuitive, and self-evident to the theorist herself or rhetorically effective for some time among a certain broader group, that, *as such,* will eradicate or transcend other people's significantly *different* identities/economies/perspectives and will make them, autonomous subjects that they *also* are, willing to forgo their own interests, desires, and advantages.[27]

It is, of course, recognition of the latter difficulty that has historically motivated the search for some set of interests and perspectives which transcend all particularity, which belong to all human beings by virtue of the fact that they are human, and which, when known and duly acknowledged, would necessarily take priority over—subsume, absorb,

177

or neutralize—all otherwise individually different interests and perspectives. Hence the relation of political theory to traditional axiology. And hence also the collapse of axiological political theory into an abyss of infinite regresses, however concealed or patched up by the hopeful theoretical machinery of Kantian transcendental analysis. It is always possible to posit what seem to be "natural," "reasonable," or otherwise objectively grounded universal interests and consequent "natural" or "rational" goals for humanity at large: universal individual freedom, global peace and prosperity, the continuation of the species, and so forth. As the long histories of these various candidates demonstrate, however, the positing of any one of them inevitably invites the citation of contrary cases and leads, accordingly, to the familiar regresses of judgment and justification. For example, there will always be someone, such as Freud or Bataille, who will note death wishes, the economy of loss, and the desire for sacrifice, bondage, war, self-annihilation, and so forth; or it will be noted, by theologians or others, that perhaps it is personal spiritual immortality, and not physical survival or the historical continuation of the species, that we all fundamentally do or should want. Or it could be suggested that what we all really want is any number of mutually incompatible things. Moreover, given the inevitable vagueness or generality of candidates for transcendental interest or universal value, there will always remain the question of how to *interpret* them in relation to specific practices and conditions, and how to *implement* them or even conceive of them in relation to specific goals.

Are we to take the not especially inspiring history of various proselytizing creeds in these regards as evidence only that these transcendent interests have *not yet* been correctly identified? Or does it attest only to the blindness, stubbornness, and inhuman selfishness of certain people (Jews and pagans, for example, in the case of Christianity; or technocrats, systems theorists, aesthetes, and nihilists in the case of neo-Marxist critical theory) to agree to their interpretation and specific implementation? Why is "man," in spite of his underlying essential nature, so exasperatingly different from himself? Is it that some external force remains potent, or is it the product of some deformity deep within us, some original flaw that is as much an underlying universal of human behavior as the alleged universal desire for peace, harmony, and nondominant intersubjective mutuality? Perhaps we need a savior to cut through the mess, or an arbiter or committee of the elect to give the right interpretation and implementation. But how will we know that the savior is not the antisavior? And, in the meantime, who will decide, and how will it be decided, who should be Arbiter or serve on the Committee? And so the infinite regress continues infinitely.

The history of the West, and also the East or any civilization that joins theory with power, seems to consist of a fitful alternation between intellectual/political totalitarianism (the effort to identify the presumptively universally compelling Truth and Way and to compel it universally) and the struggle to secure a freedom that consists in the opportunity for individual agents and sets of agents to assess conditions and explore resources in relation to their particular interests and projects, and to act out their particular choices accordingly. So it seems. But it must be acknowledged that the lessons of History are themselves intractably divergent: from some perspectives, what these alternatives reveal is that we must press even harder for an ultimately universal Truth and Way; from others, my own included, that we must create and maintain structures and procedures that give as much scope as possible to the laborious working out, individually and in concert, of courses of action that are the "best" (all things considered . . .) for each, and each set, of us.

It seems unlikely that there can be a world altogether free of conflicts of interests or of disparities of resources among individual subjects and different sets, tribes, or communities of subjects: conflicts and disparities that are structural and systemic, the residue of history, the traces of what there is and how it has been, and the product also of what is differently remembered and imagined as *otherwise*. This is *not at all* to say that the poor will always be with us or that any current disparities of resources—those, for example, along sexual or racial lines—are natural or inevitable. It is to say, rather, that "the best" is always both heterogeneous and variable: that it can never be better than a state of affairs that remained more or less that good *for some people*, or got considerably better for many of them *in some respects*, or became, *for a while*, rather better on the whole. If, as I believe, there can be no total and final eradication of disparity, variance, opposition, and conflict, and also neither perfect knowledge nor pure charity, then the general optimum might well be that set of conditions that permits and encourages, precisely, *evaluation*, and specifically that continuous process described here in relation to both scientific and artistic activity: that is, the local figuring/working out, as well as we, heterogeneously, can, of what seems to work better rather than worse.

179

Conceptual Tastes and Practical Consequences

Having been perhaps persuaded that relativism does no particular harm, students, colleagues, and other audiences seem eager to hear what benefits it bestows, how it can be applied, how they can buy some of it and take it home. And, having gone through the always arduous task of showing that it probably will not bring the world to an end, or at least not any faster than any other conceptualization, I am often tempted to oblige them with a show of the utility, practical power, and palpable profit of these views—a demonstration that they are precisely what is needed and what everyone has been looking for. Although the temptation will be resisted here (as it is always more or less resisted elsewhere), I would like to offer some related points, of which three are especially significant.

The first is that conceptualizations of the world, in the combined sense of states of mind, processes of thought, and theoretical constructs, do not usually originate in a will to value—that is, in some subject's personal desire to do some general good or to make something generally useful or profitable—but, rather, as ongoing responses to more or less ad hoc emergent conditions, including prior and ongoing conceptual conditions. The second, however, is that unless a theoretical construct can be applied or appropriated in *some* way, unless it can turn *some* coin, it will dissolve or be radically transformed. (Objectivism and traditional axiology have obviously turned handsome profits in the past, and still do.) The third, accordingly, is that, although there is no specific agenda or heuristic—no set of practical things to be done, or method for doing specific things the right way—that follows from this study per se, it may be worthwhile to indicate some general activities through which the views it presents often exhibit themselves and some tendencies that they appear to encourage.

When the necessity or desirability of consensus, norms, and standards is invoked, such views alert one to the inevitability and value, including communal value, of difference, variety, and innovation. They discourage utopianism, nostalgia, and apocalyptic reaction—the positing of "ideal" conditions, the lament for "lost" ones, the anxious delineation of Falls and Declines—in favor of an analysis of conditions and of *accordingly* responsive actions. In the classroom, as anywhere else, they are "applied" case by case or, rather, they encourage the handling of each case, each occasion for critical judgment and pedagogic action, in specific rather than categorical terms—which is not to say, of course, in

180

relation to short-term as distinct from long-term considerations but, rather, in relation to historically, culturally, institutionally, and otherwise *individuated* goals, stakes, means, and consequences rather than to putative transcendentally *universalized* ones.

According to the analyses presented in this study, when someone or some group of people insist(s) on the *objective* necessity or propriety of their own social, political, or moral judgments and actions, and deny the *contingency* of the conditions and perspectives from which those judgments and actions proceed, it must be—and always is—a move to assign dominant status to the *particular* conditions and perspectives that happen to be relevant to or favored by that person, group, or class; it must be—and always is—simultaneously a move to deny the existence and relevance, and to suppress the claims, of *other* conditions and perspectives. While all this seems to occur everywhere and all the time, it sometimes happens that the subordinated members of a community question and actively oppose the claims of "necessity" and "naturalness" made for the conditions and perspectives of the dominant, pointing out the existence of other conditions, namely those relevant to their lives, and other perspectives, namely their own. This sort of questioning and opposition are politically significant actions, and a theoretical analysis such as the present one may encourage and strengthen their occurrence in the fields of cultural/aesthetic norms specifically discussed here.

The political effectiveness of theoretical analysis in this and (as stressed above) perhaps any domain is, however, *limited*. The situations, felt as inequitable and oppressive, that give rise to some people's opposing the normative dominance of other people are rarely changed through argument alone and, it may be suspected, are never changed as a consequence of theoretical analysis alone in the sense of someone's just producing or invoking such an analysis, no matter how rigorous and persuasive it may, from certain perspectives, appear to be. Rather, because situations of normative dominance emerge from particular *sociopolitical conditions and dynamics* and give distinct *advantages* to those who are dominant, such situations can be changed only through a specifically motivated and directed change of *those conditions* or through an intervention in the operation of *those dynamics*. Moreover, although they are sometimes joined by those who are otherwise unsettled (for example, cognitively or aesthetically) by the inequities in question, the most energetic agents of such changes and interventions are usually those who are actually put at a disadvantage by those conditions or dynamics. In other words, a theoretical analysis such as the present one can do some things, but not *everything*, for some people, but not *all* people.[28]

A further word on the theory and politics of normativity may be added here. I have spoken of situations in which communal norms that tacitly privilege the conditions and perspectives of *some* members of a community have effects that are felt to be inequitable and oppressive by *other* of its members. It may be objected that not all norms are inequitable or oppressive in that way. Certain norms and standards, it may be said—for example, standardized units of measurement, industrial safety standards, or certification standards for registered nurses—are not like customs or laws regarding eligibility for marriage. The former, it might be thought, are based on conditions that really *are* objective; or, it may be said, the establishment of such norms and standards, even when not so based, will benefit *everyone* in the community. (Hume appealed to comparable cases, we recall, in claiming that it was "natural" to seek a standard of aesthetic taste.) In a certain sense, this is true: that is, while all norms and standards are conventional in the sense that they are based on arbitrarily privileged conditions and perspectives, it may be acknowledged that some phenomena occur under a quite broad range of conditions and appear, if not quite the same, then at least similar enough "for all practical purposes" from the perspective of all concerned. Although such *relative* uniformities and constancies are just that and therefore not, strictly speaking, absolute, nevertheless, to the extent that they operate within some community as *in effect* unconditional and universal, they may be said to be "contingently absolute," and norms based on them can be said, accordingly, to be "contingently objective." Lest this be taken, however, as just what is needed to move right back into traditional objectivist/axiological formulations or neo-objectivist/ communitarian ones, it must be remembered that a community is never totally homogeneous, that its boundaries and borders are never altogether self-evident, that we cannot assume in advance that certain differences among its members are negligible or irrelevant, and that the conditions that produced the relative unconditionality, local universality, and contingent objectivity are themselves neither fixed forever nor totally stable now. Moreover, in view of the evident recurrence of the sociopsychological dynamics through which self-privileging/other-pathologizing norms emerge, and also in view of readiness with which any social dominance becomes self-confirming and self-protecting, it seems desirable to maintain a generalized theoretical and political wariness on all these matters.

"Relativism" in the sense of a conception of the world as continuously changing, irreducibly various, and multiply configurable does not conceive of itself as a logical deduction, or as an inescapable conclusion drawn either from personal experience or scientific experiment, or as an insight into the underlying nature of things, or as a transcendental revelation. Rather, it conceives of its own conception of the world as the contingent product of many things: *contingent* in the sense that it is a function not of "the way the world is" but of the states of numerous particular systems interacting at a particular time and place. This conception of the world requires that there be "something" other than itself, other than the process of conceiving-the-world; but it cannot conceive of a single other thing to say, or way to think, about that "something"—not a single feature to predicate of it, or any way to describe, analyze, or manipulate any of its properties—that would be *independent* of that process.

Being not a conviction but a conceptualization, relativism in this sense is not a proselytizing position, and, given especially the arduous conceptual and practical *work* that its thinking-out and living-out require, its alleged current "spread" must be quite confined and its ultimate "triumph" very much to be doubted. Like any other cognitive taste, however, it prefers self-stabilizing confirmation to self-destabilizing contradiction; and, insofar as its theoretical/discursive articulation is played out institutionally and thus—as in a market, game, or battle—competitively, it must, to stay in the running, have something to show and also must play to win. Relativism, in the sense of a *contingent* conceptualization *that sees itself and all others as such,* cannot found, ground, or prove itself, cannot deduce or demonstrate its own rightness, cannot even lead or point the way *to* itself. In view of the interests and pressures just mentioned, it will, of course, often attempt to point the way quite energetically. It recognizes, however, that "the way" will be perceived and pursued differently by each to whom it is pointed out. Self-consistently, it conceives of itself as continuously changing, of all conceptions of the irreducibly various as irreducibly various, and of the multiply configurable as always configurable otherwise.

Since the relativist knows that the conjoined systems (biological, cultural, ideological, institutional, and so forth) of which her general conceptual taste and specific conceptualization of the world are a contingent function are probably not altogether unique, she expects some other people to conceptualize the world in more or less the same ways she does and, like her, to find objectivist conceptualizations more or less cognitively distasteful, unsatisfactory, and irritating along more or less similar lines. She may have found it worth her while to seek out such fellow relativists, to promote conditions that encourage their emergence, and, where she has had the resources, to attempt to cultivate a few of them herself: "worth her while" because, since she cannot herself live any other way, she's glad for a bit of company.

Notes
Index

Notes

1. Fixed Marks and Variable Constancies

1. The first part of this chapter was prepared for delivery at a session of the Modern Language Association titled "Evaluating Shakespeare's Sonnets." Its convenor had suggested that the panelists focus their remarks on Sonnet 116:

> Let me not to the marriage of true minds
> Admit impediments: love is not love
> Which alters when it alteration finds
> Or bends with the remover to remove.
> O no, it is an ever fixèd mark
> That looks on tempests and is never shaken;
> It is the star to every wandering bark,
> Whose worth's unknown although his height be taken.
> Love's not Time's fool, though rosy lips and cheeks
> Within his bending sickle's compass come;
> Love alters not with his brief hours and weeks,
> But bears it out even to the edge of doom.
> > If this be error and upon me proved,
> > I never writ, nor no man ever loved.

2. Stephen Booth was a copanelist.
3. *Anatomy of Criticism* (Princeton, N.J., 1957), p. 18.
4. For two recent descriptions and assessments of the classical axiological arguments (plus their updated versions and associated fallacies: emotivism, prescriptivism, intuitionism, naturalism, panaestheticism, methodological relativism, relative absolutism, sociohistorical relationism, and so forth), see Stefan Morawski, *Inquiries into the Fundamentals of Aesthetics* (Cambridge, Mass., 1974), pp. 1–57, and Zdzislaw Najder, *Values and Evaluations* (London, 1975), esp. pp. 51–74. Both of these are adaptations from studies originally published in Poland and, in fact, a number of unusually inter-

esting inquiries into aesthetic value have been pursued in Eastern Europe (either as developments of or "in dialogue with" classical Marxist thought), among the most original and penetrating of which is Jan Mukařovský's *Aesthetic Function, Norm and Value as Social Facts* (Prague, 1936), tr. Mark E. Suino (Ann Arbor, Mich., 1970).

5. These observations are elaborated in Barbara Herrnstein Smith, *On the Margins of Discourse: The Relation of Literature to Language* (Chicago, 1978), pp. 116–124.

2. The Exile of Evaluation

1. The most recent of these include E. D. Hirsch, Jr., *The Aims of Interpretation* (Chicago, 1976), esp. the essays "Evaluation as Knowledge" (1968) and "Privileged Criteria in Evaluation" (1969); Murray Krieger, "Literary Analysis and Evaluation—and the Ambidextrous Critic," in *Criticism: Speculative and Analytic Essays,* ed. L. S. Dembo (Madison, Wis., 1968); a number of brief essays by Anglo-American as well as continental European theorists in *Problems in Literary Evaluation,* ed. Joseph Strelka (University Park, Pa., and London, 1969); and the chapters on value and evaluation in John Ellis, *The Theory of Literary Criticism* (Berkeley and Los Angeles, 1974), in John Reichert, *Making Sense of Literature* (Chicago, 1977), and in Jeffrey Sammons, *Literary Sociology and Practical Criticism* (Bloomington, Ind., and London, 1977). All of them either participate directly in the self-justifying academic debates outlined below or are haunted by them into equivocation.

2. F. R. Leavis, *Revaluation: Tradition and Development in English Poetry* (London, 1936; New York, 1963), pp. 5–6.

3. See esp. A. J. Ayer, *Language, Truth, and Logic* (London, 1936).

4. Yvor Winters, *The Function of Criticism* (Denver, 1957), p. 17.

5. W. K. Wimsatt, Jr., *The Verbal Icon* (Louisville, Ky., 1954), p. 250.

6. Cf. the discussions of David Hume in Chapters 3 and 4, below.

7. I. A. Richards, *Principles of Literary Criticism* (1924; London, 1960), pp. 5–6. "The two pillars upon which a theory of criticism must rest," Richards declared, "are an account of value and an account of communication" (p. 25). It was, of course, the latter that subsequently became the overriding concern of critical theory.

8. Ibid., p. 206.

9. Northrop Frye, *Anatomy of Criticism: Four Essays* (Princeton, N.J., 1957), pp. 18, 19; all further references to this work, abbreviated *AC,* will be included in the text.

10. It should be recalled that, like many others (e.g., E. D. Hirsch, Jr.), Frye continued to maintain that *interpretive* criticism could lay claim to objectivity. See his remarks in a paper delivered in 1967: "The fundamental critical act . . . is the act of recognition, seeing what is there, as distinguished from merely seeing in a Narcissus mirror of our own experience and social and moral prejudice . . . When a critic interprets, he is talking about his poet;

when he evaluates, he is talking about himself . . ." ("Value Judgments," in *Criticism: Speculative and Analytic Essays,* p. 39).

11. Hirsch, *The Aims of Interpretation,* p. 108.

12. In a more recent essay, "Literary Value: The Short History of a Modern Confusion" (unpub., 1980), Hirsch argues that although literary *meaning* is determinate, literary value is not. With respect to the latter, however, he concludes that "there are some stable principles"—namely ethical ones— "that escape the chaos of purely personal relativity" (p. 22). As will be seen in the analysis below, "personal relativity" neither produces chaos nor is in itself chaotic.

13. See Jurij Tynjanov, "On Literary Evolution" (Moscow, 1927), tr. L. Matejka and K. Pomorska, in *Readings in Russian Poetics,* ed. Matejka and Pomorska (Cambridge, Mass., 1971); Mikhail Bakhtin, *Rabelais and His World* (Moscow, 1965), tr. Helene Iswolsky (Cambridge, Mass., 1968); and Jan Mukařovský, *Aesthetic Function, Norm and Value as Social Facts* (Prague, 1936), tr. Mark E. Suino (Ann Arbor, Mich., 1970).

14. For surveys and discussions, see Sammons, *Literary Sociology and Practical Criticism,* and Rien T. Segers, *The Evaluation of Literary Texts: An Experimental Investigation into the Rationalization of Value Judgments with Reference to Semiotics and Esthetics of Reception* (Lisse, The Netherlands, 1978). For a recent study of considerable interest, see Jacques Leenhardt and Pierre Józsa, *Lire la lecture: Essai du sociologie de la lecture* (Paris, 1982). See also Pierre Bourdieu's extensive and very important series of studies on the social dynamics of cultural value and evaluation which include, most relevantly for the issues considered in this chapter, "The Production of Belief: Contribution to an Economy of Symbolic Goods," *Media, Culture and Society* 2, no. 3 (July 1980): 261–293; "The Field of Cultural Production or the Economic World Reversed," *Poetics* 12, nos. 4–5 (November 1983): 311–356; "Le Champ littéraire," *Lendemains* 36 (1984): 5–20; "The Market of Symbolic Goods," *Poetics* 14 (1985): 13–44; and the massive study *Distinction: A Social Critique of the Judgement of Taste,* tr. Richard Nice (Cambridge, Mass., 1984).

15. It is not mentioned as such, for example, in Jonathan Culler's *Structuralist Poetics: Structuralism, Linguistics, and the Study of Literature* (Ithaca, N.Y., 1975).

16. See, e.g., the thoroughly equivocal discussions of "objective value" in Stefan Morawski, *Inquiries into Fundamentals of Aesthetics* (Cambridge, Mass., and London, 1974), and the revalorization of the standard Eng. Lit. canon in Terry Eagleton, *Criticism and Ideology: A Study in Marxist Literary Theory* (London, 1976), pp. 162–187. "[Is] value," Eagleton asks rhetorically, "to be abandoned to some mere ideological relativism, some 'solipsism of the citizen' in which any discourse of 'objective merit' or 'false estimation' is to be jettisoned as immanentist and idealist?" (p. 168). His answer is a strained attempt to justify *"the* value" of Jane Austen, W. B. Yeats, and the whole Leavisite canon on Marxist (specifically, Althusserian) grounds. For

Marxism & Aesthetics

other discussions of the point, see Hans Robert Jauss, "The Idealist Embarrassment: Observations on Marxist Aesthetics," *New Literary History* 7 (Autumn 1975): 191–208; Raymond Williams, *Marxism and Literature* (Oxford, 1977), esp. pp. 45–54 and 151–157; Tony Bennett, *Formalism and Marxism* (London, 1979), esp. pp. 172–175; and Peter Widdowson, " 'Literary Value' and the Reconstruction of Criticism," *Literature and History* 6 (1980): 138–150.

More recent Anglo-American neo/post-Marxist accounts of literary value and evaluation include Evan Watkins, *The Critical Act: Criticism and Community* (New Haven, 1978); John Fekete, *The Critical Twilight: Explorations in the Ideology of Anglo-American Literary Theory from Eliot to McLuhan* (London and Boston, 1977); and Eagleton's own modified—certainly more enlightened though otherwise still limited—account in *Literary Theory: An Introduction* (Minneapolis, 1983), pp. 10–16.

17. For a sophisticated exploration in a Derridean framework, see Arkady Plotnitsky, *Constraints of the Unbound: Transformation, Value, and Literary Interpretation*, diss., University of Pennsylvania, 1982.

   The period during which the Anglo-American literary academy assigned to oblivion not only almost all continental philosophy but also its own most decisively postaxiological modern philosopher, John Dewey, coincided with the years of the exile of evaluation chronicled above. That oblivion has been lifted and exile increasingly revoked during the past decade, during which time (and certainly not coincidentally) there has also been evidence of increasingly strong interest in the thought and writings of both Nietzsche and Dewey. See Richard Rorty, *Philosophy and the Mirror of Nature* (Princeton, 1979), and idem, *Consequences of Pragmatism: Essays* (Minneapolis, 1982), for Dewey's significance for contemporary thought. See Daniel T. O'Hara, ed., *Why Nietzsche Now?* (Bloomington, 1985), and Alexander Nehamas, *Nietzsche: Life as Literature* (Cambridge, Mass., 1985), for recent Anglo-American essays on Nietzsche; and John Rajchman and Cornell West, eds., *Post-Analytic Philosophy* (New York, 1985), for a general review of these and related developments during this period. The developments themselves should not, however, be exaggerated: there is no sign that the Anglo-American philosophic *or* literary academic mainstreams will soon be flowing toward or incorporating "posts" of any kind.

18. A similar point has been made by Annette Kolodny in "Dancing through the Minefield: Some Observations on the Theory, Practice and Politics of Feminist Literary Criticism," *Feminist Studies* 6 (Spring 1980): 1–25, esp. pp. 7 and 15.

19. Attempts at such analysis are found later in this chapter and elsewhere in this study.

20. Onwuchekwa Jemie, *Langston Hughes: An Introduction to the Poetry* (New York, 1976), p. 184.

21. C. W. B. Bigsby, "Hand in Hand with the Blues," *Times Literary Supplement*, 17 June 1977, p. 734.

22. Chinweizu, letter to the editor, *Times Literary Supplement*, 15 July 1977, p. 871.

23. Thus, Sammons, in his embattled book, writes of "the elements . . . in the canon of great literature" to which we should be attentive so that, faced with charges of elitism, "we will not have to stand mute before claims that inarticulateness, ignorance, occult mumbling, and loutishness are just as good as fine literature" (*Literary Sociology and Practical Criticism*, p. 134).

24. Elements of this description anticipate self-refutationists: that is, those who complacently dismiss any challenge to traditional absolutist/objectivist formulations as necessarily self-exempting and thus self-contradictory. See Chapters 5 and 7 for further discussions of the self-refutation argument.

3. Contingencies of Value

1. For related discussion of the linguistic and intellectual history of the term/concept "value," see Barbara Herrnstein Smith, "Value/Evaluation," in *Critical Terms for Literary Study*, ed. Frank Lentricchia and Thomas McLaughlin (Chicago: University of Chicago Press, forthcoming).

2. The interrelations among human "needs and wants," cultural practices, and economic production are examined in Marshall Sahlins, *Culture and Practical Reason* (Chicago, 1976); Mary Douglas, *The World of Goods* (New York, 1979); Jean Baudrillard, *For a Critique of the Political Economy of the Sign* (Paris, 1972), tr. Charles Levin (St. Louis, 1981); and Pierre Bourdieu, *Distinction: A Social Critique of the Judgement of Taste* (Paris, 1979), tr. Richard Nice (Cambridge, Mass., 1984). Although Baudrillard's critique of the concept of "use value" and, with it, of "sign value" is of considerable interest, his effort to develop "as a basis for the practical overthrow of political economy" (p. 122) a theory of a value "beyond value" (created out of what he calls "symbolic exchange") is less successful, partly because of its utopian anthropology and partly because the value in question does not escape economic accounting. See Chapter 6, below, for further discussion of Baudrillard in relation to anti-utilitarian cultural theory.

3. For an excellent analysis of the relation between classification and value, see Michael Thompson, *Rubbish Theory: The Creation and Destruction of Value* (Oxford, 1979), esp. pp. 13–56. The phenomenology and transformations of these classifications are also examined by Susan Stewart in *On Longing: Narratives of the Miniature, the Gigantic, the Souvenir, the Collection* (Baltimore, 1984).

4. The magnetism or recurrent mutually metaphoric relation between economic and aesthetic—especially literary—discourse is documented and discussed by Marc Shell in *The Economy of Literature* (Baltimore, 1978), and by Kurt Heinzelman in *The Economics of the Imagination* (Amherst, Mass., 1980).

5. Andrew Harrison, *Making and Thinking* (Indianapolis, 1978), p. 100.

6. See George J. Stigler and Gary S. Becker, "De Gustibus non est disputan-

dum," *American Economics Review* 67 (March 1977): 76–90, for an ingeni-
ous and influential attempt (at the opposite extreme, perhaps, of Baudrillard's) to demonstrate that differences and changes of behavior (including
aesthetic behavior) that appear to be matters of "taste" and, as such, beyond explanation in economic terms can be accounted for (a) as functions
of subtle forms of "price" and "income" and (b) on the usual economistic
assumption that we always behave, all things considered, so as to maximize
utility. As Stigler and Becker acknowledge, however, recent experimental
studies of "choice behavior" in human (and other) subjects suggest that this
latter assumption itself requires modification. These points are discussed
further in Chapter 6.

7. See Robert Fagan, *Animal Play Behavior* (Oxford, 1981), pp. 248–358, for
an extensive analysis of "intrinsically rewarding" physical activities and a
suggestive account of the kinds of evolutionary mechanisms that could
produce and sustain them.

8. See the related discussion of "cognitive play" in Barbara Herrnstein Smith,
On the Margins of Discourse: The Relation of Literature to Language (Chicago,
1978), pp. 116–124.

9. Monroe Beardsley's "instrumentalist" theory of aesthetic value in *Aesthetics: Problems in the Philosophy of Criticism* (New York, 1958), pp. 524–576,
and Mukařovský's otherwise quite subtle explorations of these questions in
Aesthetic Function, Norm and Value as Social Facts (Prague, 1936), tr. Mark E.
Suino (Ann Arbor, Mich., 1970), do not altogether escape the confinements and circularities of formalist conceptions of, respectively, "aesthetic
experience" and "aesthetic function."

10. Barry Barnes and David Bloor, "Relativism, Rationalism and the Sociology
of Knowledge," in *Rationality and Relativism,* ed. Martin Hollis and Steven
Lukes (Cambridge, Mass., 1982), pp. 25–26.

11. *"Of the Standard of Taste" and Other Essays,* ed. John W. Lenz (Indianapolis,
1965), pp. 8–10, emphasis added.

12. I. A. Richards, *Principles of Literary Criticism* (1924; London, 1960), pp. 202–
205.

13. See Morse Peckham, *Explanation and Power: The Control of Human Behavior*
(New York, 1979), for an account of deviance (or what he calls "the delta
effect") as the product of the relation between cultural practices and the
randomness of behavior and, more generally, for a highly original discussion
of the processes and institutions of cultural channeling.

14. See, in Chapter 4, the section entitled "Three Postaxiological Postscripts"
for further discussion of this account of tastes and of a set of related arguments repeatedly raised in defense of the asymmetrical account.

15. Speaking so, that is, describing these fluid and usually "unconscious"—or,
in the term to be used below for both, *inarticulate*—processes in terms
associated with political economy, requires special commentary: see the
discussion of "economic metaphorics" in Chapter 5 and of the "double
discourse of value" in Chapter 6.

16. The eighteenth-century phrase here anticipates the discussion of David Hume's essay "Of the Standard of Taste" in Chapter 4 and is intended to suggest a structural/dynamic homology between individual and social conflicts of preference.

17. Pierre Macherey and Etienne Balibar analyze some aspects of this process in "Literature as an Ideological Form: Some Marxist Propositions," tr. James Kavanagh, *Praxis* 5 (1981): 43–58. See also Bourdieu, *Distinction,* pp. 230–244, for a related analysis of what he refers to as "the quasi-miraculous correspondence" between "goods production and taste production."

18. For a description of some of the specific constraints that shape both the process and its termination and, more generally, for a useful account of the ways in which artworks are "produced" by social networks, see Howard Becker, *Art Worlds* (Berkeley, Los Angeles, and London, 1982), pp. 198–209.

19. For a related discussion of the continuities among theoretical, critical, and aesthetic activities, see Barbara Herrnstein Smith, "Masters and Servants: Theory in the Literary Academy," *Explorations in Music, the Arts and Ideas: A Festschrift for Leonard B. Meyer,* ed. Eugene Narmour (forthcoming).

20. For a well-documented illustration of the point, see Nina Baym, "Melodramas of Beset Manhood: How Theories of American Fiction Exclude Women Authors," *American Quarterly* (Summer 1981): 125–139. In addition to anthologies, Baym mentions historical studies, psychological and sociological theories of literary production, and particular methods of literary interpretation.

   Since the time the original version of this section was written, there has been an enormous expansion of the study of the role of academic institutions in the process of literary canon formation and, more generally, in the activities of value marking and value transmission. For other studies relevant to the present discussion, see Peter Uwe Hohendahl, *The Institution of Criticism* (Ithaca and London, 1982); Edward Said, *The World, the Text, and the Critic* (Cambridge, Mass., 1983); Paul Lauter, "Race and Gender in the Shaping of the American Literary Canon: A Case Study from the Twenties," *Feminist Studies* 9 (Fall 1983): 435–463; Jane Tompkins, *Sensational Designs: The Cultural Work of American Fiction, 1790–1860* (New York and Oxford, 1985); and Gerald Graff, *Professing Literature: An Institutional History* (Chicago, 1987).

21. Here and throughout this study the term "desired/able" indicates that the valued effect in question need not have been specifically desired (sought, wanted, imagined or intended) as such by any subject. In other words, its value for certain subjects may have emerged independent of any specific human intention or agency and, indeed, may have been altogether a product of the chances of history or, as we say, a matter of luck.

22. For a careful neo-Marxist analysis of the continuous historical "rewriting" of the Homeric texts, see John Frow, *Marxism and Literary History* (Cambridge, Mass., 1986), pp. 172–182.

23. *Truth and Method* (orig. pub. as *Wahrheit und Methode,* Tübingen, 1960; tr. New York, 1982), pp. 257–258.

24. Ibid., p. 255.

25. For a somewhat unguarded example of such claims, see Leonard B. Meyer, "Some Remarks on Value and Greatness in Music," in his *Music, the Arts and Ideas* (Chicago, 1967). See also Gerda Smets, *Aesthetic Judgment and Arousal* (Louvain, 1973), and Sven Sandström, *A Common Taste in Art: An Experimental Attempt* (Lund, 1977), for two studies sympathetic to the project of empirical aesthetics but relatively sophisticated about the implications of its data.

4. Axiologic Logic

1. *"Of the Standard of Taste" and Other Essays,* ed. John W. Lenz (Indianapolis, 1965), p. 3. Subsequent references to this edition of the essay, abbreviated *ST,* will be given in the text.

2. That force is demonstrated as well in the examples Hume chooses to illustrate what he sees as the contrast between the historical mutability and variability of *cognitive* tastes and the stability and universality of *aesthetic* ones: "Nothing has been experienced more liable to the revolutions of chance and fashion than these pretended decisions of science. The case is not the same with the beauties of eloquence and poetry . . . Aristotle, and Plato, and Epicurus, and Descartes, may successively yield to each other: but Terence and Virgil maintain an universal, undisputed empire over the minds of men" (*ST,* p. 18).

3. Like so many after (and no doubt also before) him, Hume evidently believed that true value is revealed by the supposedly impersonal "filtering" operations of time itself. Although he does not use the expression "test of time," the metaphor of test and crucible is clearly operating here. In our own era, the metaphor often merges with a survival-of-the-fittest model of cultural history that ignores the dynamics of natural selection as developed by Darwin and offers instead a social-Darwinist vulgarization.

4. Or—since the relevant phrase bears an alternate reading—who do not in fact acknowledge what is universally acknowledged to be the superior judgment ("preference") of certain men.

5. Immanuel Kant, *Critique of Judgment,* tr. J. H. Bernard (New York and London, 1951), section 7. Subsequent references to the *Critique* in this translation and edition will be indicated in the text by *section* number.

6. Contemporary axiological appeals to language frequently recall or duplicate Kant's. Thus, Alisdair MacIntyre has recently developed the remarkable suggestion that even if, in a world gone all subjectivist and individualistic, *nobody* has thoughts of justice or duty anymore, those *words* still mean those things in themselves and, when uttered, make moral claims independently of their speakers. Cf. MacIntyre, *After Virtue: A Study in Moral Theory,* 2nd

ed. (Notre Dame, Ind., 1984), esp. pp. 8–10, and the discussion in Chapter 5, below.

7. These other forms of analysis are cited here only to help characterize the distinctive aspects of Kant's method and are not being recommended per se; nor, for that matter, could it be said that what are termed in our own time "phenomenological" or "empirical" aesthetics are themselves free of apriorism.

8. "Sensation/judgment" is necessary here because, given Kant's analysis, what *has* validity is the "sensation" but what *claims* validity is its "judgment," the latter in the sense both of the mental act of discriminating the sensation and also the verbal expression or "giving out" of that mental act.

9. I summarize here, as we *now* explain them, things that Kant explained in terms of the then-current models of human perception and cognition, including of course his own models.

10. The "system" spoken of here *always* includes (though "inclusion" is not really the proper term here) the subject's "body" and is *never* confined only to that part of it which is above the neck. My concern here is the tendency in genteel aesthetics and post-Kantian critical theory to distinguish among experiences on the basis, it seems, of just that sort of dividing line. See, for example, W. K. Wimsatt's allusion to our being "amorphously rubbed against" things as distinguished from our experiencing them through vision or hearing (*The Verbal Icon: Studies in the Meaning of Poetry* [Louisville, Ky., 1954], p. 238), a distinction itself related to Kant's own hierarchy of the senses in relation to their mediated distance from the source of stimulation. The revulsion against the bestial/bodily involved in this tradition is examined by Jacques Derrida in "Economimesis," tr. Richard Klein, *Diacritics* 11 (Summer 1981): 3–25, and by Pierre Bourdieu in *Distinction: A Social Critique of the Judgement of Taste* (Paris, 1979), tr. Richard Nice (Cambridge, Mass., 1984), esp. pp. 487–491. For its relation to The-Other's-Poison Effect, see the discussion below.

11. Contrary to his own claims on the evidence of his own introspections, it may be supposed that even for Kant, as for any other human creature—that is, a creature characteristically haunted by images, ideas, words, and verbally encoded memories—the experience of "beauty" and "pure form" must have had some mnemonic, verbal, and conceptual stuff sticking to it. Indeed, it may be suspected that it was for this very reason—that is, the fact that his sensations and concepts could *not* be "separated off" from each other—that Kant's consciousness supplied him with introspections of pure sensations of beauty in such good accord with his own conceptual model of the mental faculties: a model, that is, in which sensations and concepts *could* be "separated off." It appears, in other words, that Kant's sensations were conditioned by his concepts to appear unconditioned by concepts.

12. In "Economimesis," Derrida discusses the comparable series of distinctions and exclusions through which, especially in the "Analytic of the Sublime," Kant develops the opposition/relation of art and nature.

13. The cited passage appears not in the "Analytic of the Beautiful" but in a later section of the *Critique,* the "Dialectic of the Aesthetical Judgment," where Kant resumes the axiological analysis and where the perplexity remarked above appears even more intractable. Observing that "we can do nothing more than remove the conflict between the claims and counterclaims of taste," that is, between *everyone has his own taste* and *there is no disputing about taste* (statements that Kant takes to be making diametrically opposed claims for reasons that are, to say the least, strained), he goes on as follows: "It is absolutely impossible to give a definite objective principle of taste in accordance with which its judgments could be derived, examined, and established, for then the judgment would not be one of taste at all. The subjective principle, viz. the indefinite idea of the supersensible in us, can only be put forward as the sole key to the puzzle of this faculty whose sources are hidden from us" (sect. 57). Here and elsewhere, Kant's rigorous efforts to solve the central logical problems of the demonstration and to tie up its evident incoherences appear to have repeatedly created further logical problems and incoherences that required further rigorous working out. (The general point is made implicitly, but not quite faced, by Paul Guyer in his painstaking but ultimately *un*critical exegesis, *Kant and the Claims of Taste* [Cambridge, Mass., 1979].) It is, perhaps, this very combination of rigor and incoherence that is so addictive to commentators, the rigor continuously attracting their intellectual energies and the incoherence continuously eluding their exegetical skills. It is as if the *Critique* were always *on the verge* of making the most utterly airtight sense, if only one worked at it a bit harder. For other recent efforts, see *Essays in Kant's Aesthetics,* ed. Ted Cohen and Paul Guyer (Chicago, 1982).

14. Conflicts among the latter trio over the determination of aesthetic value are reported regularly in the popular press and have become quite familiar. Cf. the litigation over Richard Serra's sculpture "Tilted Arc," and related reports and discussions in a revealingly diverse array of publications, including: "Wailing at the Wall," *Newsweek* 105 (May 13, 1985): 94; Calvin Tompkins, "Tilted Arc," *New Yorker* 61 (May 20, 1985): 95; Margaret Moorman, "Arc Enemies," *Art News* 84 (May 1985): 13; "Public Art: Moving the Not-So-Great Wall," *Time* 125 (June 10, 1985): 35; Arthur C. Danto, "Public Art and the General Will," *Nation* 241 (Sept. 28, 1985): 288; Andrew Decker, "Serra Goes to Court," *Art News* 86 (April 1987): 29. The postaxiological study of public art or art in public places, with attention to the disputes between experts deploring philistine taste and citizens outraged by expenditures of communal funds on what they see as nonuplifting, depressing, insulting, and/or ridiculous objects, remains to be pursued.

15. For Hume's own observation of intellectual fashions, see n. 2, above.

16. For a corrosive discussion of the appeal to intuitions of reality in contemporary philosophy, see Richard Rorty, *Consequences of Pragmatism: Essays, 1972–80* (Minneapolis, Minn., 1982), pp. xxi–xxxvii.

17. Martin Jay, *Adorno* (Cambridge, Mass., 1984), p. 17. For an account of

Adorno's critique of mass culture in the context of Frankfurt School cultural criticism, see also Jay's *The Dialectical Imagination: A History of the Frankfurt School and the Institute of Social Research, 1923–50* (Boston, 1973), pp. 173–218.

18. For influential statements earlier in the century, see José Ortega y Gasset, *The Revolt of the Masses* (1930; New York, 1957), and Herman Broch, "Notes on the Problem of Kitsch," in *Kitsch: The World of Bad Taste*, ed. Gillo Dorfles (New York, 1969), pp. 49–76. See also Theodor W. Adorno, *Negative Dialectics*, tr. E. B. Ashton (Frankfurt am Main, 1966; New York, 1973); Herbert Marcuse, *One-Dimensional Man* (Boston, 1964); idem, *The Aesthetic Dimension* (Boston, 1978); Dwight MacDonald, "Masscult and Midcult," in MacDonald, *Against the American Grain: Essays on the Effects of Mass Culture* (New York, 1962); André Malraux, "Art, Popular Art, and the Illusion of the Folk," and Clement Greenberg, "Avant-Garde and Kitsch," both of which are in James B. Hall and Barry Ulanov, eds., *Modern Culture and the Arts* (New York, 1967).

For more recent versions, see Barbara Tuchman, "The Decline of Quality," *New York Times Magazine*, Nov. 2, 1980, pp. 37–41, 102 (and Nov. 30, 1980, p. 170, for the full page of largely supportive letters to the editor in response to the article); Murray Krieger, *Arts on the Level: The Fall of the Elite Object* (Knoxville, Tennessee, 1981); Denis Donoghue, "The Promiscuous Cool of Postmodernism" *New York Times Book Review*, June 22, 1986, p. 1; Jean Baudrillard, *Simulations*, tr. Paul Foss, Paul Patton, and Philip Beitchman (New York, 1983); idem, *In the Shadow of the Silent Majorities*, tr. Paul Foss, Paul Patton, and John Johnston (New York, 1983); Richard Wolin, "Modernism vs. Postmodernism," *Telos* 62 (Winter 1984–85): 9–29; Jürgen Habermas, "Modernity versus Postmodernity," *New German Critique* 22 (Winter 1981): 3–14; E. D. Hirsch, Jr., *Cultural Literacy: What Every American Should Know* (Boston, 1986); and Allan Bloom, *The Closing of the American Mind: How Higher Education Has Failed Democracy and Impoverished the Souls of Today's Students* (New York, 1987). For a documentary history of the American literary academy's self-defining resistance to mass and popular culture, see Gerald Graff, *Professing Literature: An Institutional History* (Evanston, Ill., 1986). For a useful examination of Frankfurt School cultural theory in relation to comparable apocalyptic analyses in Western intellectual history, see Patrick Brantlinger, *Bread and Circuses: Theories of Mass Culture and Social Decay* (Ithaca and London, 1983), pp. 222–248.

There are, of course, important exceptions to these general tendencies. For recent sophisticated studies of mass and popular culture, see Susan Stewart, *Nonsense: Aspects of Intertextuality in Folklore and Literature* (Baltimore, 1979); idem, *On Longing: Narratives of the Miniature, the Gigantic, the Souvenir, the Collection* (Baltimore, 1984); Janice A. Radway, *Reading the Romance: Women, Patriarchy, and Popular Literature* (Chapel Hill, 1984); and Jane Tompkins, *Sensational Designs: The Cultural Work of American Fiction, 1790–1860* (New York, 1985). See also Fredric Jameson's canny though deeply ambivalent essay "Postmodernism, or The Cultural Logic of Late Capitalism," *The New Left Review* 146 (July–August 1984): 53–92.

19. Martin Jay, *The Dialectical Imagination*, p. 187.

20. As Bourdieu puts it: "Taste classifies, and it classifies the classifier. Social subjects, classified by their classifications, distinguish themselves by the distinctions they make" (*Distinction*, p. 6). Although he is not altogether evenhanded in the tone of his analyses, describing working-class practices rather sympathetically and reserving his most elaborate satire for the self-privileging *grand bourgeois*, hapless *petit bourgeois*, and "mis-recognitions" of intellectuals and academics, Bourdieu neither privileges nor pathologizes any practices theoretically and accounts for all cultural preferences symmetrically by reference to general sociological dynamics.

21. Cf. Herbert Gans, *Popular Culture and High Culture: An Analysis and Evaluation of Taste* (New York, 1975), esp. pp. 67–118.

22. Questions may be raised concerning the extent to which the generality of the observations and conclusions in *Distinction* are historically, culturally, and perhaps even nationally limited by Bourdieu's data (two surveys conducted in France, largely in Paris, during the 1960s). They may also be raised about its implication (by omission) that sociological dynamics alone can account for all variations among human tastes and preferences. The crucial questions here, however, are whether the methodological limits of the study compromise either the power of Bourdieu's critique of traditional aesthetic axiology or the suggestiveness of his analyses for postaxiological explorations of the social economics of culture, and whether, for those factors that he omits, their inclusion would revalidate the traditional asymmetrical accounts of the phenomena of taste in terms of objective standards, intrinsic value, natural powers of discrimination, and so forth. The answers to these latter questions are, I believe, clearly negative.

23. For a general description of such processes and the suggestion that social and political theory must develop new models to make them intelligible, see Niklas Luhmann, *The Differentiation of Society*, tr. Stephen Holmes and Charles Larmore (Columbia, 1982), esp. pp. 229–254.

24. See, for example, R. C. Lewontin, Steven Rose, and Leon J. Kamin, *Not in Our Genes: Biology, Ideology, and Human Nature* (New York, 1984); Jean Grimshaw, *Philosophy and Feminist Thinking* (Minneapolis, 1986), esp. pp. 130–133; and, for an exceptionally subtle analysis and, in effect, deconstruction of the traditional categories and oppositions discussed here, Susan Oyama, *The Ontogeny of Information: Developmental Systems and Evolution* (Cambridge, 1985).

25. Comparable and comparably dubious arguments for universals of moral judgment and objective moral value have been drawn from research on the alleged "stages" of moral development of children. For example: "Our psychological theory claims that individuals prefer the highest stage of reasoning they comprehend, a claim supported by research. This claim of our

psychological theory derives from a philosophical claim that a later stage is 'objectively' preferable or more adequate by certain *moral* criteria." Lawrence Kohlberg, "The Claim to Moral Adequacy of a Highest Stage of Moral Judgment," *Journal of Philosophy* 70 (1973): 633. As this passage from Kohlberg suggests, there is some question as to what "supports" what, what is "derived" from what, and whether everything is not bootstrapped into existence in the usual fashion of neo-Kantian transcendental logic. For a shrewd critique of such studies in connection with Jürgen Habermas's appeals to and appropriations of them, see Thomas McCarthy, "Rationality and Relativism: Habermas's 'Overcoming' of Hermeneutics," in *Habermas: Critical Debates*, ed. John B. Thompson and David Held (Cambridge, Mass., 1982), pp. 57–78, in which the passage from Kohlberg just quoted is cited and discussed (pp. 289–290).

26. The fact that someone who, as child, loved bright colors, strong rhythms, and nonsense verse now, in middle age, seeks out muted colors, mimimalist music, and biographies of Lincoln can certainly be attributed in part to changes of that kind—though, as I emphasize above, by no means completely accounted for by them.

27. Herbert Gans, *Popular Culture and High Culture: An Analysis and Evaluation of Taste* (New York, 1974), p. 127. Further page references will be cited in the text.

28. Neither comprehensiveness nor informativeness is, of course, an intrinsic or objective property of objects. At the time Gans was writing, empirical aesthetics was still beguiled by an information-theory model and norm of aesthetic value, in relation to which "informational richness" could be seen as an objective property. See, for example, Leonard B. Meyer, "Some Remarks on Value and Greatness in Music," in his *Music, the Arts and Ideas* (Chicago, 1967).

29. Gans's specific suggestions here, namely "incremental aesthetic reward" or "the extent to which each person's choice adds something to his or her previous experience and his or her effort toward self-realization" (*Popular Culture and High Culture*, p. 127), combine the clichés of 1950s and 60s social-scientific liberal uplift and a perhaps more fundamental Kantian-plus-American *puritanism* that cannot acknowledge the possibility that the "gratification" sought and found by both high- and low-culture persons might be a state of quite ephemeral pleasure that was noncumulative and not only nonutilitarian but altogether unedifying.

5. Truth/Value

1. The view or alleged view that equates the two and which is thus supposedly refuted is called, in Anglo-American philosophy, "emotivism": "alleged" because any account that questions the concept of objective value and, with it, the machinery of traditional axiology is commonly seen as, and said to

be, "emotivist." The allegation illustrates the general tendency of objectivist thought to generate phantom heresies out of its own inversion. Its consequences are examined at length in Chapter 7, below.

2. *After Virtue: A Study in Moral Theory*, 2nd ed. (Notre Dame, 1984). Page references to the book, abbreviated *AV*, will be cited in the text.

   I shall not be concerned here with the specifically *historical* dimension of MacIntyre's narrative or its governing idea, namely that there has been a continual erosion of moral authority and moral consensus in Western thought and life beginning, it appears (MacIntyre's dating is vague and not altogether consistent), with the Reformation and accelerating from the time of the Enlightenment. I would note, however, that, like many others who chart the Decline of the West along such lines, he underestimates the extent of the ranges and varieties of discourse and practice in any era, culture, or "community," and, especially through contrasts posed in such terms as "our predecessor culture," "the present age," and "modern life," obscures crucial and relevant differences—such as those of class, gender, place, race, and historical experience—that cannot readily be seen as matters of degeneration, loss, failure, or fragmentation.

3. As can be seen in the passages quoted above, MacIntyre uses terms such as "expression" and "statement" in such a way that it is never altogether clear whether he is talking about abstract verbal *forms* or about particular *utterances* (of a certain form) produced in specific (if hypothetical) contexts. Indeed, it appears that he does not recognize the difference or its significance for the questions at issue here.

4. According to MacIntyre, a few philosophers such as G. E. Moore have understood what modern people were really *doing* when they *said* "It is good," but those philosophers have tried only to make postlapsarian life more comfortable for the fallen by maintaining that objective standards and wholesome moral discourse never existed anyway, or that appeals to them were always manipulative: hence the emotive theory (*AV*, pp. 14–20). It should be observed, however, that MacIntyre's own account of moral discourse participates in the same dualism that produces both the standard axiological account and, as its self-inversion, the so-called emotive theory. Indeed, his "hypothesis" and its narrative development consist simply of the *temporalization* of that dualism. Whereas the alleged emotivist allegedly says, "Since there are no objective standards, all judgments, including ostensibly impersonal ones, are nothing more than expressions of personal preference," MacIntyre says, "Since people *no longer* believe in objective standards, all judgments must *now* be—at heart, if not in form—nothing more than expressions of personal preference." Here, as elsewhere, the temporalization of a dualism yields a myth of the Fall.

5. See the related discussion of proverbs, maxims, and "sayings" in Barbara Herrnstein Smith, *On the Margins of Discourse: The Relation of Literature to Language* (Chicago, 1978), pp. 69–73.

6. MacIntyre writes of "the larger totalities" in which our moral concepts and

their corresponding expressions were "originally at home" and of which they are now "deprived" (*AV*, p. 10). He fails to add the necessary corollary of this, which is that, if they remain available as concepts and continue to be used as expressions at all, it must be because they are now "at home" in *other* totalities. The latter may, of course, be more heterogeneous than those "original" ones, or coexistent with more alternatives.

7. "Appropriability" here and below is not the extent to which an utterance would secure explicit agreement but, rather, the extent to which people other than the speaker could, so to speak, "make it their own"—that is, use it or apply it to themselves in some way. It should be emphasized in relation to later discussions that this is always a way *more or less* different from how the speaker applies it to herself and wants them to, or believes they would, apply it to themselves.

8. For other works in the same mode, see Robert Bellah et al., *Habits of the Heart: Individualism and Commitment in American Life* (Berkeley, 1985); and Charles Taylor, "Interpretation and the Sciences of Man," in Taylor, *Philosophy and the Human Sciences: Philosophical Papers*, vol. 2 (Cambridge, 1985), pp. 15–57. For other critiques along the lines offered here, see Niklas Luhmann, *The Differentiation of Society* (New York, 1982); and William Connolly, *Politics and Ambiguity* (Madison, Wis., 1986). Michael Walzer attempts to develop a positive pluralistic alternative in his *Spheres of Justice: A Defense of Pluralism and Equality* (New York, 1983). See also the discussion of "community" and "solidarity" in Chapter 7, below.

9. Among the most recent of those—of course quite diversely produced, articulated, and circulated—demonstrations (and critiques of those attempted rehabilitations) are Jacques Derrida, *Of Grammatology*, tr. Gayatri C. Spivak (Baltimore and London, 1974); idem, *Margins of Philosophy*, tr. Alan Bass (Chicago, 1982); Nelson Goodman, *Ways of Worldmaking* (Indianapolis, 1978); Richard Rorty, *Philosophy and the Mirror of Nature* (Princeton, 1979); idem, *The Consequences of Pragmatism: Essays, 1972–1980* (Minneapolis, 1982); Gonzalo Munévar, *Radical Knowledge: A Philosophical Inquiry into the Nature and Limits of Science* (Indianapolis, 1981); Barry Barnes, *T. S. Kuhn and Social Science* (New York, 1982); and David Bloor, *Wittgenstein: A Social Theory of Knowledge* (New York, 1983).

10. For an interesting approach to such an account, see Humberto R. Maturana and Francisco G. Varela, *Autopoiesis and Cognition: The Realization of Living* (Dordrecht, Holland, and Boston, 1980).

11. Having particular *effects* rather than performing particular functions is a more suitable unpacking in many cases.

12. As a current rating service puts it: "CONSUMER GUIDE knows what a challenge it is to pick the 'best buy' that meets your requirements . . . So we call in the experts to do the comparison shopping for you." *Consumer Buying Guide* (Skokie, Ill., 1987), p. 4.

13. The relation of scientific practice to evaluation will be examined further below, but the following summary of why, contrary to standard views of

scientific method, the *replication* of a "finding" does *not* constitute a test of truth in science is relevant here: "The problem is that, since experimentation is a matter of skillful practice, it can never be clear whether a second experiment has been done sufficiently well to count as a check on the first. Some further test is needed to test the quality of the experiment—and so forth . . . The failure of these 'tests of tests' to resolve the difficulty demonstrates the need for further 'tests of tests of tests' and so on—a true regress." H. M. Collins, *Changing Order: Replication and Induction in Scientific Practice* (London, Beverly Hills, New Delhi, 1985), p. 2.

14. The force of J. L. Austin's insight that there are other measures (e.g., "felicity") has been all but lost in the objectivist appropriation of his work in socalled speech-act theory. It may be noted as well that Austin appreciated, though he did not pursue his own emphasis of it, the radical contingency of "truth": "It is essential to realize that 'true' and 'false' . . . do not stand for anything simple at all; but only for a general dimension of being a right or proper thing to say as opposed to a wrong thing, in these circumstances, to this audience, for these purposes and with these intentions." *How to Do Things with Words* (New York, 1962), p. 144.

15. Jürgen Habermas, "What Is Universal Pragmatics?" in *Communication and the Evolution of Society,* tr. Thomas McCarthy (Boston and London, 1979).

16. See Smith, *On the Margins of Discourse,* pp. 77–106, for an earlier version. Other accounts along these lines include Erving Goffman, *Strategic Interaction* (Oxford, 1970); idem, *Relations in Public* (New York, 1971); and Morse Peckham, *Explanation and Power: The Control of Human Behavior* (New York, 1979). Pierre Bourdieu develops a somewhat different but compatible sociological analysis of "the linguistic marketplace" in "The Economics of Linguistic Exchange," *Social Science Information* 16 (1977): 645–688.

17. *Consumer Buying Guide,* p. 4.

18. Thus, readers of the *Consumer Buying Guide* are assured: "Our experts are also careful to match the products to the changing needs of consumers, including, for instance, downsized appliances for small households" (p. 4).

19. The mission of disciplinary science is also the production of appropriable *technical skills* and the two may not always be separable, but, in connection with questions of verbal communication and the value of "propositions," our focus here is on its verbal/conceptual products: reports, statements, writings, theories, measurements, models, and so forth.

20. For recent discussions of the structure and operation of social and institutional constraints in disciplinary science, see David Bloor, "Essay Review: Two Paradigms for Scientific Knowledge?" *Science Studies* 1 (1971): 105–115; Pierre Bourdieu, "The Specificity of the Scientific Field and the Social Conditions of the Progress of Reason," *Social Science Information* 14 (1975): 19–47; Barry Barnes, *T. S. Kuhn and Social Science,* esp. pp. 64–93; H. M. Collins, *Changing Order: Replication and Induction in Scientific Practice,* esp. pp. 129–168; Bruno Latour and Steve Wolgar, *Laboratory Life: The Social Con-*

struction of Scientific Facts (Beverly Hills and London, 1979), esp. pp. 151–186; and Bruno Latour, *Science in Action: How to Follow Scientists and Engineers through Society* (Cambridge, Mass., 1987), esp. pp. 21–62.

21. For a recent attempt to analyze the good-true-beautiful relation in modern theoretical physics, see Paul Davies, *Superforce: The Search for a Grand Unified Theory of Nature* (New York, 1984), pp. 50–69.

22. My account here shares many elements with the analysis by Paul Davies in *Superforce*. Davies points out, for example, that the "rightness" of certain highly abstract features of a theory cannot be a matter of their validation "by concrete experience," that "beauty in physics is a value judgment involving professional intuitions," and that, with regard to theories, "better" means not truer (he does not, in fact, use the term) but more "useful," "more economical," "smoother," "more suggestive," and so on (pp. 66–69). He nevertheless moves repeatedly toward gratuitously objectifying formulations (e.g., "Nature *is* beautiful" and "Nevertheless the aesthetic quality *is there* sure enough"—pp. 68, 69) that obscure the significance of the relationship, here emphasized, between the scientist's intuitive sense of the "beauty" of a theory and its suitability for appropriation by the members of a relevant community.

23. I am ignoring here the other parameters of goodness and badness—"comprehensibility," "syntactic well-formedness," "felicity," and so forth —that are sometimes proposed, typically *in addition to* "truth-value," as required for or presupposed by effective (or, as in Habermas, "genuine") communication. Setting aside the serious questions of conceptualization and determination that might be raised concerning each of these criteria, one can grant that defects of roughly these kinds may occur, in which case the speaker (for example, one who mumbles, stutters, speaks "broken English," or produces malapropisms) would certainly be at a competitive disadvantage in the linguistic market, and the economics of his or her individual verbal transactions would be affected accordingly. Such criteria can be ignored here, however, since they are always said by those who invoke them to be irrelevant to truth-value and are also irrelevant to the specific kinds of negative value noted above. Thus, someone's evaluation of an artwork may be exquisitely well-formed as well as earnest, but *still* excruciatingly uninteresting to her listeners, and a political prisoner's extorted report may be pronounced altogether felicitously and "accurately," so that it is readily understood and effectively appropriated by his questioners, but *still* at considerable cost to himself.

24. *May,* not *must:* this is certainly not to suggest that every verbal transaction or other form of social interaction is a zero-sum game.

25. "Speakers" here are those who produce verbal forms in any mode or medium; "listeners" are those who respond to (*not* who simply "receive") such forms.

26. The adversarial quality described here coexists with whatever mutual be-

nevolence otherwise and simultaneously characterizes the relation between the parties: it does not contaminate the latter, but neither does the latter transcend it.

27. The term and concept "information" and also its traditional conceptual syntax ("getting," "having," "giving," "transmitting" it, and so on) are among those by which traditional discourse segments, arrests, and hypostasizes the complex processes through which our behavior is modified by our interactions with our environments. In an account more rigorous than that offered here, the entire problematic terminology of "information" would be replaced by a description of the specific dynamics of such interactions.

28. The present account does not exclude what are called moral or ethical (inter)actions though it would, in any elaboration, necessarily reconceptualize their dynamics.

29. Habermas, "What Is Universal Pragmatics?" p. 3.

30. Ibid., p. 41.

31. Mary Louise Pratt mounts a critique of the utopian models of verbal exchange in speech-act theory in "Ideology and Speech-Act Theory," *Poetics Today* 7, no. 1 (1986): 59–72. Observing that such models characteristically project an idealized ("Western liberal") conception of exchange as a relation of equality, reciprocality, and cooperation, she notes that they thereby obscure the significance of power relations among the parties both in literal markets and in verbal interactions. Pratt's critique, which is spirited and incisive, is properly directed against models of communication such as those of Paul Grice and Habermas but is not properly directed against the account outlined here, which not only stresses the significance of those power relations but insists on the inevitable asymmetries and inequalities—as well as inevitable differences—of motives, means, and consequences among the parties in every other aspect of verbal exchange. The point needs emphasis in view of the fact that Pratt, observing that "Grice's formulations now function widely . . . as the norm for non-literary verbal interaction" (p. 65), cites without further comment my earlier study, *On the Margins of Discourse*. As in the present study, however, the model of verbal exchange first developed in that book is quite otherwise inspired and its formulations are crucially different from those of Grice, especially with respect to the points at issue, that is, whether verbal interactions can be appropriately described as governed by categorical maxims and whether they exhibit the behavior of rational agents.

The issue is complicated, of course, by the existence of a number of different—and to some extent contradictory—relevant senses of "rational." Thus, Pratt, having examined several notions of communication as exchange, observes that the speech-act theorist's view of language as "essentially a *cooperative* form of behavior, in which participants work together *rationally* to achieve common goals," is decisively contradicted by the routine violation of Grice's conversational maxims in "almost any press conference, board meeting, classroom, or family room in the country" (p. 66, emphasis added). No matter how *unruly* it is, however, in the sense of either obstreperous or non-rule-governed, and also no matter how self-serving, competitive, exploitative, and downright bestial, the behavior of verbal agents may still be described as *rational* in the familiar economistic sense of either self-consistent or as-if-utility-maximizing. To be sure, Grice's Cooperative Principle and associated maxims (be brief, be sincere, be relevant, be clear) are altogether dubious: not, however, because verbal behavior is *not* "rational" in the latter sense, but because, being cast and conceived in terms of neo-Kantian ethics, such principles and maxims neither capture nor account for the force of verbal reciprocality, which, as I explained above, is the fact that the "things" that speakers and listeners "do" to and for each other are, for better and worse, *interdependently consequential.* (Significantly, Grice's maxims are addressed only to speakers: like Habermas and speech-act theorists generally, he does not recognize that listeners are also agents or that they do anything other than listen and "understand." See Paul Grice, "Logic and Conversation," in *Syntax and Semantics III: Speech Acts,* ed. Peter Cole and Jerry Morgan [New York, 1975], pp. 41–58). Whether verbal agents are properly described as "rational," then, depends on the sense in which the term is taken. The behavior of speakers and listeners could certainly be seen as "rational" in the economistic sense indicated above, though someone who saw it thus might be inclined to redescribe Grice's conversational maxims not as general principles governing and presupposed by all speech acts but, rather, as patterns of effective social interaction under certain, limited, conditions in certain, historically particular, verbal communities. If, on the other hand, one takes the term "rational" in the philosophical/ethical sense of behaving in accord with "good"—meaning, it seems, logically articulatable, morally justifiable, and/ or otherwise transcendentally proper—"reasons," one could either note, as Pratt does, the typical *non*rationality of actual (as opposed to idealized) verbal interactions or one could insist, as does Habermas, on a strict (and, in my view, altogether question-begging) distinction between "truly rational"—and presumably ethical—communicative agents and those who pursue effectiveness and thereby exhibit only "instrumental rationality." I will return to the question of human rationality in general in Chapter 6.

32. Thus M. F. Burnyeat reformulates and reaffirms Plato's alleged demonstration that Protagoras's "Man is the measure of all things . . ." is self-refuting: "No amount of maneuvering with his relativizing qualifiers will extricate Protagoras from the commitment to truth absolute which is bound up with the very act of assertion. To assert is to assert that p— . . . [i.e.] that something is the case—and if p, indeed if and only if p, then p is true (period). *This principle, which relativism attempts to circumvent, must be ac-*

knowledged by any speaker." "Protagoras and Self-Refutation in Plato's *Theaetetus,*" *Philosophical Review* 85, no. 2 (April 1976): 195, emphasis added.

33. For the view that we underestimate the communicative subtlety of our interactions with animals, see Vicki Hearne, *Adam's Task: Calling Animals by Name* (New York, 1987). For a suggestive theory of the evolution of animal communication as strategic interaction, see John T. Krebs and Richard Dawkins, "Animal Signals: Mind-Reading and Manipulation," in *Behavioral Ecology: An Evolutionary Approach,* ed. J. R. Krebs and N. B. Davies, 2nd ed. (Sunderland, Mass., 1984), pp. 380–402.

34. See Mary Louise Pratt, "Ideology and Speech-Act Theory," and the discussion in note 31, above.

35. Insofar as this second objection also reflects the idea that the validity of a model or analogy remains limited to the specific site of its derivation, it misunderstands the nature and operation of models, analogies, and metaphors. If someone uses a current account of the motion of Saturn's rings to clarify his description of how the telephone system operates, he is not limited to describing how people telephone each other *on Saturn;* nor, if the latter account comes into disfavor among astrophysicists, is the value of his own description of the telephone system thereby undermined. Similarly, even if there are no marketplaces in Bongo-Bongo, a marketplace analogy could still illuminate how people communicate there. (The idea that how people interact verbally is affected by the particular economic systems in which they live is not to be dismissed out of hand, but is not self-evident and *also* not to be assumed in advance). And, of course, even if it was conclusively demonstrated that neoclassic economics described nothing on the face of the earth, its structure might still operate as a productive and otherwise effective metaphor in a description of the dynamics of human communication.

36. For representative discussions of the controversies mentioned, see Karl Polanyi, "Our Obsolete Market Mentality, *Commentary* 3 (1947): 109–117; Cyril Belshaw, "Theoretical Problems in Economic Anthropology," in Maurice Freedman, ed., *Social Organization: Essays Presented to Raymond Firth* (Chicago, 1968); George Dalton, "Theoretical Issues in Economic Anthropology," in *Economic Anthropology and Development: Essays on Tribal and Peasant Economies* (New York and London, 1971); Harold K. Schneider, *Economic Man: The Anthropology of Economics* (New York and London, 1974); Marshall Sahlins, *Stone Age Economics* (Chicago, 1972); and idem, *Culture and Practical Reason* (Chicago, 1976).

37. For an early and influential outline of social-exchange theory, see George Homans, *Social Behavior: Its Elementary Forms* (New York, 1961; rev. ed., New York, 1974). For recent studies in decision science, see Daniel Kahneman, Paul Slovic, and Amos Tversky, eds., *Judgment under Uncertainty: Heuristics and Biases* (Cambridge, 1982). For game theory, see Anatol Rappaport et al., *Prisoner's Dilemma: A Study in Conflict and Cooperation* (Ann

Arbor, 1965); and, more recently, Robert Axelrod, *The Evolution of Cooperation* (New York, 1984).

38. As has recently and increasingly been documented and explored, the most historically significant and conceptually powerful related critique is that of Nietzsche. For a useful bibliography and collection of pieces by, among others, Martin Heidegger, Gilles Deleuze, Maurice Blanchot, and Sarah Kofman, see David B. Allison, ed., *The New Nietzsche: Contemporary Styles of Interpretation* (New York, 1977).

39. Samuel Weber, "Reading and Writing—Chez Derrida," *Tildschrift voor Filosofie* 45, no. 2 (March 1983): 41–62, reprinted in Weber, *Institution and Interpretation* (Minneapolis, 1987). I initially presented this discussion as a response to the version that Weber delivered at the Conference on Deconstructive Theory, Temple University, Philadelphia, March 26, 1983.

40. The latter phrase is Derrida's, quoted and translated by Weber from *La Carte postale* (Paris, 1980), p. 305. Elsewhere in this paragraph and in the two that follow, I freely paraphrase Weber's text (which itself, at many points, both incorporates and paraphrases Derrida's texts) and also, in the course of giving my own version of the tale he tells, resituate a number of his evocative phrases and rearrange some links in his artfully forged chains of metaphors.

41. I shall not attempt to summarize here that very thick cluster or tangle of concepts, metaphors, and conceptual/textual moves that Derrida reveals, analyzes, and disassembles—that is, deconstructs—as "the metaphysics of presence." For the reader not otherwise familiar with Derrida's work, however, it may be noted that it includes what I describe above as (a) the telegraphic model of communication, particularly insofar as such a model posits an ideal of the duplicative transmission of messages in which *sameness* is preserved perfectly across some channel or from one "medium" to another, (b) the epistemology in which that model is embedded, that is, a concept of knowledge as an interiorization or mental mirroring of an external reality that is both immediately available and also independently determinate, and (c) the tendency to absolutize, binarize, polarize, and hierarchize arrays of relative differences.

42. Jacques Derrida, *Positions,* tr. Alan Bass (Chicago, 1980), p. 26.

43. Weber, "Reading and Writing—Chez Derrida," p. 55.

44. Francis Bacon, *Novum Organum,* ed. Thomas Fowler (Oxford, 1878), Book I, Aphorisms 38–59.

45. I speak here of contemporary philosophy of science, particularly the text entitled *Against Method* (London, 1975), by Paul Feyerabend.

46. For an interesting discussion of the point, see A. Newell and H. A. Simon, *Human Problem-Solving* (Englewood Cliffs, N.J., 1972).

47. This appears to be implied by the theory of the emergence of organic systems proposed by Manfred Eigen and Paul Schuster in *The Hypercycle: A Principle of Natural Self-Organization* (Berlin, Heidelberg, and New York, 1979).

48. For a nice meditation on the relation between the imperfect operations of natural selection and those of the tinkerer (as opposed to the engineer), see François Jacob, "Evolution and Tinkering," *Science* 196 (June 10, 1977): 1161–66.

49. For other examples, see Hillel J. Einhorn, "Learning from Experience and Suboptimal Rules," in *Judgment under Uncertainty: Heuristics and Biases*, ed. Daniel Kahneman, Paul Slovic, and Amos Tversky (Cambridge, 1982), pp. 268–283. As is indicated by the other studies collected in this instructive volume, there are numerous cognitive processes ("heuristics") that, as the editors put it, "are highly economical and usually effective, but . . . lead to systematic and predictable errors" (ibid., p. 20).

50. Thus is *"différance"* characterized in Derrida's essay of that title in his *Speech and Phenomena*, tr. David Allison (Evanston, Ill., 1973), p. 130.

6. The Critiques of Utility

1. Although technical definitions of "utility" in contemporary mathematical economics (for example, the concept of a "utility function" as a representation of an ordered assembly of "displayed preferences") have historical and other connections with both the assumption of utility-maximization in classic economic theory and the greatest-good-for-the-greatest-number utilitarianism of Jeremy Bentham and other political theorists, the former operational and indeed tautologous senses of "utility" should be distinguished from both of the latter, especially in relation to the more or less philosophical critiques of "utility theory" examined below. For informative discussions of the history of these terms and theories, see R. Duncan Luce and Howard Raiffa, *Games and Decisions: Introduction and Critical Survey* (New York, 1957), pp. 1–38; and Ross Harrison, *Bentham* (London, 1983).

2. For significant recent studies and surveys, see Herbert A. Simon, "A Behavioral Model of Rational Choice," *Quarterly Journal of Economics* 69 (1955): 99–118; idem, "Theories of Decision-Making in Economics and Behavioral Science," *American Economic Review* 49 (June 1959): 253–283; Amartya Sen, "Rational Fools," reprinted in his *Choice, Welfare and Measurement* (Oxford, 1982); George Akerlof, "Labor Contracts as Partial Gift Exchange," *Quarterly Journal of Economics* 97 (1982): 543–569; Daniel Kahneman, Paul Slovic, and Amos Tversky, eds., *Judgment under Uncertainty: Heuristics and Biases* (Cambridge, 1982); Robert P. Abelson and Ariel Levi, "Decision-Making and Decision Theory," in *Handbook of Social Psychology*, ed. G. Lindzey and E. Aronson (Reading, Mass., 1983); and Amitai Etzioni, "Rationality Is Anti-Entropic," *Journal of Economic Psychology* 7 (March 1986): 17–36.

3. The broader division would actually be economics and axiology more generally. My focus here, however, is designed to engage current theory and analysis in the literary academy and cultural studies, from the perspective of which the "humanistic" disciplines are commonly seen as those concerned

primarily with texts and other cultural products. From other perspectives, "the humanities" could be seen to center on philosophy and religious studies where, of course, aesthetics is traditionally secondary to ethics in the broader discursive domain of axiology.

4. That is, an ordered assembly of a subject's preferences (however specified or ascertained) among some set of things is taken as a representation of the relative utility of each of those things to that subject. The strict operationality—and thus substantive generality or indeed vacuousness—of this notion of utility has been emphasized as follows: "In this theory it is extremely important to accept the fact that the subject's preferences . . . came prior to our numerical characterization of them. We do not want to slip into saying that he preferred *A* to *B* because *A* has the higher utility; rather, because *A* is preferred to *B*, we assign *A* the higher utility." (Luce and Raiffa, *Games and Decisions*, p. 22.)

5. The alternate (nondualistic) conceptions of *utility* outlined above are not themselves without problems, including problems shared with various formulations of classic utility theory. The crucial question here, however, is not the validity (or utility) of any specific theory of utility but, rather, whether the most extensive and corrosive detailing of the individual and shared problems of all such theories would, in itself, necessarily underwrite the definitively humanistic *anti*-utilitarianism described here and, with it, the entire dualistic conceptualization of value in which it is embedded and which it perpetuates. For a set of unusually sophisticated critiques of current economic conceptions of utility, see the essays assembled in *Utilitarianism and Beyond*, ed. Amartya Sen and Bernard Williams (New York, 1982). In view of the title of that volume, we could restate the question here as whether "beyond" utilitarianism can only be equivalent to *back to* essentialist and dualistic conceptions of value.

6. Such studies—e.g., Stephen R. G. Jones, *The Economics of Conformism* (Oxford and New York, 1984), and those by Loomes and Sugden cited in note 7 below—as opposed to the critical ones cited above in note 2, offer to rehabilitate the conventional assumptions of rationality and utility-maximization apparently undermined by various inconsistencies, irregularities, and other types of puzzles observed in people's economic and political behavior.

7. See, for example, G. Loomes and R. Sugden, "Regret Theory: An Alternative Theory of Rational Choice under Uncertainty," *Economic Journal* 92 (1982): 805–824; idem, "Regret Theory and Measurable Utility," *Economics Letters* 12 (1983): 19–21; idem, "A Rationale for Preference Reversal," *American Economic Review* 73 (1983): 428–432; R. Sugden, "Regret, Recrimination and Rationality," *Theory and Decision* 19 (1985): 77–99; and Richard E. Nisbett, Eugene Borgida, Rick Crandall, and Harvey Reed, "Popular Induction: Information Is Not Necessarily Informative," in Kahneman, Slovic, and Tversky, *Judgment under Uncertainty*, pp. 101–116.

8. As might be expected, these explorations are to some extent Marxist in

inspiration and orientation but by no means exclusively so and, in any case, by no means confined to the economic determinism of classical Marxist cultural analysis.

9. The concept of the sacred as a distinct realm of value set apart from the profane was developed most notably by Emile Durkheim in *The Elementary Forms of the Religious Life* [*Les Formes élémentaires de la vie religieuse*] (Paris, 1912), tr. Joseph Ward Swain (Glencoe, Ill., 1947). Much of Durkheim's deeply and, indeed, emphatically dualistic conceptualization is retained in Marshall Sahlins's important critique of Marxist and other forms of economistic "naturalism," *Culture and Practical Reason* (Chicago, 1976), and, combined with the related analyses developed by Marcel Mauss, in the essay by Georges Bataille examined below. For an excellent recent discussion of sacralization and commoditization that emphasizes their *dynamic* aspects (but retains a gratuitous culture-nature opposition), see Igor Kopytoff, "The Cultural Biography of Things: Commoditization as Process," in *The Social Life of Things: Commodities in Cultural Perspective*, ed. Arjun Appadurai (Cambridge, 1986).

10. However ridiculous in relation to the large social and political struggles of the first half of the century, the anti-Semitism of T. S. Eliot, Ezra Pound, et al. was neither incidental nor extraneous to the development and articulation of contemporary Anglo-American humanism. For a study of the moral-allegorical force of images of Mammon's agents in English literature, see Kurt Heinzelman, *The Economics of the Imagination* (Amherst, Mass., 1980).

11. Cf. Pierre Bourdieu's discussion of what he terms "mis-recognition" and associates with the high culture "disavowal [*dénégation*] of the 'economic,'" characterized as a "collective repression of narrowly 'economic' interest and of the real nature of practices revealed by 'economic' analysis." Bourdieu, "The Production of Belief: Contribution to an Economy of Symbolic Goods," tr. Richard Nice, *Media, Culture and Society* 2 (1980): 261–293; orig. pub. in *Actes de la Recherche en Sciences Sociales* 13 (1977): 3–43. Of course, as already noted, it is in the nature of the conflicts described here (or the mis-recognitions that Bourdieu himself delineates) that there must always be a question of which description of these practices is to be privileged as revealing their "real nature."

12. See Anne Chapman, "Barter as a Universal Mode of Exchange," *L'Homme* 20, no. 3 (July–Sept., 1980): 33–83; Fernand Braudel, *The Wheels of Commerce* [*Les Jeux de l'échange*] (Paris, 1979), tr. Sian Reynolds (New York, 1982); J. W. Leach and E. Leach, eds., *The Kula: New Perspectives on Massim Exchange* (Cambridge, 1983); Pierre Bourdieu, *Distinction: A Social Critique of the Judgement of Taste* (Paris, 1979), tr. Richard Nice (Cambridge, Mass., 1984); and, especially, the excellent discussion by Arjun Appadurai, "Introduction: Commodities and the Politics of Value," in *The Social Life of Things*, pp. 1–63, from which a number of elements in the following account have been drawn.

13. The general principle here was examined in Chapter 5 as "Value always cuts both, or all, ways." Cf. also " 'Tis an ill wind that blows no man good."

14. For the marketplace as a site of spectacle, subversion, carnival, and transformation, see Peter Stallybrass and Allen White, *The Politics and Poetics of Transgression* (Ithaca, 1986), esp. pp. 27–43; and Jean-Christophe Agnew, *Worlds Apart: The Market and the Theater in Anglo-American Thought, 1550–1750* (Cambridge, 1986).

15. See *Distinction* for Bourdieu's extensive discussion of the complex relations among cultural, social, and economic value and power.

16. For discussion of the crucial significance of classification in relation to value and, in particular, the value of "literature" and "art," see Chapter 3. See also Michael Thompson, *Rubbish Theory: The Creation and Destruction of Value* (Oxford, 1979).

17. "The Notion of Expenditure" ["La Notion de dépense"] (1933), in Bataille, *Visions of Excess: Selected Writings, 1927–1939*, tr. Allan Stoekl, with Carl R. Lovitt and Donald M. Leslie, Jr. (Minneapolis, 1985), p. 116. Page references for subsequent passages are given in the text.

18. A number of these paths are usefully traced by Michèle H. Richman in *Reading Georges Bataille: Beyond the Gift* (Baltimore and London, 1981).

19. "Utility theory" so defined is, however, fairly remote from any formulations produced by the classic eighteenth- and nineteenth-century utilitarians or operating in modern economics.

20. Along with a need for expenditure and absolute loss, he posits a desire for "violent, orgiastic pleasure" in opposition to what he sees as the privileging of "moderate" pleasure by utilitarianism. Also, as the metaphorics of the essay implies and as Bataille makes more or less explicit at various points, he associates utilitarianism with the official social theory of the (bourgeois) *father* (God) while the posited "principle of loss" is associated with the actual practices of the (prodigal) *son* (Satan).

21. Recurrences of economic accounting in discourses that seek either to indicate its specific irrelevance or, as in Shakespeare's sonnet and Bataille's essay, to escape it altogether, are common. For a recent attempt by a noted political economist to establish a category of activities not explicable in utilitarian/instrumentalist terms, see Albert O. Hirschman, "Against Parsimony: Three Easy Ways of Complicating Some Categories of Economic Discourse," *Economics and Philosophy* 1 (1985): 7–21. In elaborating and exemplifying this category, Hirschman repeatedly invokes the terms of the very economic ("cost-benefit") analysis that he seeks to exceed, as in the following passage, where he reflects on activities that recall Pascal's observation that "the hope Christians have to possess an infinite good is mixed with actual enjoyment" (*Pensées*, 540, Hirschman's translation): "This savoring, this fusion of striving and attaining, is a fact of experience that goes far in accounting for the existence and importance of noninstrumental activities. *As though in compensation* for the uncertainty about the outcome, and for the strenuousness or dangerousness of the activity, the striving effort

is colored by the goal and in this fashion makes for an experience that is very different from merely agreeable, pleasurable, or even stimulating: *in spite of* its frequently *painful character* it has a well-known, *intoxicating quality*" (pp. 13–14, emphasis added). The discussion of "intrinsically rewarding" activities in Chapter 3, above, is relevant here as well.

22. For a noneconomistic analysis of expenditure that does not reproduce these dualisms, see Clifford Geertz's account of the complex social dynamics and diverse stakes of Balinese cockfighting in his classic essay "Deep Play: Notes on the Balinese Cockfight," in *The Interpretation of Cultures* (New York, 1973), esp. pp. 432–436, for his discussion of gambling in relation to Bentham and utility theory.

23. His notion of "heterogeneity" is elsewhere elaborated accordingly: compare the discussion in Richman, *Reading Georges Bataille,* pp. 40–60; and in Jacques Derrida, "From Restricted to General Economy: A Hegelianism without Reserve," in Derrida, *Writing and Difference,* tr. Alan Bass (Chicago, 1978).

24. The kind of "calculation" indicated here and below need not be and usually is not *verbally articulated*—or, as is said, "conscious"—but, rather, what I described in Chapter 3 as the continuous process of inarticulate and intuitive cost-benefit analysis that can be seen as characterizing the *systemic* behavior of all responsive organisms.

25. The idea of *measure of relative positivity* has been associated with the terms "value" and "worth" (and their cognates in other European languages) from the time of their first recorded occurrences.

26. *Distinction,* p. 55. It should be emphasized that Bourdieu is concerned here with how patterns of cultural consumption operate agonistically between classes and what he calls "class fractions" in, presumably, *any* stratified society; as the quoted passage indicates, he does not duplicate Bataille's theoretically and empirically dubious oppositions between the noble, courageous economic practices of an original primitive society and the degenerate styles of consumption and expenditure in our own postlapsarian "moldy society." Indeed, Bourdieu also calls attention to the agonistic social and economic functions of the very aristocratic/aesthetic ethos through which Bataille frames his own analysis: "The tastes of freedom can only assert themselves as such in relation to the tastes of necessity, which are thereby brought to the level of the aesthetic and so defined as vulgar . . . This means that the games of artists and aesthetes . . . are less innocent than they seem" (*Distinction,* pp. 56–57).

27. Alfred Gell, "Newcomers to the World of Goods: Consumption among the Muria Gonds," in Appadurai, *The Social Life of Things,* p. 131.

28. Cf. John Dewey, *Theory of Valuation* (Chicago, 1939), pp. 40–50, for a demonstration of the infinitely regressible alternation of means and ends whereby that which is said to be an end is always redescribable as a means.

29. Marcel Mauss, *Essai sur le Don* (1925), which, it may be noted, is itself a retelling of ethnographic material collected by other anthropologists. Au-

thenticity or reliability of ethnographic data is not, however, at issue here.

30. I refer to the implications of deconstruction or poststructuralist thought generally, but Derrida's discussion of dubious anthropological paradigms is especially relevant here. See Jacques Derrida, *Of Grammatology,* tr. Gayatri Chakravorty Spivak (Baltimore and London, 1976), pp. 95–140. See also the discussion of Alisdair MacIntyre's Myth of the Fall in Chapter 5, above.

31. Richman speaks of the "tension" in Bataille's work between "nostalgia" and "critical thought." As she puts it: "The heuristic contribution of anthropological data must be safeguarded from ideological appropriation. Yet it is precisely the sense of deprivation motivating nostalgia which draws individuals together and constitutes the impetus for collective criticism of the status quo" (*Reading Georges Bataille,* p. 139).

32. The "reasoning that balances accounts" is encountered in other neo/post-Marxist texts: for example, in Frankfurt School theory—initially in Adorno and Horkheimer, later in Habermas—under the name "instrumental reason." Habermas's effort to constitute "genuine communication" as a transaction free of instrumentality is, of course, related to this conception.

33. See Bourdieu's exploration of the general dynamics of cultural *agon* in *Distinction,* pp. 56–57, for a comparable analysis. Although the relation between the two is not clear (Bataille is nowhere explicitly mentioned by Bourdieu), much of the latter's study could be read as an elaboration— minus the myth of the Fall and in a (relatively) less sensational idiom—of just this insight.

34. This process is seen as "facilitated [in the United States] by the preliminary existence of a class [namely, blacks] held to be abject by common accord" (p. 126).

    We might note also that it becomes hard to see what claim "workers" per se have to any special regard under an account in which "unproductivity" is posited as fundamental to human life and, more generally, that Bataille is caught repeatedly in the contradictions—or, in Richman's words, "tensions"—produced by his Marxian self-identifications and his simultaneous attachment to an aristocratic ethos that valorizes "honor and glory."

35. Cf. again the concluding line of Sonnet 146: "And Death once dead, there's no more dying then." There is, of course, a historical continuity between the transcendental arithmetic of Christianity and that of Marxist redemptionism, and the fact that Bataille took neither his (ex-)Catholicism or (vagrant) Marxism straight did not make him immune to their classic formulations.

36. The quotation marks here are mysterious, since Bataille invokes the concept of human nature repeatedly throughout the essay without problematizing it. See, for example, the quite comparable invocation of "human life" in the passage quoted just below.

37. In a familiar move (cf. Dostoevsky's "Notes from Underground"), irrationality, self-destruction, perversity, and so forth are taken as the signs of a *theologically* defined free will or what Bataille names "the sovereign opera-

tion." This is not a move that could be found in Nietzsche and one may, accordingly, question any facile assimilation of "sovereignty" to the latter's "will to power."

38. The evocation of a totally disassembled or nihilistic perspective on human activity or all activity has its purposes in certain theoretical discourses, and it is evidently thus that Derrida would restate and thereby conserve the value and productivity of Bataille, translating his paradoxes and absolute inversions into a neutral nihilism: "What has happened? In sum, nothing has been said" ("From Restricted to General Economy," p. 274). The neutrality itself or, as Derrida writes, "from left to right or from right to left, as a reactionary movement or as a revolutionary movement, or both at once" (ibid., p. 276), is a theoretical position that Bataille indeed seems always on the verge of occupying but from which, nevertheless, he repeatedly retreats to both left (that is, revolutionary Marxism) and right (that is, the reactionary aristocratic/aesthetic ethos repeatedly noted above).

39. My concern here is to question the decisive *break* that Bataille and humanistic anthropology generally mark between "primitive societies" and modern ones after the Fall into Commerce, not to suggest that there are no differences among societies in relation to economic organization and practice. The discussion in Chapter 5 of contemporary controversies in economic anthropology is relevant here as well.

40. These and comparable principles are the subject of research and theoretical development in contemporary evolutionary biology. For an interesting discussion of the analogical relation between the conditioning of individual organisms and the mechanisms of natural selection, see B. F. Skinner, "Selection by Consequences," *Science* 196 (June 10, 1977): 1161–66.

41. This appears to be the conception of "good" proposed in G. E. Moore, *Principia Ethica* (New York, 1959; orig. pub. 1903).

42. The extent to which these are historically confined and otherwise specific matters (that is, Western, European, etc.) remains a question for another type of exploration. See Chapter 7, below, for a related discussion of Richard Rorty's suggestion that "true" (or, presumably, some counterpart wordform) is a universal term of commendation for beliefs.

43. If "the good" is not simply tautologously constituted as whatever "seems good to" or "is good for" the subject or, in an only slightly alternative formulation, as what benefits or has some sustaining or stabilizing "function" for the community or "the species," then it is constituted as something objective or absolute to which the subject's desires and welfare must be or should be subordinate, and which—if the "must" or "should" is pressed—yields either a tautologous restatement of the objective/absolute goodness of the objective/absolute good (an infinite regress of goods) or some arbitrarily selected ultimate good.

44. See Jean Baudrillard, *For a Critique of the Political Economy of the Sign*, tr. Charles Levin (St. Louis, Mo., 1981), for a related and comparably strained

attempt to demonstrate the existence of a value "beyond value" (*au-delà de la valeur*). Referring to this value-free value as "symbolic exchange" and exemplifying it with personal reciprocal exchange, that is, gift giving, Baudrillard comments:

> The objects involved in reciprocal exchange, whose uninterrupted circulation establishes social relationships, i.e., social *meaning,* annihilate themselves in this continual exchange without assuming any value of their own (that is, any appropriable value) . . . [However,] once symbolic exchange is broken, this same material is abstracted into utility value, commercial value, statutory value. The symbolic is transformed into the instrumental, either commodity or sign. Any one of the various codes may be specifically involved, but they are all joined in the single form of political economy which is opposed, as a whole, to symbolic exchange. (p. 125)

> The symbolic is not a value (i.e., not positive, autonomisable, measurable or codifiable). It is the ambivalence (positive and negative) of personal exchange— and as such it is radically opposed to all values. (p. 127)

Among the questions raised here are whether anything, including any of the examples given, actually exemplifies "symbolic exchange" *so defined* and how or in what sense objects "annihilate themselves." And among the questions begged are whether *no* value really is assumed thereby (that is, whether no exchange value or use value is produced in and through the very *act* of gift giving), whether "social meaning" is itself without value, and, finally, whether these values are really immeasurable and the meanings thereby established really not themselves "codifiable." Cf. Marshall Sahlins's analysis of gifts as disguised exchanges in *Stone Age Economics* (Chicago, 1972), pp. 149–183; and Bourdieu's analysis of gifts as temporally deferred exchanges in *Outline of a Theory of Practice,* tr. Richard Nice (Cambridge, 1977), pp. 3–9.

45. Thus Bataille titles the first section of "The Notion of Expenditure" (p. 116).
46. Indeed, the notion of "system" here is itself no more than a theoretically enabling construct: there are no observer-independent or theory-independent boundaries to that or any other system. While certain tendencies within this interplay of forces may be described from various perspectives and articulated in the terms of various classic or current conceptual structures (Bataille's anthropological economics or, alternately, Christian-Aristotelian ethics, Freudian psychology, sociobiology, etc.), it is obvious that these perspectives and descriptions do not "converge" on each other and cannot be hierarchically ordered: that is, they are not simply a matter of different "levels" of description, and they are otherwise irreducibly various.
47. See Humberto Maturana and Francisco G. Varela, *Autopoesis and Cognition: The Realization of Living* (Dordrecht, Holland, and Boston, 1980), for an analysis of reflection or self-description as an activity of certain living systems.

7. Matters of Consequence

Epigraph: "Questions of Method: An Interview with Michel Foucault," in *After Philosophy: End or Transformation?* ed. Kenneth Baynes, James Bohman, and Thomas McCarthy (Cambridge, Mass., 1987), p. 114.

1. For the phrase and characterization, see W. J. T. Mitchell, "The Good, the Bad, and the Ugly: Three Theories of Value," *Raritan* 6, no. 2 (Fall 1986): 63–76. Other specific objections and examples cited in this chapter are drawn from the queries and comments of respondents, reviewers, and others who have read or heard parts of this book over the past ten years or so.

2. It readily accommodates the idea, however, that some things change more slowly than others and that some varieties and configurations are more recurrent, widespread, and stable than others.

3. "Relativists" in the general sense just indicated are rarely self-designated. Notable contemporary exceptions are Paul Feyerabend, whose spirited and free-spirited discussions of "The Spectre of Relativism" in his *Science in a Free Society* (London, 1978) can, in some respects, hardly be bettered; Nelson Goodman, who in his *Ways of Worldmaking* (Indianapolis and Cambridge, Mass., 1978) refers to his carefully articulated (and, in relation to this study, congenial) views as "Radical Relativism"; and the group at the University of Edinburgh associated with the "strong programme" in the philosophy and sociology of science. The latter include Barry Barnes and David Bloor, whose "Relativism, Rationalism and the Sociology of Knowledge" is the only instance of unqualified self-labeling in the influential collection *Rationality and Relativism,* ed. Martin Hollis and Stephen Lukes (Cambridge, Mass., 1982).

   Other recent studies and collections include Michael Krausz and Jack W. Meiland, eds., *Relativism: Cognitive and Moral* (Notre Dame, 1982); Richard J. Bernstein, *Beyond Objectivism and Relativism: Science, Hermeneutics, and Praxis* (Philadelphia, 1983); and *The Monist* 67, no. 3 (1984), on the topic "Is Relativism Defensible?" Although Anglo-American philosophers on the whole regard what they name "relativism" as an unmitigated menace and folly, a small number of them, including Joseph Margolis, in *Pragmatism without Foundations: Reconciling Realism and Relativism* (Oxford and New York, 1986), and Bernard Williams, in "The Truth in Relativism," *Proceedings of the Aristotelian Society* 75 (1974–75): 215–228, give highly qualified endorsement to various deeply hedged positions under that label. What Bernstein offers as "beyond" objectivism and relativism is a precariously poised neo-objectivism pieced together from salvaged remnants of the thought of Popper, Gadamer, and Habermas. Bernstein reports and to some extent echoes critiques of these works and also of classic epistemology but does not acknowledge the intellectual *force* of those critiques for the questions at issue and moves repeatedly toward reaffirmations of orthodoxy.

   For a wide-ranging, sharp-shooting rejoinder to several of the essays in the Hollis and Lukes collection (and others elsewhere), see Clifford Geertz, "Anti-Anti-Relativism," *American Anthropologist* 86, no. 2 (June 1984): 263–278. (It must be added that Geertz's views on these issues are complex and apparently ambivalent, as will be seen below.) For a skeptical assessment of Margolis's versions of relativism, see Joseph Valente, "Against Robust Relativism," *Philosophical Forum* 17, no. 4 (Summer 1986): 296–321.

4. For a lucid discussion of the charge of self-refutation in relation to Nietzsche's "perspectivism," see Alexander Nehamas, *Nietzsche: Life as Literature* (Cambridge, Mass., 1985), pp. 65–68.

5. The phrase "anything goes" is associated with Feyerabend's critique, especially in his *Against Method* (London, 1975), of traditional conceptions of scientific methodology. His own comments on the phrase and association are very pointed and altogether pertinent here. Referring to the historical case studies he offers in the book, Feyerabend writes (*Science in a Free Society*, p. 188):

> I not only try to show the *failure* of traditional methodologies, I also try to show what procedures *aided* scientists *and should therefore be used. I criticize some procedures but I defend and recommend others* . . . I point out that it is such a study of concrete cases rather than the arid exercises of rationalists that should guide a scientist and I argue for an anthropological and against a logical study of standards . . . None of these suggestions seem to have been noticed by my reviewers and this despite the fact that their discussion fills more than half of my book. All they notice are my somewhat ironical summaries and the only positive statement they find [, which they] immediately elevate into a "central thesis," or a "principle" of "[Feyerabend's] methodology [,]" is the slogan "anything goes." *But "anything goes" does not express any conviction of mine, it is a jocular summary of the predicament of the rationalist:* if you want universal standards, I say, if you cannot live without principles that hold independently of situation, shape of world, exigencies of research, temperamental peculiarities, then I can give you such a principle. It will be empty, useless, and pretty ridiculous—but it will be a "principle." It will be the "principle" "anything goes."

6. Hilary Putnam, "Why Reason Can't be Naturalized," in Baynes et al., *After Philosophy*, pp. 240–241. Putnam is specifically concerned here with the invocation, by W. V. Quine and others, of Alfred Tarski's "disquotational" theory of truth. The passage continues: "But it is pointless to make further efforts in this direction. Why should we expend our mental energy in convincing ourselves that we aren't thinkers, that our thoughts aren't really *about* anything . . . that there is no sense in which any thought is right or wrong (including the thought that no thought is right or wrong) beyond the verdict of the moment, and so on? This is a self-refuting enterprise if there ever was one!" (pp. 241–242).

7. Putnam reports, with mixed bafflement and gratification, that Quine has *repeatedly* said (apparently in private conversation and one can only imagine

with what weariness) that "he didn't mean to 'rule out the normative' " (ibid., p. 239).

8. In view of the gravity of the charge, one may ask by exactly what mechanisms the denial of orthodox objectivism, per se, is supposed to have yielded the death camps. In the absence of any precise specification of such mechanisms, the association must be regarded as classic *scapegoating:* a dangerous pastime, even among philosophers, and also an evasion of the difficult tasks of political analysis and corresponding political action described below.

9. Richard Rorty, "Solidarity or Objectivity?" in *Post-Analytic Philosophy,* ed. John Rajchman and Cornell West (New York, 1985), p. 6. Page references to the essay will be cited in the text.

10. Rorty's account of "truth" in this essay is, at points, more positive than he acknowledges, as in his quasi-empirical observations suggesting a universal usage of "true" as "commendatory." "[It] means the same in all cultures," he remarks (as do, he claims, "here," there," "good," "you," and "me"), though it has "diversity of reference among them." In view of the fact that even *within* our "culture" (that is, the Anglophone verbal community), the "reference" of the term "true" is diverse or, as I think it better to say here, the *conditions of its usage* are *irreducibly various,* this must be seen as a crucial oversimplification. Moreover, it is no quibble to note that most "cultures" or verbal communities do not have the term "true" at all. For to imply that *different wordforms* are *the same ''term''* is to make a key move in the related debates over (un)translatability and (in)commensurability and, one would think, just the move that Rorty should *not* be making here. (See, e.g., Donald Davidson, "On the Very Idea of a Conceptual Scheme," in his *Inquiries into Truth and Interpretation* [Oxford, 1984], an important piece but considerably more elusive and equivocal than one would suspect from its frequent citation as decisive on these matters.) Although Rorty clearly rejects the objectivist correspondence-to-reality criterion of "truth," he does not sufficiently problematize the term/concept itself; that is, retaining Frege's highly questionable distinctions, he also retains the idea that "true," even if it "refers to" diverse things, still "means" *some single thing in particular.* It is just the latter idea, however, and the semantic theory in which it is embedded, that must be rejected in the development of alternative, nonobjectivist accounts of "truth" and, more generally, of "meaning," "language," and "communication." To the extent that Rorty's pragmatist retains that idea and theory in his discussions of truth, he encourages the confusions of his realist adversary.

11. Value in all these instances can, of course, be *dis*value: thus, frequently cited along with the unappreciated objective goodness or betterness of reading Seneca's *Medea* or studying ancient languages is the unrecognized objective badness or worseness of wife beating, bride burning, clitoridectomy, and watching television crime-dramas. The added piquancy of examples in which the victims are female can hardly be missed.

12. For a recent example of charges of academic relativism, quietism, and "lax-

ity," coupled with more or less egregiously reactionary proposals, see Allan Bloom, *The Closing of the American Mind: How Higher Education Has Failed Democracy and Impoverished the Souls of Today's Students* (New York, 1986).

13. The items in these two series have not been chosen in flagrant disregard of "fundamental distinctions" but to emphasize that the value of authority, like the value of anything else, cuts both (or all) ways, an important principle obscured by the usual examples of altogether benevolent parents and teachers, and altogether malevolent institutional officials—with missionaries, serving as the hinge here, historically invoked as both.

14. Rorty makes a similar point forcefully: "To say that [cultures] have 'institutionalized norms' is only to say, with Foucault, that knowledge is never separable from power—that one is likely to suffer if one does not hold certain beliefs at certain times and places. But such institutional backups for beliefs take the form of bureaucrats and policemen, not of 'rules of language' and 'criteria of rationality.' To think otherwise is the Cartesian fallacy of seeing axioms where there are only shared habits, of viewing statements which summarize such practices as if they reported constraints enforcing such practices" ("Solidarity or Objectivity?" p. 9).

15. In "The Truth of Relativism," Williams argues for the necessity of distinguishing between "real" and "notional" conflicts or "confrontations" of ethical judgment. The distinction moves in a useful direction, but not far enough, for the real/notional dualism itself obscures the range of dimensions along which conditions relevant to disparities of judgment may *vary* and also the range of their individual *modulations* and mutual *interactions*. Indeed, Williams's distinction continuously hedges the issue of ethical relativism and ultimately operates to deny the radical contingency of ethical judgment and action. It is disappointing but not altogether surprising to find him, in a later discussion of the point, explicitly recanting its more radical implications. Cf. Bernard Williams, *Ethics and the Limits of Philosophy* (Cambridge, Mass., 1985), pp. 160 and 220.

16. The relativist may, even when sorely baited, forbear entering into serious arguments with other people when she recognizes that the stakes would be much greater for *them* than for *her:* for example, their continued conviction of their personal salvation and immortality or the value of their life's work versus her relatively superficial pleasure in self-confirmation or in the exercise of skill or power. Forbearance under such conditions is not, of course, restricted to relativists, but only in them is it taken as a sign of intellectual torpor rather than of human charity.

17. These formulations speak of *individual* agents for the sake of clarity and vividness, not in order to obscure—or as a consequence of forgetting—the possibility and necessity of *communal* action. Just as "the other fellow" is always pluralizable here (extendable, in other words, into "other people" or other *communities:* societies, nations, entire cultures, and so forth), so also, to the extent that the relativist acts as a member of a group of agents, "she" is herself pluralizable here.

219

18. The challenge of "how one answers the Nazi," and, as discussed above, one of the ways of replying (namely, "It *depends*") are obviously relevant here.

19. Clifford Geertz, "The Uses of Diversity," *Tanner Lectures on Human Values,* vol. 7 (Cambridge, 1986), pp. 272–273.

20. I. A. Richards, *The Principles of Literary Criticism* (1924; London, 1960), p. 206.

21. I would myself also maintain an attitude of skepticism toward all appeals to putatively redemptive sacrifices and sufferings, but Rorty's pragmatist and I may well differ deeply here.

22. Geertz's own resolution to the anthropologist's related "relativism"/ "ethnocentrism" predicament is to reject the latter as a dangerous surrender to "the pleasure of invidious comparison" but, like Rorty, to declare the former, which Geertz glosses here as "counsels of indiscriminate tolerance," to be necessarily *insincere* ("The Uses of Diversity," p. 274). The sentiment through which Geertz frames his own recommended alternative, "We must learn to grasp what we cannot embrace," is certainly unexceptionable, but one must wonder if any of the cultural relativists of anthropological shame and philosophical scandal—Ruth Benedict, for example—would have said anything different or, indeed, if they *meant* anything different by the tolerance they urged. For there remains the question, of course, of what, once it was clear one could not *embrace* it, one should *do* with what one had "grasped"; and there is no reason to think that in every case "indiscriminately," including the *ad horrendum* case of Nazism in 1939 (which is when Benedict's *Patterns of Culture,* with its memorable "counsels of tolerance," appeared), those relativists would have counseled just putting it down gently and letting it go its way.

23. Charles Levin, "Introduction," in Jean Baudrillard, *For a Critique of the Political Economy of the Sign* (St. Louis, Mo., 1981), p. 7.

24. Ibid., p. 12.

25. Cf. the classic Marxist analysis of surplus value and exploitation in which capitalism is seen as objectively unjust because the relation of profits to production costs is, in effect, mathematically unequal. For discussion of the analysis in relation to contemporary economic theory, see G. A. Cohen, "The Labour Theory of Value and the Concept of Exploitation," *Philosophy and Public Affairs* 8, no. 4 (1979), repr. in Ian Steedman et al., *The Value Controversy* (London, 1981), pp. 202–223.

26. Although the concept of "interest" is not innocent, its guilt is not as redemptive as is sometimes claimed; for the mere fact that the term has had a particular intellectual history, or even that it has kept bad theoretical company (specifically eighteenth- and nineteenth-century classic economics), does not in itself validate such reactive notions as a will to transcendent nonmaterial sovereignty or a fundmental human impulse to self-sacrifice. Baudrillard's critique of "use-value" in *For a Critique of the Political Economy of the Sign* has evident affinities to that of Bataille, discussed earlier in relation to such reactive redemptionist notions. For the history of the notion

of "interest" in relation to economic theory, see Albert O. Hirschman, *The Passions and the Interests: Political Arguments for Capitalism before Its Triumph* (Princeton, N.J., 1977). For a shrewd discussion of ambivalent invocations of (and attacks on) "interests" by contemporary political theorists and political historians, see T. J. Jackson Lears, "The Concept of Cultural Hegemony: Problems and Possibilities," *American Historical Review* 90, no. 3 (June 1985): 567–593, esp. 579–586.

27. Although this account is designed to apply to any sort of oppositional political theory and action, its specific relevance to contemporary feminist theory and politics is intentionally highlighted by the pronouns.

28. Stanley Fish has notoriously observed that theory has no consequences; see Fish, *Is There a Text in This Class? The Authority of Interpretive Communities* (Cambridge, Mass., 1980), pp. 370–371. This is right, in the sense that a new analysis of institutional practices does not in itself change those practices and (as Fish evidently wishes to assure his audiences) that the familiar world, under a novel and unorthodox description of it, does not disappear. It does not follow from the former, however, nor does Fish himself claim, that theories have no consequences whatsoever; and it does not follow from the latter ("We have everything that we have always had—texts, standards, norms . . . and so on"—p. 367) that he is especially eager to preserve the status quo. For not only do theories have, along the lines described above, considerable *rhetorical* power (a form of practical efficiency which, given the centrality of "persuasion" versus "demonstration" in his own analyses, Fish could hardly regard as inconsequential), but even more significantly, and in accord with his own antiobjectivist formulations, in changing—in some places—the ways in which "the world" is conceptualized and perceived, *theory,* including Fish's own, also and thereby changes, precisely, *the world.*

Index

Index

Homer, 15, 35, 36, 48, 52–53

Horkheimer, Max, 213n32

Human nature: universals of, 14–15, 67, 135, 174; and tastes, 15, 37, 59–63, 77–81; Bataille on, 134–144, 145; conceptions of, 134, 144–149; as scrappy, 148, 165, 167; and political theory, 154, 174–179; and ethics, 161–163. *See also* Subject

Humanism: and literary academy, 18–20, 22, 26; and economism, 115; and anti-utilitarianism, 125–134; and anti-Semitism, 210n10

Hume, David, 15, 26, 38, 41, 83, 170, 182, 188n6, 193n16, 194nn2–3, 196n15; on standard of taste, 36–37, 55–64; compared to Kant, 65, 69–70, 71, 72; and Other's-Poison-Effect, 74

Information: and aesthetic value, 51–52; in verbal transactions, 108–109, 204n27

Interests: and value, 31, 32, 34, 46, 51; and evaluation, 43, 100; and politics, 176, 177; concept of, 220–221n26

Interpretation: and evaluation, 7, 10–11, 22, 49–51; and critical theory, 17–18, 23. *See also* Meaning

Intuitions: linguistic, 66–67, 86, 90; and axiologic logic, 73–74

Jacob, François, 208n48

Jameson, Fredric, 197n18

Jauss, Hans Robert, 190n16

Jay, Martin, 75, 196–197n17, 197n19

Jemie, Onwuchekwa, 26–27, 190n20

Johnson, Samuel, 4, 19, 25

Jones, Stephen R. G., 209n6

Józsa, Pierre, 189n14

Judgment Day, 149

Judgments: of taste, 64–72; and language, 85–102, 107; typology of, 85–93, 101; moral, 86–90, 162, 164–166, 198n25, 219n15; and truth, 94–101; validity of, 104–107; and relativism, 158–161. *See also* Criticism; Evaluation

Justification: infinite regress of, 63, 100, 178; and relativism, 159–166; Rorty on, 170–173; and politics, 173–179

Kahneman, Daniel, et al., 206n37, 208n49, 208n2, 209n7

Kamin, Leon J., 198n24

Kant, Immanuel, 26, 33, 34, 35, 36, 37, 42, 55, 86, 92, 194nn5,6, 195nn7–12, 196n13; on judgments of taste, 64–72

Kantianism, 75, 113, 178, 199n25, 205n31

Keats, John, 5, 21, 25, 81, 82

Kilmer, Joyce, 25

Kofman, Sarah, 207n38

Kohlberg, Lawrence, 199n25

Kolodny, Annette, 190n18

Kopytoff, Igor, 210n9

Krausz, Michael, 216n3

Krebs, John T., 206n33

Krieger, Murray, 188n1, 197n18

Language: and aesthetics, 33–36, 59; and axiology, 66–67, 85–96, 194n6; and value judgments, 85–93; norms in, 109; economics of, 113–114; and evolution, 122–123. *See also* Communication; Intuitions, linguistic; Judgments; Value, discourse of

Latour, Bruno, 202n20

Lauter, Paul, 193n20

Lears, T. J. Jackson, 220n26

Leavis, F. R., 19, 188n2; 189n16

Leenhardt, Jacques, 189n14

Lenz, John W., 58, 194n1

Levin, Charles, 173

Lewontin, R. C., 198n24

Literary academy: and critical theory 17–24; and standards, 41; and value, 43–44, 45–47; and canon-formation, 49–50

Literary criticism, 1–16, 24–27, 45–47, 58–59. *See also* Critical theory; Evaluation; Judgments

Literary theory, 16, 17–18, 23–24. *See also* Critical theory

Literature: evaluation of, 1–16, 19, 21–23, 26–28; as classification and label, 14, 32, 43–44, 47; and canon-formation, 47–53

Logic: in axiological arguments, 38, 54–84, 174; tastes in, 72–73

Loomes, G., 209n6

Luce, Duncan, 208n1, 209n4
Luhmann, Niklas, 198n23, 201n8
Lukes, Steven, 192n10, 216–217n3

MacDonald, Dwight, 197n18
Macherey, Pierre, 193n17
MacIntyre, Alisdair: on value judgments, 86–94, 194n6, 200nn2–4,6, 212n30; on communities, 93–94, 172
Malraux, André, 197n18
Marcuse, Herbert, 173, 197n18
Margolis, Joseph, 216–217n3
Marx, Karl, 135
Marxism: and aesthetics, 23, 188n4, 189n16, 190n16, 209–210n8; and cultural criticism, 75; and redemptionism, 130, 213n35; and Bataille, 140, 214n38; and political theory, 174, 175, 178; and economic theory, 220n25
Mass media, 37–38, 75, 77
Maturana, Humberto, 201n10, 215n47
Mauss, Marcel, 135, 140, 141, 210n9, 212n29
McCarthy, Thomas, 199n25, 216
Meaning: and value, 48, 49; and linguistic usage, 89–90, 92. *See also* Interpretation
Meiland, Jack W., 216n3
Meyer, Leonard B., 194n25, 199n28
Michelin guides, 93, 103
Monist (journal), 216n3
Moonmen, 164–165
Moore, G. E., 214n41
Moral value. *See* Ethics; Judgments, moral
Morawski, Stefan, 187n4, 189n16
Mukařovský, Jan, 23, 188n4, 192n9
Munévar, Gonzalo, 201n9

Najder, Zdzislaw, 187n4
Nazism: and relativism, 153–155, 220n18
Nehamas, Alexander, 190n17, 217n4
New Criticism, 17, 20
Newell, A., 207n46
Nietzsche, Friedrich, 23, 135, 144, 171, 190n17, 207n38, 217n4
Nisbett, Richard E., et al., 209n7
Norms: and standards, 37, 40–41, 181–183; and communities, 40, 93–94, 131, 181–183; and institutions, 43; in language, 109–110; and relativism, 153–154, 162, 180–182

Objectivism, 98, 101, 113–114; and relativism, 150–173, 180–184
Objectivity: of value, 11, 101; in literary study, 19–20, 22, 28; apparent, 40, 92, 93; of judgments, 70, 101–102, 103–104; Rorty on, 167; and standards, 182
Ortega y Gassett, José, 197n18
Other's-Poison-Effect, The, 26, 74–77
Oyama, Susan, 198n24

Peckham, Morse, 192n13, 202n16
Plato, 120, 205n32
Platonism, 113
Plotnitsky, Arkady, 190n17
Polanyi, Karl, 115, 206n36
Political theory: and relativism, 154–155, 173–179; and communitarianism, 168–169, 171–173; and Marxism, 174, 175, 178
Politics: and literary criticism, 24–27; and MacIntyre, 93–94; and Rorty, 168, 170–171; and justification, 173–179; and personal economies, 175–178
Pope, Alexander, 36, 61
Popular culture: I. A. Richards on, 37–38; vs. high, 74–77, 81–84
Postaxiology, 75, 77, 190n17, 196n14
Pound, Ezra, 210n10
Pragmatism: and validity, 106; Rorty's, and relativism, 155–165, 166–173
Pratt, Mary Louise, 204–205n31, 206n34
Preferences. *See* Tastes
Protagoras, 205n32
Putnam, Hilary, 153–154, 217nn6,7

Quietism, 150; and relativism, 151–152, 153–155, 156–166
Quine, W. V., 217nn6,7

Radway, Janice A., 197n18
Raiffa, Howard, 208n1, 209n4
Ransom, John Crowe, 4
Rappaport, Anatol, 206n37
Rationality: economic, 99, 126, 136, 209n6; concept of, 147–148, 204–205n31; and relativism, 163–166
Reason, 71, 74, 164